STILL ME

The world held its breath when Christopher Reeve struggled for life on Memorial Day, 1995. On the third jump of a riding competition, Reeve was thrown headfirst from his horse in an accident that broke his neck and left him incapable of movement. Since then, Reeve has not only survived, but has fought for himself, for his family, and also for the hundreds of thousands of people with spinal cord injuries around the world. And he has written a heartbreaking, funny, courageous and hopeful autobiography. *Still Me* is the story of his life: the early success on Broadway, the adventure of filming *Superman*, the dazzling years of stardom that followed—and his heroic journey to rebuild his life after the accident. With dignity and sensitivity, he describes the journey he has made—physically, emotionally and spiritually. Deeply moving and inspiring, *Still Me* is a testament to the human spirit.

STILL ME

Christopher Reeve

CHIVERS PRESS
BATH

First published 1998
by
Century
This Large Print edition published by
Chivers Press
by arrangement with
Random House UK Ltd
1999

ISBN 0 7540 1289 1

Copyright © Cambria Productions, Inc. 1998

Christopher Reeve has asserted his right under the
Copyright, Designs and Patents Act, 1988 to be
identified as the author of this work.

All rights reserved

British Library Cataloguing in Publication Data available

Printed and bound in Great Britain by
REDWOOD BOOKS, Trowbridge, Wiltshire

*For everyone
whose life has been touched by disability*

The marvelous richness of human experience would lose something of rewarding joy if there were not limitations to overcome. The hilltop hour would not be half so wonderful if there were no dark valleys to traverse.

—HELEN KELLER

ACKNOWLEDGMENTS

At Random House, Harry Evans gave me the opportunity to write about the past when I was extremely uncertain about the future. Wanda Chappell, Ruth Fecych, and Ann Godoff came aboard and have taken this project to the finish line.

Barbara Walters, Katie Couric, and others in the media have not only listened, but have helped to inform the public about spinal cord injury.

I am especially indebted to June Fox, who became much more than a transcriber of my thoughts. I literally could not have written this book without her.

Dan Strone, my literary agent, was always there to help.

Scott Henderson, my long-time friend and agent; Joel Faden, my business manager; and Lisa Kasteler, my publicist, are members of a rare breed of generous and fiercely loyal allies in a business replete with fleeting associations. Each has stood by me through thick and thin.

Marsha and Robin Williams, Steven Spielberg, the gang at HBO, as well as friends and colleagues too numerous to mention have helped me break through boundaries both real and imagined.

My personal assistants, Michael Manganiello, Sarah Houghton, and Rachel Strife, found photos, helped me proofread, and worked tirelessly managing daily crises, which allowed me to shut the door and concentrate on this book.

I am lucky to have an outstanding team of

nurses, aides, equipment vendors, and accessibility advisers without whom I could not live my daily life, let alone write about it.

I would like to thank my family, who have so often gone out of their way to visit even for a few hours, but mostly for providing historical details and indulging me in my perspective.

And, most important, my eternal gratitude and love to Dana, Matthew, Alexandra, and Will, whose unconditional love, humor, joy, and appetite for life inspire me daily.

CHAPTER ONE

A few months after the accident I had an idea for a short film about a quadriplegic who lives in a dream. During the day, lying in his hospital bed, he can't move, of course. But at night he dreams that he's whole again, and is able to do anything and go everywhere. This is someone who had been a lifelong sailor, and who had always loved the water, and he had a beautiful gaff-rigged sloop. Not like my boat, the *Sea Angel*, which was modern and made of fiberglass. In the story the boat is a great old wooden beauty, whose varnish gleams in the moonlight.

In his dream he sails down the path of a full moon, and there's a gentle breeze, perfect conditions—the kind of romantic night sailing that anyone can imagine. But by seven in the morning, he's back in his bed in the rehab hospital and everything is frozen again.

The dream is very vivid. And as time passes it becomes even more vivid. At first it's just a dream, and he recognizes it as such. But suddenly one night he finds himself actually getting out of bed and leaving the hospital, fully aware of walking down the corridor and out the door, then into the boat, which, magically, is anchored not far away.

And he gets on board and goes sailing, long into the night and the moonlight. Soon these voyages become so real to him that when he wakes up in his bed at seven in the morning, his hair is soaked. And the nurse comes in and says, 'Oh, I'm sorry. I didn't dry your hair enough last night when I gave you a

1

shampoo. You slept with wet hair.' He says nothing, but he's thinking that his hair is wet from the spray when he was out on the water. One time he comes back still wearing his foul weather gear, and he has to hide it in the hospital room closet because the nurses are going to wonder where it came from.

Now his wife and family, his wife and children, have been very distressed all along because, since he became paralyzed, he has not been able to pull out of a serious depression. He has shut them out of his life. His children are afraid of him because he is not himself and they don't know how to be with him, and his wife has been talking to the doctors and the psychologists at the hospital about what to do because he is apparently unable to cope or to come out of his shell.

But as he continues to go sailing in his dreams and as these dreams become more and more real, his mood begins to improve and he seems less withdrawn. In the mornings he is more content and much more communicative. His wife notices the change, but she can't understand it, and he won't explain it. It's not something that he can talk about. He's not sure if he's going crazy. He thinks that he may be losing his mind. But since the family is feeling the benefit of his improvement, his dreams are making their life together happier.

He sails in Tenants Harbor, or a similarly idyllic spot in Maine, and there's a fellow there, an older man, who always turns on the light in his cabin down by the water when our man is sailing. He doesn't sleep very well, and he always gets up to watch the younger man go out in the wooden boat. Sometimes he comes down to his dock, and we can tell from the yearning in his eyes that the sailboat is something he loves and admires. Not that he's jealous, but he never misses a chance to see the boat sailing so beautifully in the moonlight.

Well, there comes a time when our protagonist realizes that these voyages offer a way of escaping from his paralyzed condition, that he could just sail and sail on happily—it's what he loves most in the world—until one night he would go out into the middle of the ocean, and he wouldn't take supplies or anything. He would just sail until he dropped. And he would die happy. He would just go sailing down the path of the moon, as far as he possibly could go, and leave everything and everyone behind him.

And one night he starts to do that. He just decides he's going to go, with no idea where; he is going to sail away forever. But then, as he is heading out to sea, he starts to think about what he has in his life, how grateful he is for his wife and his children. Because, during the days, you see, he's changed. His kids are less afraid of him, and they're playing with him, and his wife . . . they're clearly in love. He is coming out of his depression.

So here he is doing the thing that he loves most for himself, thinking that he could sail on and forget the world. But along the way he begins to realize what he is leaving behind. He turns the boat around and comes back. And he goes straight to the dock of the older man who has always loved this boat. He ties up right at the dock, and when the old man comes down to greet him, our man says, 'Here, this is for you.' He gives up the boat. He no longer needs it. And he goes back to the hospital, and he wakes up, and he's frozen and he's a quadriplegic again. But he has an entirely new

3

basis for the future with his family and toward recovery.

That's the gist of it. Of course the story comes from my experience, but it's not my story. I'm different from this man because my family saved me at the very beginning. When a catastrophe happens it's easy to feel so sorry for yourself that you can't even see anybody around you. But the way out is through your relationships. The way out of that misery or obsession is to focus more on what your little boy needs or what your teenagers need or what other people around you need. It's very hard to do, and often you have to force yourself. But that is the answer to the dilemma of being frozen—at least it's the answer I found.

Yet these dreams of being able to move and to live again in your former life can be very real, very powerful. When I was in denial about my condition, they were even stronger. And it's always a shock in the morning when you wake up and realize where you are. You think: This can't be my life. There's been a mistake. It took a lot of adjustment. It still does. Less so now than it did.

I wake up in the morning. I sleep with my mouth open, so my throat is excruciatingly dry because of the drugs I'm on and the lack of humidity in the room. I may have spasmed to a very uncomfortable place, and my neck is often twisted into a painful position. And I'm lying in this narrow bed, alone, because it's not big enough for Dana to share, though she always sleeps in the same room with me. She has a single bed next to me so we can be near each other and talk and wake up and know we're together.

4

*   *   *

On Memorial Day 1995 I was headed down to Culpeper, Virginia, with my horse, Buck, to compete in a combined training event. I was getting to be a pretty good rider; I had taken up the sport about ten years earlier, when I was cast as Vronsky, a captain in the cavalry in a film version of *Anna Karenina* and wanted to do some of my own riding. I had been allergic to horses since childhood, but to prepare for the part I loaded up with antihistamines and took daily lessons at a barn on Martha's Vineyard, where I usually spent part of the summer. By the end of a month of intensive training, I could walk, trot, canter, and gallop fairly respectably. The horse was a huge Trakehner stallion named Good Boy; but when Charlotte, my instructor, would say 'good boy' in a praising tone, she wasn't talking to me.

I went off to Budapest in the fall of 1984 to begin filming and quickly discovered that the other riders in the movie were members of the Hungarian national equestrian team. One of the highlights of the story is a steeplechase in which Captain Vronsky's horse is injured and he has to shoot him on the spot. I didn't feel quite ready (to say the least) to jump four-foot hedges at twenty-five miles an hour, but I did feel prepared to gallop on the flat along with the team rather than use a double. In the nineteenth century races had no starting gates; the riders walked their horses around in a circle, and when the starter dropped the flag everyone turned from the position he was in and started down the track. I asked the team coach how I would know when to start if I was

5

facing away from the flag, and he replied, in his thick, broken English, 'When your horse sees others are going, he is going too.' This proved to be a major understatement. The cameras rolled; the flag dropped; the professional riders spurred their horses; and suddenly I was flying down the course in the middle of the group, going so fast we outran the camera truck that was supposed to keep pace alongside us. After a couple of takes the director gave the truck more of a head start.

The whole experience was absolutely exhilarating; I was bitten by the riding bug. I realized I had been in over my head in Hungary, so when I came home I decided to take up the sport properly. I began to train at a small barn in Bedford, New York (where we have our home today), and to build up time in the saddle with good friends in Williamstown, Massachusetts, where I often appeared at the theater festival. In the fall we would usually go up to Woodstock, Vermont, for three days of trail riding in the Green Mountains. I learned a lot from riding many different horses, especially from Hope, a mare I rode briefly who was one of the meanest and most unpredictable four-legged creatures I've ever come across. Whenever I came into her stall to feed her or put on the saddle, she would turn around, stick her rear end in my face, and pin her ears back—a sure sign that she was about to kick me in the teeth. Once in Vermont I sat quietly on a hilltop waiting for the others to catch up. As I loosened my legs and dropped my feet out of the stirrups, Hope spun around for no good reason and dumped me off her side. I began to think her name was particularly apt, because you could only hope to catch her in a good mood and have a decent ride.

By 1989 I had progressed to the point where I could consider competing in combined training events. This aspect of the sport appealed to me because it has three phases: dressage, stadium jumping, and cross-country jumping. The challenge is to develop such a strong bond between horse and rider that you can succeed in the precise maneuvers and tight control of the dressage ring, then take sizable jumps at a gallop out in the woods a few hours later, which requires speed, accuracy, and confidence. I had various horses over the years, and whenever I went on a film location I found the best trainer in the area and surreptitiously took lessons, hoping that the producers or their insurance company wouldn't catch me at it. In this way I had the benefit of working with some of the best riders and teachers in the country—Mark Weissbecker, Brian Sabo, Mike Huber, Stephen Bradley, and Yves Sauvignon, to name a few.

Each trainer had a slightly different approach. Mark Weissbecker emphasized the quality of the canter in approaching every jump: the hindquarters, the 'engine' of the horse, must be fully engaged in order to jump successfully. Brian Sabo gave me a mental image that helped build my confidence when approaching challenging fences at speed. He asked his students to imagine that there was a steel spear strapped to the breastplate of the horse, and that the rider's intention was to go at the jump and make splinters out of it with that weapon. In other words, you think of going through the jump rather than over it. This usually results in finding the perfect distance for takeoff; the horse, naturally preferring to go over the fence instead of through it, will jump nicely.

My allergies disappeared. I was smitten with riding and wanted to do it as often and as well as I could. But as I learned I always kept in mind the advice of my first flying instructor, Robert Hall, just after I received my license: 'The successful outcome of any maneuver must never be seriously in doubt.' As an avid sports enthusiast, particularly attracted to activities that some would consider risky or even dangerous, I took this almost as a mantra.

In the fall of 1994 I was filming *Village of the Damned* in Northern California, but I was desperate to compete in one more combined training event before the season was over. So I caught a plane back east and went up to Mark Weissbecker's barn in the Berkshires, where he had been training my Irish Thoroughbred, Denver, while I was away. On Saturday I took Denver to the meet at Stonleigh-Burnham. This was a competition in which all three phases are done on the same day: dressage and stadium jumping in the morning, cross-country in the afternoon. I hadn't been on Denver for more than three months, but Mark had kept him going well, and we were high in the standings before the afternoon. As we started the cross-country phase, however, I realized that Denver was reverting to one of his old bad habits: he was running with his head down as we approached the jumps instead of with his head up, which is the safe and proper way to approach an obstacle. I was not happy with the way he took the first four jumps. We got over them, but I felt that the two of us weren't connecting. I pulled him up and retired from the course rather than risk injury in the quest for a prize.

I was a good sailor, having raced or cruised in all kinds of sailboats from the age of seven. I had flown various airplanes for over twenty years and made two solo trips across the Atlantic; I had raced sailplanes, and once climbed to 32,000 feet in the powerful rising air currents over Pikes Peak in Colorado. I enjoyed scuba diving, played tennis, and was a skier as well. I never felt that I was courting danger, because I always stayed within my self-imposed limits. In all aspects of my life I enjoyed being in control, which is why my accident was a devastating shock not only to me but to everyone who knew me.

The fact that I went to Culpeper at all was a fluke. I had originally signed up to compete that weekend at an event in Vermont. I'd had success in Vermont the year before. I'd finished first in one event at Tamarack, and placed third in the Area I Championships in the fall of 1994. I'd met a lot of nice people. I also preferred the cool weather. I figured that on Memorial Day weekend, it would be more pleasant in Vermont than down in Virginia.

I also knew that this event would be the last one I could do for the season, because I was about to go to Ireland for a film. I was scheduled to leave five days later to act in *Kidnapped*, produced by Francis Ford Coppola and directed by Ivan Passer. I had been over to Ireland the week before to rent a house, and I'd found a perfect one about twenty miles south of Dublin, which just happened to be right next to a stable. I'd made arrangements to train with one of the top event riders in Ireland,

9

who was based there. I was very excited about that. I was going to be riding in the movie, too.

So my plan was to do one more event on my new horse, Eastern Express, nicknamed Buck, whom I'd bought in California during the shoot of *Village of the Damned*. He was a twelve-year-old American Thoroughbred with a lot of experience in combined training—in fact, he and his previous owner had been coached by Brian Sabo. Brian recommended the horse to me, describing him as a fearless jumper in both cross-country and stadium, big enough to carry me, though not a star in dressage. He was a light chestnut gelding with a sweet disposition, easily won over with plenty of carrots and TLC. I tried him out in all three phases at Yves Sauvignon's place, not far from the film location, and we agreed it was a good match. I felt that Denver's tendency to run on the cross-country course and occasionally knock down rails in the show-jumping phase meant I would probably not be able to move him up to the higher levels of competition. But Buck had the experience, a keen attitude, and a lot of mileage left in him.

I brought him back east after I finished the film and worked with Lendon Gray, one of the top dressage coaches in the country, whose barn is near our home in Bedford. (Dana and I left the city in 1992, ostensibly because we didn't want to bring up our new son, Will, in the Flatiron district of New York; but I was especially happy with our decision because it gave me a chance to ride six days a week.) I trained with Lendon during the winter of 1994–95 and did well. Buck's dressage was coming along nicely. I alternated work in the ring with conditioning, walking him up and down hills to

10

strengthen his hind end; he needed a stronger canter. By January I was taking blue ribbons at local dressage shows and getting higher scores than I ever had before. I was very happy with the way the horse was going and the kind of partnership Buck and I were building.

My plan was to spend the '95 season with Buck doing Training Level events and then move up to Preliminary in '96. In Training Level the jumps are never more than three feet six and the combinations are not too difficult, but the Preliminary Level is much more demanding, and you really need a brave and capable horse as well as full-time dedication to the sport. I wanted to be careful, to do everything steadily and safely, but to make progress. Novice Level was no challenge anymore, and Training Level was getting to be pretty easy. But I wanted to make sure I was prepared for Preliminary.

At an event in Massachusetts just a couple of weeks before the accident, Buck was stunning going cross-country. He just ate the course up; he had a ball, and so did I. This was very encouraging to me, because we'd missed some practice and a couple of events in April; once he had a sore back, another time he had an abscess in his foot, which kept me off him for more than ten days just at the time I would ordinarily have been shifting into high gear in preparation for the season. Perhaps I should have seen these as warning signs. But Buck was so talented and seemed to enjoy going cross-country so much and our partnership seemed so solid that I thought we were well enough prepared. Our performance at that event the weekend of May 14 seemed to confirm that all was going well.

In April I had moved to another barn in the Bedford area called Peace and Carrots (a very nice facility even though I couldn't stand the name) and was reunited with my first coach, Bill McGuinness. Most of the barns in the area concentrate on dressage or hunters or jumpers, but Bill ran the only combined training barn and had a group of half a dozen loyal clients, all of whom were as motivated as I was. They had decided to go to Culpeper for the Memorial Day weekend, and Bill invited me to come along to help keep expenses down. I knew from experience it's more fun to compete as a group, so I agreed to go and got an entry in at the last minute. I've since learned that this sort of impulsive decision is typical of many accidents. At the last minute someone decides to get in another car or take an earlier flight. I would have preferred to go to Vermont; our summer house is nearby in Williamstown, and we could have stayed there. I've often thought that if I'd stuck to the original plan nothing bad would have happened. But Dana pointed out that if we'd gone sailing that weekend instead, I could just as easily have been hit in the head by the boom, knocked overboard, and drowned. An accident can happen at any time, even to someone who is cautious and in control.

In the spring of 1995 I remember that Dana and I were very busy doing our own things. Dana, a wonderful singer and actress, had several auditions that she needed to prepare for. I was riding a lot, getting ready for the season, and also involved in helping to rewrite the script for *Kidnapped*. And there were other things—my work for The Creative Coalition (TCC), a public service organization for

12

which I served as copresident, social obligations, personal appearances, and speeches. This weekend was intended to be a family minivacation before going back to work.

The plan was that I would drive down, Buck would go in the big trailer with the other horses, and Dana would take our son, Will, to Washington by train, then rent a car, because we thought he would enjoy the adventure. We stayed at the Holiday Inn not far from the fairgrounds, which had a pool and a sloping grassy area where the three of us could kick around a soccer ball. I arrived ahead of them on Friday in time to practice that afternoon. Dressage and cross-country were going to be on Saturday, and show jumping on Sunday. Buck and I rehearsed the dressage test on Friday afternoon, and it went well. That night we all had an early dinner at the Holiday Inn.

Staying in a motel was a big deal for Will, who was nearly three. He had his own bed and his own room, and he felt very grown-up about it. When he unpacked, he put everything—clothes, shoes, toys—into one dresser drawer. We piled pillows around his bed and kept the door to his room open for safety. Of course, this meant very little privacy for us. Often we were apart on Memorial Day weekends because of our schedules. I think Dana was less than thrilled to spend this holiday watching me compete. She said to me, half-jokingly, 'Next Memorial Day, *I* get to choose what we do.' She was thinking: We really need to spend some time alone together. We'll just get through this weekend and we'll be able to reconnect again.

I got up early on that Saturday morning. My dressage time was 9:08. We did very nicely, though

13

Buck was a little tense. I felt he knew that the cross-country was coming up next, and that's what he loves best, what he was born to do. He could see the other horses warming up to go cross-country. So there was a slightly distracted quality about his dressage, as if he'd been thinking: I've got to go through this and then we get to do the fun stuff.

In spite of that we had a pretty good ride, and at the end of the dressage I was in fourth place out of twenty-seven. That gave me a good chance to move up. Somebody would probably drop a rail in show jumping; each rail means a subtraction of four points. So if you're in the top six after dressage, you're in a good position to win the event. I was happy. I cooled Buck down, put him in his stall, and went back to the Holiday Inn to spend time with Dana and Will, to chill out. At around one I changed into my cross-country equipment and headed back to the fairgrounds.

I went out and walked the course again. I had already done it twice the day before. But I walked it one more time. The first six jumps seemed very easy. Then they became more difficult until the two jumps that worried me, sixteen and seventeen. Sixteen was a water complex, where you had to jump in, change direction, and jump out of the water over a log. Then there would be a long gallop across a field to seventeen, a wide bench between two trees. By the time you got to it you'd be clipping along at a really good pace. Those were the two jumps I was concentrating on.

You walk a cross-country course to decide how you're going to take every jump. You literally write your plan down on a map of the course. You decide: Okay, when I pass that tree I'm going to

14

slow him down. When I pass that second tree there, I'm going to sit up. When I get over that jump, I'm going to look left because I've got a sharp turn to make. You decide where you're going to gallop, where you're going to slow down and show-jump it. You decide how you're going to do every jump, and you write the plan down and study it overnight. The cross-country course opens at 3:00 on Friday, and the ride is on Saturday or Sunday, so you always have time to think things through. Still, I walked the course again to be on the safe side.

When I was plotting my strategy earlier in the day, I certainly wasn't worried about the third fence on the course, which was a zigzag. It was only about three feet three, in the shape of a large W. I was mainly concerned about sixteen, the water jump, because I hadn't taken Buck through much water. And in order to take the big bench at seventeen, we'd really have to have a good rhythm going. But Buck had been so brilliant two weeks earlier that I was feeling quite confident. Plus, I'd recently had a private clinic with Stephen Bradley, one of the top event riders in the country, and that, too, had gone well. He was impressed by my horse and very complimentary about our partnership. Buck and I were really settling into a groove.

When I arrived back at the stables, I ran into John Williams, an Advanced Level rider and trainer and a good friend. He had taken care of Denver when the horse was recovering from a tendon injury in 1993. He had just come over to say hello since he lived nearby. I told him that I liked the course and was glad I'd come to Virginia, that I had a great new horse and was looking forward to a good ride. He wished me luck.

15

From that moment until I regained consciousness several days later in the intensive care unit at the University of Virginia, I have no memory of what occurred.

Later, as I tried to reconstruct the sequence of events, I was told that I finished suiting up, put on my chest protector and helmet, got Buck out of the stall, and headed out for the warm-up area. There were three practice jumps: first a crossrail, then a vertical, then an oxer—two rails with a separation between them. You have to take them all in the same direction, and you always warm up at a hand gallop; you don't trot because you want to let the horse know that now it's time to be aggressive. For vertical jumps you slow down and sit up, but because you're competing against the clock you have to move right along to make the time. Many of the jumps are wide but not very high; they're called fly fences. Those are the ones you take right in stride at a full gallop, staying well off the horse's back so that he can move freely underneath you. I was particularly careful of Buck's back, which was still somewhat tender, probably because I had been working him a little too hard to make up for lost practice time. This high position is easier on the horse but more precarious for the rider, especially a tall one, in case of a sudden stop.

The warm-up went fine. I left the starting box at exactly 3:01. The times are always that precise; another rider goes every two minutes. We made a nice strong start. Witnesses said that Buck was absolutely willing and ready. First jump, no problem. The second jump was a medium-size log pile. No problem. Then we came to the zigzag. The fence judge's report says I was going fast, not

16

excessively fast but moving right along.

Apparently Buck started to jump the fence, but all of a sudden he just put on the brakes. No warning, no hesitation, no sense of anything wrong. The judge reported that there was nothing to suggest Buck was worried about the fence. He just stopped. It was what riders call a dirty stop; it occurs without warning. Someone said that a rabbit ran out and spooked Buck. Someone said it could have been shadows.

When I went over I took the bridle, the bit, the reins, everything off Buck's face. I landed right on my head because my hands were entangled in the bridle and I couldn't get an arm free to break my fall.

I flipped over landing on the other side of the fence. My helmet prevented any brain damage, but the impact of the landing broke my first and second vertebrae. This is called a hangman's injury because it's the kind of break that happens when the trapdoor opens and the noose snaps tight. It was as if I'd been hanged, cut down, and then sent to a hospital. I was heard to say, 'I can't breathe,' and that was it.

Buck probably ducked his head right after he stopped. This often happens; the horse puts his head down because the rider is coming forward and he wants to get away from the weight. As you go over a jump you're supposed to stay in the center of the horse—in fact you should always be in the center of your horse—but if you're both committed to the jump and he suddenly refuses, it's very hard to stop your forward momentum, especially if you're well off his back the way you're supposed to be when you go cross-country. And in order to

17

protect Buck's back, I was actually riding with my stirrups a little higher than usual.

My hands probably got caught in the bridle because I was making every effort to stay on. If you fall off during your cross-country ride, you lose sixty points and have no chance of placing in the competition. If my hands had been free, my guess is that I would have broken a wrist. Or I would have just rolled over, gotten up, cursed quietly to myself, and hopped back on. Instead I came straight down on the top rail of the jump, hyperextended my neck, and slumped down in a heap. Head first, six feet, four inches and 215 pounds of me straight down on the rail. Within seconds I was paralyzed and not breathing.

In many other sports it's essential to be light on your feet. In tennis you can't be flat-footed and move effectively around the court. In skiing your weight is forward, reaching down the fall line. I remember when I was first learning to ski someone told me to try to curl my toes upward inside my boots because that forces your knees and weight forward. If you try to pull away from the mountain, if you raise your shoulders or take your weight off your downhill ski, you're going to slide and fall. The important thing is to stay forward.

Yet in riding, if you get too far forward before the horse leaves the ground you're likely to get into trouble. And that may have been what happened to me over that fence. As you go over a jump, your heels have to be thrust down and your butt should be reaching backwards to keep you in the center of the horse. This position is the opposite of what comes naturally. You have to train yourself to keep your heels down and stay in the middle. 'On your toes' in riding invites disaster.

For more than a year I wondered if my injury was purely an accident, a freakish event, or if I was responsible for what happened to me. Buck had never stopped on a cross-country course before, so what caused him to refuse this easy fence that he could probably have walked over? Rabbit or no rabbit, shadows or no shadows, I think I may have done something to cause the accident, and I have to take responsibility for it.

I often think of my friend Tim Murray, who went sailing one day in November 1994 and drowned. Why? He took the Styrofoam flotation out of his boat because he was working on it. He went out on a windy day with no life preserver, and he and his friend—both expert sailors—raised the spinnaker. Normally this wouldn't present a problem, but two miles offshore waves were building up, it was blowing twenty-five knots, and the boat swamped. The water was forty-eight degrees, and there was no way they could make it to shore. They both drowned, for all those reasons.

My friend Robbie Robertson, an exceptional pilot, won the national championship in soaring. Right after he came home he went gliding at a different airport than usual. It was a very gusty day, and he forgot to tell the tow pilot that he needed to be towed at eighty miles an hour because he was carrying a full load of water ballast in his wings. So he was towed at sixty-five, the normal speed for low-performance canvas gliders, and they ran out of runway. As the tow plane released and climbed away, Robbie tried to pull up. He went up about one hundred feet and stalled. The glider went straight into the ground. He was killed instantly.

So I come back to my own situation, approaching that third jump on May 27. I may have moved forward before I should have, which is an easy mistake to make. On the other hand, that shouldn't have been enough to cause Buck to stop. But I've learned that to speculate endlessly about what happened serves no purpose other than to torment myself. Regardless of exactly what happened, I know now that I can't relive the event forever. If I made a mistake, I've got to forgive myself for being human. I'm in the process of doing that now.

I only fell a few feet, but I shattered my first cervical vertebra as I landed on the top rail of the jump. The second vertebra was also broken, but not so badly. Then I was fighting for air like a drowning person. It's possible that as I twisted my head and fought for air the shards of my first vertebra and the broken part of the second vertebra were cutting and damaging nerves in the spinal cord. I was probably my own worst enemy at that point.

By the time the paramedics arrived at the scene, I hadn't breathed for three minutes. They stabilized my head and managed to keep me alive by squeezing air into my body with an ambu bag. Apparently I was still conscious; later they described me as 'combative.' I'm very lucky they reached me so quickly, because after four minutes of not breathing, brain damage begins. They managed to hold my head still enough to put on a collar that immobilized my neck. After I was loaded into the ambulance, they drove off the field extremely slowly, so that the rough terrain wouldn't cause further damage.

Several months later I called these paramedics and told them how grateful I was that they had saved my life. They were very matter of fact, saying that it was just part of their job. I was deeply moved by their quiet, understated response. In keeping with EMT policy, they never even told me their names.

Dana was always there when I competed, usually stationed at the more difficult jumps. Often she would videotape as much of the ride as possible, and I would spend countless evenings running the film backwards and forwards, looking for ways to improve. But this time she was still back at the Holiday Inn, where Will was having a difficult time waking up from his nap. Suddenly the phone rang. It was Peter Lazar, one of our group, and the first thing he said was, 'Now, don't panic.' Dana asked, 'What happened?' She's a doctor's daughter; in emergencies she is pretty steady. She immediately assumed that I had fallen. There would be no other reason for Peter to call and say, 'Don't panic.' When he said, 'Chris had a spill,' it occurred to Dana that this is the kind of language people use to minimize situations. (Dana's sister once crashed into a tree in a skiing accident, broke her nose, and lacerated her face: her other sister called up and said she'd had a 'skiing mishap.') Then Peter added, 'I don't know why, but they had to take him off the field on a stretcher.'

Dana took Will, who of course did not know what was happening, drove to the Culpeper hospital, and found the emergency room. A nurse came in. Dana said, 'Hi, I'm Dana Reeve. My husband is here.' And the nurse said, 'Oh, okay.' Dana asked, 'Is my husband all right? Is he okay?' The nurse would only say, 'The doctor will be out in a minute.'

21

Dana was beginning to sense that something terrible had happened. She was still very conscious of Will, who went on talking and wanting to play. There was only one other person in the waiting room. It was all quiet and sleepy; the Culpeper facility is a really small place. Then the nurse came back and said, 'The doctor will be right out.' There were the three of them sitting in silence—Dana, Will, and a woman reading a magazine.

Then she saw a helicopter landing in the courtyard, with the name *Pegasus* painted on the side. She thought: That's not for a broken arm.

Two nurses came out and told Dana the doctor wanted to see her in his office. One took one elbow and one took the other, and they walked down the hallway. Dana was carrying Will and thinking: They're holding me up. This is really serious, this is something awful.

Dr. Maloney, the admitting physician at the ER, came into the office and said he was very worried about me. But he didn't tell her I had broken my neck. Will was sitting in Dana's lap, and as Dr. Maloney was giving her the details of my injury, she felt like she was being knocked backwards with each new thing he said: I'd broken the top two cervical vertebrae (C1 and C2), I was having trouble breathing, I was on a respirator. After each new piece of information, Dana took a breath and said, 'Okay, okay, okay.' She felt as if she were being punched repeatedly and had to prepare herself each time for the next blow.

Will was sitting there squeezing Dana's nose with his fingers so that she would say 'beep.' It was one of his favorite games. He did that as Dana was hearing about my injury. She listened, and she kept

22

saying 'beep'—trying to remain the parent in control while receiving the most devastating news of her life.

She was very confused. If I was on a respirator, that meant I was practically dead but they were just keeping me breathing. She knew nothing about broken necks. She didn't understand how it all fit together. She said, 'I have to call my father.' She needed a translation.

Amazingly, Chuck Morosini was at home that holiday weekend. Dana told him, 'Chris has had a serious riding accident. It's a neck injury.' Her father said, 'Oh God.' That was enough. She knew immediately that my life was hanging in the balance. The people at Culpeper said that Dana should see me before the helicopter took off, because it might be for the last time.

Dana had to collect Will, try not to frighten him with what was happening, and check out of the motel. How she got through that afternoon, I have no idea.

She also had to cope with the public. She knew the media would be all over the story, but she didn't want to deal with anybody outside the family. She knew she had to protect Will and to protect me. Her reaction was, 'Everybody out, this is a crisis.' The only way to deal with it was to form a tight circle.

As Dana packed up my belongings, she was acutely conscious that I might never need them again. She collected my shaving things, my socks, and the rest of my clothes. She came across my map of the cross-country course, which I had been studying just a couple of hours before. But she remained composed, putting everything in the

23

suitcase, looking under the bed, in the drawers, finding keys, going through all the ordinary motions of checking out of a motel.

Will wanted to play soccer. He was clearly searching for some normality now that everything had gone haywire. Dana actually went out and kicked the ball with him a couple of times, then came back in and continued packing. 'Mommy has to finish packing. We have to go. They're taking Daddy in the helicopter. We have to go.'

Then they went to the front desk to check out. Earlier that day someone had come by and said, 'The manager would like to have dinner with you and your husband tonight, and we have baby-sitters.' As she turned in our keys, Dana said, 'Could you please tell the manager that we won't be able to have dinner tonight, and thank him very much?' The woman asked, 'Where's your husband?' And Dana said, 'He had to leave.' 'Oh,' said the woman, 'I really wanted a picture. Can I have a picture of you?' So Dana posed. She sat there with Will and posed for a picture because she just didn't want to explain.

Then she and Will drove to the University of Virginia, as I was being flown there in a helicopter named for a flying horse.

CHAPTER TWO

When Dana arrived at UVA, she still had no idea what to expect. In the ER, Dr. Nadkarni, who told her to call him Mo, came in, sat down, and said, 'I have some bad news.' She'd already had so much bad news. She didn't know whether the next thing would be: 'Your husband didn't survive the helicopter trip' or 'He's brain damaged beyond repair.'

He repeated much of what she had heard at Culpeper: I couldn't breathe on my own, I was intubated and on a respirator. But he was the first one who said, 'There's a chance he may never breathe on his own.' Dana said it was like being slammed into a wall. Her whole body and head involuntarily turned to one side, as if she had been struck.

Will was picking all of this up. For a good two weeks afterwards, he would ask Dana repeatedly, 'Why did Mo have bad news?' And she would have to tell him over and over that I had fallen off Buck, my neck was badly injured, and that this meant I couldn't move my body. Hearing this over and over again was part of his attempt to process what had happened. During my first week in the hospital, Will repeatedly reenacted the accident for himself on a hobbyhorse in the playroom of the pediatric wing. Again and again he would deliberately fall off the horse in slow motion, saying, 'Oh, my neck, my neck.' Dana would reassure him that he was fine but that, yes, my neck was injured and I wasn't able to move.

Like everyone else Mo was wonderful with Will. Later he took him to a playroom so that Dana could spend a little time with me before I went in for an MRI. He became friends with Will, and Mo was the first person outside our family that he was willing to stay with.

Dana got Will something to eat, then went back to the emergency room. It was about five-thirty,

25

still light out. Will was very hungry, and Dana was trying to keep him happy while keeping herself from falling apart.

A doctor brought her in to me. I was lying on a gurney, intubated and still unconscious. She met with the chief of neurosurgery, Dr. John Jane, and Dr. Scott Henson, his second-in-command. They told her I was extremely lucky to have survived the accident, that my head was intact, and that my brain stem, so close to the site of the injury, appeared unharmed. If there is damage to the brain stem, your face doesn't work; you can't move your mouth, can't move any of your facial muscles.

I was on morphine and Versed, completely snowed. And whenever I did become conscious for brief moments, all they could do was wash my mouth out with flavored swabs—little pieces of foam on a stick that come in cherry, raspberry, and orange. I wasn't allowed to drink or eat anything during the days before the operation. I would become semiconscious for a short time, not aware of anything much, then drift back under again. All the while Dana was sitting beside me. I felt absolutely nothing. I had no idea of my situation. Even in the brief moments when I was awake, I was still unaware.

After a few days of heavy sedation, I developed what is called ICU psychosis. When sleep patterns are disrupted for long enough, you can become disoriented and slightly psychotic. This is temporary and disappears when the patterns are restored. It has something to do with dark and light, with sleeping in the dark but sensing that you're in the light.

Apparently I would wake up suddenly, still in a

26

sort of dream, imagining wild situations. I would look at Dana and start talking—mouthing, actually, because I couldn't speak—as if we were accomplices, members of a gang. I'd tell her, 'Get the gun.' Dana would ask, 'Get the gun?' and I'd say, 'Yeah, get the gun out of the bag.' I kept saying, 'There's foul play.' 'There's foul play, they're after us.' Dana would ask, 'Who?' and I'd reply, 'The bad guys.' It was like a kids' game with cops-and-robbers talk. But I was clearly feeling persecuted and believing that people were out to get me. For Dana this was chilling. She left my room and told the doctors, 'He's really talking strangely.' They reassured her that there was no head injury. A CAT scan had shown that my brain was fine, and when I came off the drugs the hallucinations would disappear, which they did.

I was extremely lucky to have come under the care of Dr. Jane, a brilliant neurosurgeon and professor of neurosurgery. In addition to being chief of neurosurgery at UVA Hospital, he is chairman of the Department of Neurological Surgery at the University of Virginia Medical School, where he has trained many of the world's leading neurosurgeons and preeminent professors of neurosurgery. His curriculum vitae is roughly the size of a county telephone directory, listing accomplishments that seem too numerous for a single lifetime. In 1993 he was elected president of the Society of Neurological Surgeons and editor of the *Journal of Neurosurgery*; in addition he served a term as director of the American Board of Neurological Surgeons. He has lectured and taught all over the world, from the United States to Taiwan, from Stockholm and Prague to Korea. He

27

has received dozens of awards and grants to investigate cranial injuries and nerve regeneration. The coauthor of several books on the central nervous system, he has also contributed chapters in close to seventy others and published more than 260 articles in prestigious journals. It was just my great good fortune that he was at the hospital when I arrived, that he took control of my care and agreed to operate on me himself.

At the small county hospital in Culpeper, little could be done for me. But fortunately the doctors there had methylprednisolone (MP) on hand and administered it to me immediately. Methylprednisolone is a synthetic steroid, which must be given within eight hours of the injury to have any effect. Doctors discovered in the 1980s that it can help fight the inflammation that occurs immediately after a lesion in the spinal cord. Not only does the victim suffer the damage caused by the initial trauma, but soon afterwards the entire central nervous system starts to fall apart, going down rapidly like a row of dominoes. The inflammation, which in my case extended down to the seventh cervical vertebra, causes the breakdown of fats into unstable compounds called free radicals that are like acid to cell tissues. In other words, healthy nerves below the site of the injury are being eaten alive, causing further loss of sensation and motor function. But in most patients MP can reduce this inflammation by about 20 percent. This 20 percent can mean the difference between patients breathing on their own and spending life hooked up to a ventilator.

This is why being given the MP was so critical. Afterwards the staff at Culpeper could only wait for the medevac helicopter to airlift me to Charlottesville and the intensive care unit at UVA.

As soon as I arrived there, Dr. Jane had me stabilized to prevent any more compression in the spine (a result of having landed straight on my head). Compression causes electrical impulses attempting to travel through the injured area to go haywire, which leads to the death of even more nerve cells. As these cells die another wave of destruction radiates out from the damaged site. Immune cells flood in and, in a frenzied attempt to clear away the accumulated debris, begin to chew up damaged and healthy nerves alike.

So as the victim of a spinal cord injury at the C2 level lies immobilized and unconscious, inflammation is steadily destroying the essential functions of the body: breathing, bladder and bowel control, sexual response, and any motion below the neck. Only the heart and the brain continue to function normally.

Dr. Jane had me placed on a bed and implanted a metal structure into my head just above the temples. Then he attached a heavy weight behind it to keep me immobile. I was hooked up to machines that monitored my heart rate, pulse, blood pressure, and oxygen saturation levels (SATs). I continued to drift in and out of consciousness. Sometimes I would attempt to flail and jerk my head from side to side, and they would have to sedate me even more.

My lungs had begun to fill with fluid, making me highly susceptible to pneumonia. In the past doctors had no way of removing liquid from the lungs, and at this stage a patient usually died. I had pneumonia in one lung, but they managed to clear the infection with powerful antibiotics and by repeated suctioning—an extremely unpleasant experience. They stick a tube into your lungs and suck out the liquid. The tube going down your throat can be very painful, and you're off the ventilator for at least four or five breaths, which can seem like an eternity. I dreaded suctioning more than any other 'care' the entire time I was in the ICU.

After five days I became fully conscious and able to make sense. Henson and Jane came in to explain my situation. They told me in detail about the extent of my injury, and that after the pneumonia cleared from my lungs they would have to operate to reconnect my skull to the top of my spine. They didn't know if the operation would be successful, or even if I could survive it. They had a plan, but it was extremely risky and they needed my consent. Dana had insisted (over the objections of some of the family) that the doctors discuss everything with me personally and that nothing be done without my consent.

I answered somewhat vaguely, 'Okay, whatever you have to do.' Ever since childhood I'd been used to solving my problems. Whatever scrape I would get myself into, I was always sure of a way out. I'd think: I'll get out of this, I'll be okay, everything's fine. I'd survived a lot of difficult situations before, both physically and emotionally.

Once I fell out of a parasail on Martha's Vineyard because my friend who owned the boat and all the equipment probably didn't realize, and certainly didn't tell me, that the harness was certified to carry only up to 180 pounds. As the boat pulled away from the beach and I gained altitude, all four straps slipped through the buckles. I fell about ninety feet into four feet of water. Luckily I had the presence of mind to curl up into a ball and go in sideways, so I wasn't seriously injured. I coughed up a little blood, and the next day one side of my body was black and blue, but I was fine. I've broken an ankle skiing, bruised my ribs playing hockey, and contracted malaria while scouting locations for a film in Kenya. During the shooting of *Street Smart* I had an emergency appendectomy, but I was back on the set the next day. I always recovered quickly from these physical setbacks, and over time I coped successfully with the emotional challenges in my life, such as my parents' divorce, as well.

So at first I thought this was just another temporary problem. I needed some kind of surgery, but I'd be up and around before long. It was only after the doctors left that I really began to absorb what they had told me: This is a spinal cord injury, a paralyzing injury. I had the horrible realization that this was different.

The doctors had explained my condition, and now I understood how serious it was. This was not a C5–C6, which means you're in a wheelchair but you can use your arms and breathe on your own. C1–C2 is about as bad as it gets. Why not die and save everyone a lot of trouble?

Dana came into the room. She stood beside me, and we made eye contact. I mouthed my first lucid words to her: 'Maybe we should let me go.' Dana started crying. She said, 'I am only going to say this once: I will support whatever you want to do, because this is your life, and your decision. But I want you to know that I'll be with you for the long

31

haul, no matter what.' Then she added the words that saved my life: 'You're still you. And I love you.'

If she had looked away or paused or hesitated even slightly, or if I had felt there was a sense of her being—being what?—*noble*, or fulfilling some obligation to me, I don't know if I could have pulled through. Because it had dawned on me that I was going to be a huge burden to everybody, that I had ruined my life and everybody else's. Not fair to anybody. The best thing to do would be to slip away.

But what Dana said made living seem possible, because I felt the depth of her love and commitment. I was even able to make a little joke. I mouthed, 'This is way beyond the marriage vows—in sickness and in health.' And she said, 'I know.' I knew then and there that she was going to be with me forever. My job would be to learn how to cope with this and not be a burden. I would have to find new ways to be productive again.

My two older children—Matthew, fifteen, and Alexandra, eleven—my children with Gae Exton, had come over from England. I had met Gae when I was shooting the first two *Superman* films in London. Although we never married, we had been together for nearly ten years until an amicable split in February 1987. Dana had called them, and all three flew over right away. During the first three days of their visit, all they could do was come into the room and help swab my mouth with sponges or wipe my face with a damp cloth. When I finally regained consciousness, I saw them gathered around me, putting on their bravest faces. And I understood in an instant how much they needed me. In spite of the terrible condition I was in, I

32

could see how glad they were that I was still alive. Despite the ugly equipment that kept me immobilized, each one of them managed to touch me or give me a gentle hug.

At first Will was too terrified to join us in the ICU. He was even afraid of Dana visiting me. It took him several days to overcome that fear. But when he finally did come in and saw that Dad was the same, just lying down, he had a dramatic surge in bravery. It was as if he'd overcome the greatest nightmare of his life.

Soon after, Dana told me about something remarkable. I used to take Will for swimming lessons in Mt. Kisco, just after he turned two. Part of the routine there was that the kids had to jump off the side of the pool into Dad's or Mom's waiting arms. Will was afraid to jump off the side, and I'd have to really coax him to make the leap. I'd have to get closer and closer until he felt safe. But now, right after his visit with me, he was making huge jumps off the side of the pool at the Omni Hotel. He didn't want his water wings anymore, and he dared to go underwater. I watched videotapes of him swimming during that month in Virginia and was amazed to see this new courage.

In the evenings I'd watch the Stanley Cup finals. There was always somebody visiting me, and Dana was just down the hall. Alexandra and Matthew had flown back to London to finish the school year. But now Will would come in and out all the time. I was so grateful that he didn't seem to be uncomfortable or afraid of me. He'd learned all the nurses' names and made himself at home. He'd come in and I'd be connected to all kinds of IVs, tubes, and hoses and things, with a trach, a tracheotomy tube coming out of my throat, like the one I have now. But Will could look past all that and see me, and want to be with me. He would climb up on the bed and get comfortable and we'd watch the hockey games together.

This meant so much. If he'd avoided me or seemed scared or been afraid to touch, I would have felt utterly rejected. But Will's shiny little just-turned-three-year-old face coming through the door to spend time was always a great lift.

I realized: I can't drift away from this. It wouldn't be fair to my family. I *don't* want to leave. This realization, following what Dana had said, ended my thoughts of suicide.

My mother had come down from Princeton and was immediately led into the ICU. She saw me unconscious and immobilized, and was told that I had only a slim chance of survival. She became distraught and began arguing strenuously that the doctors should pull the plug. They told her to calm down, to wait and see what would happen. Of course she didn't want me to die, but she simply could not stand the thought of my living in such a terrible condition. She knew what an active life I'd always led—that for me being active and being alive were the same thing. In the past I would have agreed with her.

She kept insisting on this until a real fight erupted. She spoke to the chaplains in the hospital, and to the doctors. But she avoided confronting Dana, because she knew how strongly Dana felt that it was my decision, mine alone. At one point, in a moment of real despair, my mother told Dana's father, 'Tomorrow, we're going to do it.'

And Chuck Morosini replied, 'Wait a minute. You're not doing anything.'

In my ICU room I was protected from the drama and controversy going on outside. My younger brother, Ben, who had come down from Boston, sided with Dana and Chuck. Together they persuaded my mother to calm down and think things through.

Dana continued to take care of everything. She conferred with my agent, Scott Henderson, and my publicist, Lisa Kasteler, both good friends. She was bombarded by the media, who wanted any scrap of information about my condition. She wasn't ready to face them, so Ben held a short press conference the day after my operation, while Dana contacted more of our friends and relatives all over the country. She did all this on two hours of sleep each night.

How she held everything together during those days, I don't know, but a lot of what she did was for Will's sake. She tried to keep him from seeing the calamity written on everybody's face. Her inner strength and ability to cope with the situation still seem amazing to me. Will's third birthday was on June 7; my operation took place on the sixth. Somehow Dana organized a birthday party for him, with a hired clown and lots of nice people from Virginia who Will had never met before. They had a party and he had fun, he had a good day. Later, when I saw the videotape, I couldn't stop crying. It was excruciating to watch him celebrating without me. He should have been home with all his friends and neighbors and family, the three of us hugging one another as he opened his presents.

The staff and administration at UVA were

unbelievably kind to us. Dr. Jane offered us the use of his house in Charlottesville, and Becky Lewis, the hospital administrator, offered to move out of her apartment. Sometimes when Will came to visit, the nurses would outfit him in little scrubs, let him play with their stethoscopes, and make balloons out of rubber gloves. The staff never lost patience with the endless questions from my family and friends. We had a wing of the hospital all to ourselves and were never charged for the security personnel or the extra rooms. And they provided us with an office, where Dana was set up with phones and a fax machine. We called it the mailroom because it overflowed with thousands of letters pouring in from all over the world. Many boxes of unopened correspondence spilled out into the hallway.

Dana and Will always had plenty of food, a refrigerator full of stuff brought by friends. There was a lounge area, which was great for Will because it had a view of freight trains below and of the medevac helicopter taking off and landing, which he loved. Dana hated it—the sound of *Pegasus* bringing more sick and injured people to the hospital. Another room became Dana's bedroom, while Will slept at a nearby hotel with her parents.

In the days before the operation, I had quite a few visitors. Helen and Chuck Morosini had been the first to arrive. They reached the hospital at nine o'clock Sunday morning, having dropped everything and traveled through the night. Another early visitor was Gregory Mosher, who was producing the film of *American Buffalo* in Rhode Island with Dustin Hoffman. Greg and I had been good friends from my days as an acting student at Juilliard. Over the years we had lost touch, but

36

when he heard about the accident on the radio, he caught the first flight to Virginia. I was surprised and extremely moved.

By then I was on fewer drugs and more able to communicate. My parents, divorced for many years, were both with me. My half brother Jeff Johnson had come down from Vermont. My wonderfully kind aunt, Annie Childs, my father's younger sister, was there. My great-aunt Hellie, still beautiful in her eighties, had come. Scott Henderson was there. Everybody had gathered.

As the day of the operation drew closer, it became more and more painful and frightening to contemplate. In spite of efforts to protect me from the truth, I already knew that I had only a fifty-fifty chance of surviving the surgery. I lay on my back, frozen, unable to avoid thinking the darkest thoughts. Then, at an especially bleak moment, the door flew open and in hurried a squat fellow with a blue scrub hat and a yellow surgical gown and glasses, speaking in a Russian accent. He announced that he was my proctologist, and that he had to examine me immediately. My first reaction was that either I was on way too many drugs or I was in fact brain damaged. But it was Robin Williams. He and his wife, Marsha, had materialized from who knows where. And for the first time since the accident, I laughed. My old friend had helped me know that somehow I was going to be okay.

And then we spent time together. He said he would do anything for me. I thought: My God, not only do I have Dana and my kids but I have friends like Robin and Gregory who truly care. Maybe it can be okay. I mean, life is going to be very different, and it's going to be an enormous challenge, but I can still laugh, and there's still some joy.

One day most of the family was together in the mailroom, busily sorting through stacks of letters. Will was on the floor playing. He looked up and said, 'Mommy, Daddy can't move his arms anymore.' Dana said, 'That's right, Daddy can't move his arms.' 'And Daddy can't run around anymore.' 'That's right; he can't run around anymore.' 'And Daddy can't talk.' 'That's right; he can't talk right now, but he will be able to.' Then Will paused, screwed up his face in concentration, and burst out happily, 'But he can still smile.' Everyone put down what they were doing and just looked at one another.

More family members came down, and more friends. My half brother Mark and his wife, Tracy, from Oregon; my half brother Brock and his wife, Polly, from Massachusetts. Dana's sister Adrienne came from Cape Cod to be with her and help take care of Will. Michael Stutz, my sailing buddy from Martha's Vineyard, made the long trip. Steve Collins and his wife, Faye Grant, brought messages of hope and support from many of my friends in New York. I began to understand that there's so much love around—love waiting to be shown. As a person who tended toward privacy and keeping my feelings to myself, I'm not sure I ever understood that before.

After ten days in intensive care, I was ready for the operation. My lungs had cleared—now I would be able to lie on my stomach for seven hours without choking or suffocating. One of the greatest concerns of the surgical team was how to turn me facedown without doing further damage to my spinal cord. Eventually Dr. Henson held my head and ten people very slowly turned me over. They put me on a table with a cutout for my face. For the next eight hours they patiently worked to put me back together again.

At the time I had no idea that the kind of surgery they would perform on me had never been done before. Dr. Jane had to reattach my head to my spinal column without causing brain damage while giving me the possibility of movement. He placed wires under both laminae—the bony coverings of the spinal cord. He took bone from my hip and squeezed it down to get a solid fit between C1 and C2. Then he put in a titanium pin the shape of a small croquet wicket and fused the sublaminal wires with the first and second vertebrae. Finally, he drilled holes in my skull and passed the wires through to get a solid fusion.

What Jane did, in short, was put my head back on my body. Nearly a year later he visited me in Bedford. I said to him, 'I just have to tell you that while I was in rehab I had time to look at a real skeleton, and at the spine, and I had time to look at anatomy books and read the full discharge report of what you did during the operation. You performed a miracle. I want to thank you for giving me my life.'

I'm glad I didn't know ahead of time what they were doing. As they wired the titanium pin in place, time and time again their tools came within a sixteenth of an inch of the brain stem. But they operated flawlessly. Even now, looking back, I can hardly believe what they accomplished.

When I came out of the surgery, I looked like a

prizefighter whose face had been badly pummeled. I was almost unrecognizable. Few operations are as perilous as those dealing with a C1–C2 injury. Thirty-one pairs of nerves sprout from the spinal cord. Closest to the brain are the eight cervical nerves that process information to the neck, shoulders, arms, and hands. Before the operation I could only move my head, but head-turning muscles are controlled by nerves within the brain, not the spinal cord. A year later I was able to shrug my shoulders and breathe on my own for short periods of time, meaning that nerves at the level of my first, second, and third cervical vertebrae had begun to function again. Most spinal cord patients can expect to 'descend' (to recover function) two levels below their injury.

And that is about where I am now. Movement of my biceps may come if nerves at the fifth cervical vertebra recover, some hand function would come with the sixth, triceps with the seventh, and, with the eighth, more hand functions—those involved in picking up a knife and fork. If nerves at C11 were restored, I could move my torso, and control of the hips and legs would return with recovery of nerves in the five lumbar vertebrae.

But all of this would require tremendous progress in spinal cord research. As of now, no C1–C2 has progressed beyond the C4 level. Without nerves working in the sacral area of the spinal cord, I cannot control bowel or bladder movements and have little sexual function aside from involuntary contractions. Yet I'm very lucky. If the paramedics hadn't arrived so quickly, if I had come to UVA when Dr. Jane was away, if I had had a less brilliant surgeon, if I had gone to compete in

Vermont and suffered the same injury, I would not have survived.

The staff at UVA continued to be extremely attentive to Dana and Will and to me. The nurses were so gentle. I still remember their sweet southern voices, trying to strike the correct balance between being sympathetic and being straightforward. One morning a favorite nurse, Joni, arranged for me to be taken up on the roof of the hospital to watch the sunrise. The orderlies and security people stood back respectfully as Dana and I held hands and watched the sun come up over Charlottesville.

My family began to read me some of the letters that were pouring into the hospital. The accident had been on the news pretty extensively. There were telegrams from heads of state. There was a letter from Bill Clinton.

In fact, the president had called the hospital to speak to Dana and convey best wishes to me. At the time Dana was in the ICU with me and couldn't break away, so she asked if he could call back in five minutes. Then the phone rang—the only one on our floor—and it was my half sister Alison calling from Albuquerque. Dana said, 'Hi, glad you called, but I can't talk now, I'm waiting for the president.' Undaunted, Alya replied, 'Oh, that's great, terrific, so how's Toph—and what's happening? What are the doctors saying?' Dana kept telling her, 'President Clinton is calling.' But Alya was very concerned about me, and wouldn't get off the phone. Five minutes went by, then ten, and the president of the United States couldn't get through. He finally had to give up and get back to running the country.

He ended up writing a letter. Ever since then he and Hillary have stayed in touch with greetings, encouragement, and birthday messages. And whenever we've called the White House, we've had far less trouble getting through than the president did in Virginia.

Greetings came from England, from Australia, from everywhere—from people I'd known since third grade, people I hadn't thought about in years, people I had never realized had any interest in me. Eventually we received over 400,000 letters. People are amazingly kind.

I was particularly grateful to my aunt Annie. After the operation, I was losing weight fairly rapidly. I had no appetite, but I really needed to eat. I'd had nothing but flavored swabs, and now I needed something more. Since my arrival at the hospital, I had lost nearly fifteen pounds. A test to see if my swallowing mechanism worked showed that it did. I was able to eat, but the hospital food was too unappealing.

Annie and Faye Grant arranged with a local restaurant to prepare whatever I wanted. The chef couldn't have been more accommodating, promising, 'I'll stay late, I'll come in early, I'll cook him anything.' He wouldn't let us pay for any of it either; he just wanted to give something. Annie and Faye would come back with a piece of fish or a dish of pasta—food that I could tolerate—and Annie would feed me.

It took a while to get used to the idea of being fed. It's very, very hard not to feed yourself. You begin to realize how much you have to depend on other people—when you want a sip of water, when you need to scratch your nose, everything. It takes time, even though everybody is so willing to help.

So Annie would feed me, and everyone took turns reading me the mail. There was a genuine outpouring of concern and, more than that, of real affection coming from very unexpected places. And it buoyed me up. I would get through the day carried by those letters and that love.

A security guard was stationed outside the wing. And there was always somebody sitting outside the double doors that separated the wing from the rest of the floor. Dana would wait for Will to fall asleep at the hotel and then come stay with me in the ICU. She talked to me and sang to me, even though I was often sedated. She sang all the songs that we used to sing together as a family: 'This Pretty Planet' and 'Home on the Range' and 'Red River Valley.' Will and I used to sit at the piano singing and playing, and Dana would come in with that beautifully clear voice of hers and sing harmony. We had always loved making music together.

Dana had very little privacy; she constantly had to deal with friends, family, and the media, still there in force. She answered all the phone calls from friends. The day after the accident there were thirty-five messages on the machine at home. She called our business manager to make sure that all of our wills and finances and insurance were in order. We had just done a lot of insurance work, including getting a disability plan, which was to prove very helpful because it provided some cash every month. We had no idea yet what insurance problems lay ahead. Dana took care of hundreds of details while we all waited to see what would happen next.

43

As I was recovering from the operation, Dr. Jane and his team came in to assess my condition, to find out what sensations and function I was left with. They pricked me with a safety pin to test for possible motor response, and brushed me with a Q-tip to evaluate sensation. These tests helped them determine what my prognosis was likely to be.

Some doctors believe that what you come out with after the operation basically remains your condition for the rest of your life. Others say that you can get recovery six months down the line, a year down the line, eighteen months down the line. One surgeon told me that five years after the operation, one of his patients suddenly could move his foot. The spinal cord is such a strange and unpredictable thing, and people's responses are so unique, that two individuals with the same injury can have entirely different results. I heard about two patients in the same room at the same hospital with the same injury. One ended up walking, the other did not. The person relating the story concluded that one patient had more faith than the other. It's tempting to believe that, and I do think a positive attitude helps tremendously. But I don't believe that faith alone can put a broken spinal cord back together again.

Dr. Jane is a very kind man, practically central casting's idea of a doctor. He's in his sixties and sort of stocky, with a gentle face, warm and modest about his skills. And he was extremely caring, but perhaps he tried to protect me too much.

I got the feeling that he so wanted me to be well, to be better off than I was, that whenever he came to talk to me after the operation, he would sugarcoat the situation a bit. He said that I was

44

incomplete, that I would probably descend a couple of levels. He said there was a very good chance I could get off the vent, because the phrenic nerve (which controls the impulse to breathe) was intact and the diaphragm hadn't been damaged. I felt uplifted by all this, especially when he told me that I only had a hemorrhage in my spinal column at C2, just in the left half of the spine. There was swelling, which was to be expected, down to the C6-C7 level, but as it went down and the hemorrhage cleared up, I could get significant return of sensation and function.

A C2 incomplete means that the spinal cord is still intact, and one might have more recovery over time. Complete means there will be no further recovery because the spinal cord has been transected or so badly damaged that there is no hope for repair. At C2 you can move your head and you can talk; at C3 you can breathe a little bit; at C4 you can breathe normally; at C5 you gain some use of your arms; at C6 you might begin to get use of your hands. So when someone injures their spinal cord, the first question is: What level? Because this will give you an idea what their future is. You will know what kind of chair they're going to be in, whether they're going to be on a vent or not. When I heard about Travis Roy, the Boston University hockey player who injured his spinal cord in a game, my first question was: What level? And when I heard that he was a C4, I thought: Great, he's going to breathe. The definition of complete and incomplete had changed at a medical convention in 1992. Until then, if your spinal cord wasn't severed, you were considered incomplete. But since the convention a spinal cord injury is only termed incomplete if the patient has sensation at the very base of the spine. I had none.

Nevertheless, Dr. Jane continued to see the glass as at least half full. He kept coming into my room with good news. 'You're doing great. You're going to get more recovery. You'll get off the respirator. You've got some movement in your trapezius now. It won't be long before you'll get deltoids, and then you'll be using your arms.' And so forth. I began to suspect that Dr. Jane simply wanted us both to feel better.

Then one night an intern came in, to check on me. We got to talking and I asked, 'So what about this bleeding that's been in my spine? After that goes down, there'll be a return of sensation, right?' And she said, 'You don't have any bleeding in your cord. You hardly bled at all.' I was shocked and upset. But when I questioned Dr. Jane the next day, he was annoyed. 'Are you going to listen to an intern, or are you going to listen to me?'

My spirits during those days were on a roller coaster ride. There were moments when I would feel so grateful—when a friend would come a long way to be with me, to talk to me, to cheer me up. And my family, of course, and the letters still pouring in. I used to love to listen to the people in the letters.

But the time would come when everybody would have to go. I'd be given a sleeping pill at about ten-thirty or eleven o'clock, but by one or two it would wear off. I'd wake up and be staring at everything, staring at the wall, staring at myself, staring at the future, staring in disbelief.

The thought that kept going through my mind was: I've ruined my life. I've ruined my life, and

46

you only get one. You can't say, 'I've spoiled this one, so can I have another one, please?' There's no counter you can go up to and say, 'I dropped my ice cream cone; could I please have another one?' I thought, I've ruined not only my own life but everybody else's as well. I've ruined Dana's life, I've ruined Will's life, I've ruined Matthew's and Alexandra's. This is going to be a huge burden on everybody. It's not *my* injury, it's *our* injury. Our entire family is hurt. We've all been destroyed by this stupid thing that happened. Over a nothing jump. For some reason, I didn't get my hands down and break my fall. I'm an idiot. I've spoiled everything. Why can't there be an appeal? Why isn't there a higher authority you can go to and say, 'Wait a minute, you didn't mean for this to happen to *me*. This kind of thing doesn't happen to *me*.'

I was still in a state of disbelief and very afraid. A large part of the fear was because I couldn't take a single breath on my own. And the connections of the hoses on these ventilators are tenuous at best. The nurses put tape over the joints, but they don't always hold very well, and you lie there at three in the morning in fear of a pop-off, when the hose just comes off the ventilator. I had several. After you've missed two breaths, an alarm sounds. You just have to hope that someone will come very quickly, turn on the lights, figure out where the break is, and put it back together. But it's not like holding your breath underwater. I can't hold my breath. In my case, there's no breath left in my body. When I exhale, the breath is gone.

So when you have a pop-off, there is no air in your lungs except for a tiny amount in the nooks and crannies. If you're pretty healthy, the percentage of oxygen that is getting to your brain can probably stay in the seventies, which means you can last a couple of minutes, but those are very, very anxious minutes. The nurses' station was not far away, but I was never sure how closely they were paying attention. They had many patients, I was alone in my room, and I had absolutely no control. The feeling of helplessness was hard to take.

Becoming completely dependent on other people is a terrible adjustment to make. I lay there for a month floating among various moods and feelings—gratitude, horror, self-pity, confusion, anger. There was one doctor at UVA who was the bane of my existence. She came in at all hours of the day and night to poke and prod, and I realized I didn't have any sensation below the trapezius level, just outside my neck muscles. She would also talk to me as if I were three. Finally, I couldn't stand it anymore. I yelled, 'Fuck you, I'm a forty-two-year-old man. You treat me like one or don't come in this room again.' That chastened her a little bit. I know she intended no harm or discomfort, but she increased my feelings of despair and loss, humiliation and embarrassment.

I know it may seem odd that I felt humiliation and embarrassment. But those are the emotions I tend to feel whenever something goes seriously wrong in my life. On my first flight across the Atlantic, I was given an incorrect ground speed readout by a radar controller in Greenland. He had misread the data on his screen. But the professional tone of his voice was completely convincing, and I never thought to question him. If his information had been accurate, I would have run out of fuel 200 miles west of Iceland and crash-landed in the ocean at night. That would have been the end. I expected to die, and my first thought was: I've done something stupid, and it will be really inconvenient for people.

The same thought occurred when this injury happened: 'How embarrassing.' Back in the *Superman* years, I always used to joke about needing to be very careful because I didn't want to read a headline in the *New York Post* like '*Superman* Hit by Bus.' This accident was humiliating and embarrassing. How could I have let it happen?

So now I felt embarrassed because my body was failing. The doctors would poke and prod, but I already knew the facts. All they could do was make me feel worse.

And then my stepmother, Helen, came in. She is always well meaning, and I love her very much. But she showed me a letter from somebody who had a high-level injury like mine and was writing about things he'd been able to do; that he really liked his wheelchair and really liked his van, and that he could go for fifteen hours on his ventilator without recharging. In an unintentionally patronizing tone, she said, 'You see, there are still lots of options open to you, so many things you can do.' I lost my temper and asked her to leave the room. I just wasn't ready to hear that. I hadn't accepted that I was a quadriplegic. I was still in denial, still thinking, There's been a big mistake here. Any minute someone's going to come in and say, 'Sorry, wrong person; they meant somebody down the hall. It's not you, you're free to go.'

So sometimes having relatives come to visit was hard on me, and other times it was great. Often I was angry because a few of them were talking to the press without consulting me first. There was some disagreement about what to do next, about where I should go for rehabilitation. It was a hugely stressful time. I had to get used to so many new and unpleasant things.

There were physical therapists in the ICU. About a week after the surgery, they began to move my head a little bit with isometric pressure, even though I was still in a collar all the time. And then there was the ordeal of getting up. I had to wear special stockings, called T.E.D.s. They come up over your knees, like support hose. I hated them. I thought: Old ladies wear those things. Again: This can't be me. Then Ace bandages over the T.E.D.s, and a binder around my waist. They would slide me into a wheelchair and sit me up very slowly, taking my blood pressure the whole time, because as I sat up my body was too weak to force the blood back up into the heart. Then I'd be wheeled down the hall to the mailroom or a little visiting room that they had set up. I could look out the window at the trees, a nice change of view from the rooftops I could see from my room.

The days were tolerable, but the nights were still awful. The demons kept coming after me. I would torment myself, my head full of fear and self-recrimination. I never called a nurse in just to say, 'I'm lonely and I'm upset.' I didn't know how to do that. I assumed they had other, more important things to do. As I lay there I often remembered going to a state fair in New Jersey when I was a child. One of the main attractions was 'The Man in the Box.' He had been placed in a wooden box and buried six feet in the ground with a tube coming up to the surface so he could breathe. For the price of admission you could look down at him through a little glass window. All you could see was his face. His eyes staring back at you and occasionally blinking were the only signs that he was alive. As you left the exhibit you could put your name and address on a card and place a bet as to how long he could stay down there.

When I would finally fall asleep, I'd be whole again. I'd go off and do wonderful things. I'd be riding again, or I'd be with Dana and Will, or I'd be in Maine, or I'd be acting in a play. Then suddenly I would wake up and look at the upper-right-hand corner of my room and see the screen with all my vital signs going across it—my heart rate, my blood pressure, my oxygen SATs. And I'm lying there all too alert, just staring at the numbers on this screen. Little purple beeps going along. A little blue graph shifting underneath it. Very pretty colors. And I'm thinking: I'm tied to all of this, and I can't get free. I'm tied. I'm grounded. I won't be able to fly, won't be able to sail, won't be able to ride, won't be able to ski, won't be able to make love to Dana, won't be able to throw a ball to Will, won't be able to do a fucking thing. I'm just taking up space.

It's three in the morning and there's no help. A nurse enters. Oh, here comes somebody to suction me. Now I've got to go through that pain again as they try to take more water out of my lungs. Well, at least that's going to allow another twenty minutes to pass. Sometime, somehow, morning is going to come. No, it's never going to come. It's still only 4:15. Why is there a clock on the wall? They should take the clock out of here. Time doesn't mean anything. It only measures the intervals between suctioning and being turned so my skin won't break down. I don't want to watch TV, there's nothing on TV, I'm not going to spend my time watching some stupid movie at four in the morning, especially if I'm in it.

And my eyes. I was afraid to have the bed turned away from the monitor with the heart rate and the SATs on it. I became terrified if I went below about 97 percent. I thought: Oh no, the SATs are going to drop, I won't be able to breathe, I'm going to die. They won't come in here and fix me, they won't be able to do anything for me. They're just humoring me. My thoughts would get more and more paranoid and out of control.

When I was a kid my great heroes were Harry Houdini and Charles Lindbergh. Lindbergh because he did something against overwhelming odds: On a couple of tuna sandwiches and sheer determination, he flew for thirty-three hours across the ocean. Imagine staying awake and flying an airplane nonstop for thirty-three hours. My grandmother had been staying with the Annenbergs in Paris for a year abroad in 1927, and she rode with them out to Le Bourget and brought Lindbergh back to the house. She had seen Lindbergh, she had touched him. I'd always thought: God, there's a hero, there's somebody who can do it. He beat the limitations of the body, the vagaries of the weather. He got out of a difficult situation, he pulled it off.

And Harry Houdini. You put him in a straitjacket and he could contort his shoulders and get out of it. In the middle of the night, sometimes at three in the morning, I'd think, I'm in a straitjacket, my whole body's in a straitjacket, I

52

can't move anything. I can't contort my shoulders. This isn't a trick, there's nothing I can do, there's no key, nothing I can do with my body. I'm just lying here in this bed staring at the monitor.

I'd try to go back to sleep, but it wouldn't work, and I'd start to think again, the same tormenting thoughts. It always began with: This can't be me. Then it went to: Why me? Then to: There's got to be a mistake. Then finally: Oh God, I'm trapped, I'm in prison. I've got a life sentence here. I'm stuck, I'm never going to get out of this. I'm not going to survive. I can't do this and I can't do that. I can't stand up, can't move. I'm pathetic. What am I going to do with myself? I'm forty-two. I've got no life. I'm just going to be a charity case. Into my head came the desperate plea: Somebody, please, let me out. Just let me out.

I mentioned that a C1–C2 injury is like being hanged. And I remember thinking that if you survive, they let you go. They only try once; they don't pick you up off the ground and carry you back up and retie the noose. These melodramatic thoughts would play on me. My mind would race through all kinds of absurd scenes and ideas. It would have been nice if I could have used those hours between 2:00 and 7:00 A.M. productively, but I couldn't. I was barely coping. I tried to focus on all the love and support that was coming to me. But much of the time I thought to myself: I don't care if anybody likes me or doesn't like me. I want to walk. I'll trade all this affection just to walk up a flight of stairs. The body and mind, in trying to survive, can be totally selfish. You say, Screw the rest of the world, take care of *me*. Me first. This is not fair to *me*, you know.

53

I think these selfish thoughts are part of the survival mechanism. That 'me-me-me' is an inevitable first response. And then you need to evolve to higher thoughts—a different way of thinking. For some people this comes through religion; they're able to subsume the self into their faith. But that didn't work for me, although I tried. I'm not a religious person, but I thought: I have to develop a relationship with God right now, otherwise I'm lost. There were some nights when I would pray, but I felt like a terrible phony. I felt that I was performing, that it wasn't really coming from the center of my being, from a genuine place. My friend Bobby Kennedy once said to me, 'Just fake it till you make it. The prayers will seem phony, but one day they'll become real, and your faith will become real.' But something different happened to me. I began to think: Whether or not there is a God is not so important. Spirituality itself, the belief that there is something greater than ourselves, is enough.

Dana was going through the same process. She had been raised as a Catholic but found she could not accept formal religion. After my injury she read *When Bad Things Happen to Good People*, written by Rabbi Harold Kushner, a man whose son had progeria, a terrible disease in which the victim ages rapidly and dies in adolescence. Here was a man of God, who served God, and who couldn't reconcile the fact that this could happen to him. But he finally reached a conclusion that both Dana and I could accept—that God doesn't make these things happen. We were given free will, and everything obeys the laws of nature. If you are flung over a horse's head, you very well might break your neck.

It just happens. But where God comes in, where grace enters, is in the strength you find to deal with it. You may not know where it comes from, but there's an enormous power at work.

And so you may find that you try to behave in the best manner you possibly can, the most loving way you can manage at any given moment. I think that old adage 'God is love' is literally true, whether or not you actually believe in God. Thinking that way helped me get past the 'me-me-me'—my body, my problems, my condition, myself.

Three weeks after the operation it was time to think about rehab. I had to pick a place. People had told me—and I felt this was right—that the rehab facility is important, but that it's even more important to be near people you care about, friends and family. This pointed to the Kessler Institute for Rehabilitation in West Orange, New Jersey. Most of my family lives within a reasonable distance from there. My mother's in Princeton. Dana and Will were in Bedford, only an hour away. Almost everybody else in my family lives in New England, except for my half brother Mark, who lives in Oregon, and my half sister Alya in New Mexico.

One day in late June Dr. Marcalee Sipski, the director of the spinal cord unit at Kessler, came down to UVA with a pulmonologist, Dr. Doug Green, to see if I was ready for rehab. Dr. Sipski used her safety pin and prodded around, but I had very little feeling anywhere. I could feel along my shoulders, but that was about it. I had a little feeling in the bottom of my left foot; when somebody would do deep massage on my left foot, I could feel it. Otherwise, nothing. I really couldn't feel anything below my shoulder blades.

And then Dr. Sipski said, 'I need to see whether you're complete or incomplete.' So that issue resurfaced; it had never actually been resolved. I told her that I had been classified as incomplete, but she replied that she needed to do her own assessment. She inserted a rectal tube, but I didn't even feel it. I felt absolutely nothing. Then she made the pronouncement, 'Well, you're a C2 complete.' This was devastating to me. How could Dr. Jane and the people at UVA have kept telling me I was incomplete, and I was going to descend to C4, and I would get off the vent, and my phrenic nerve was working? Yes, it is working, I thought, but it's not doing anything. It may be intact, but it's not working. Intact and working are two different concepts.

Again I plummeted. I felt such loss, such confusion, such a sense of doom. The demons continued to attack—thoughts of hopelessness and despair and being in a straitjacket and not being Harry Houdini, not being a magician who could get out of it. They came at me more ferociously than ever. I felt I'd been betrayed. All these nice people with their gentle southern voices had been torturing me with lies. Sometimes I even thought that it wasn't worth going to rehab. I should just be parked someplace. If anyone wanted to talk to me, they would know where to find me, because I would be living out my days staring out the window.

So it went. Fearful thoughts, serene thoughts, spiritual thoughts, morbid, self-pitying, pathetic thoughts. After Dr. Sipski spoke to me, I felt the truth had been told. Why did everyone else keep lying? Did they think I couldn't handle the truth?

56

Or was it just too personally painful to them to face the fact that I was a C2 complete? I couldn't figure it out, couldn't understand it. But Dr. Jane stuck to his position. He kept coming into the room, always with that sunny disposition, and he'd pat me on the shoulder and say, 'I think you're going to get some deltoid soon. And if you can get your deltoid muscles back, you can begin to move your arm. It's also a sign that you've got some C4, you'll be able to breathe.' And I would just look at him but couldn't confront him. Somebody of his standing and reputation. I was in a quandary.

The letters began to mean more than ever. One came from Deborah Huntington, who was our neighbor when we were growing up in Princeton. Because there weren't enough boys in the neighborhood, we recruited Deborah and her sisters to play baseball with us. She wrote me a five-page letter about those times—remembering me making spectacular catches in the outfield, often hitting the ball over the fence into the neighbors' yard. She recalled that she held me in a certain kind of awe in those days, casting me as a sort of neighborhood hero.

I would get letters from fellow students at Cornell, or a letter from a former schoolmate at Juilliard. There were many letters from people who were spinal cord injured, telling me to fight on. I received a long, compassionate letter from a woman who said she could identify with me completely because for many years she had suffered from chronic indigestion. There were letters from people telling me about a favorite moment in a movie or play. People recalled having seen me on the stage in Williamstown or on

Broadway. They were a lifeline, those letters. I needed support, I needed something positive. I would tell Dana, 'Read me another one, take me somewhere. Let me go back in time, let me go back and relive those moments when I could do things.'

And there were letters that said, 'You're going to go through a very morbid, self-pitying stage. But stay with it, you'll come out the other side. You'll find that a life is possible.' I couldn't believe it, especially after Dr. Sipski had been there and I'd learned about the new definition of complete. Her parting words had been: 'We'll do what we can for you.' All I had to look forward to was learning how to operate a wheelchair with my mouth. And maybe learning how to use a computer with my voice.

But slowly I began to come up again, as one does from a dive in deep water. I gradually stopped wondering, What life do I have? and began to consider, What life can I build? Is there a way to be useful, maybe to other people in my predicament? Is there a way to be creative again? A way to get back to work? Most of all, is there a way to be there for Dana and Will and Matthew and Alexandra, to be a husband and father again? No answers came, but raising the questions helped.

There was one strong image I would cling to when I was alone. Someone, a stranger, had sent me a picture postcard of a Mayan temple in Mexico, the Pyramid of Quetzalcoatl. There were hundreds of steps leading up to the top. And above the temple were blue sky and clouds. I taped this postcard to the bottom of the monitor, where it was always in view. I let it become a metaphor for the future. Even as I watched all those sobering numbers on the screen, I began to imagine myself climbing those steps, one at a time, until finally I would reach the top and go into the sky.

CHAPTER THREE

When Dana said, 'You're still you, and I love you,' it meant more to me than just a personal declaration of faith and commitment. In a sense it was an affirmation that marriage and family stood at the center of everything, and if both were intact, so was your universe. Many people have known this all their lives. I did not. Up to the time I met Dana—from early childhood until I was nearly forty—I didn't believe in marriage, although I had always yearned for a family. The idea of home was confusing to me, too, because I had grown up between two families, and neither one ever seemed truly secure. This contributed to my developing a fierce independence, which had many positive aspects. But a part of me always looked longingly at other families, where there was communication, respect, and unconditional love, which provided a solid foundation for the children as they grew up.

I was born on September 25, 1952, at Lenox Hill Hospital in New York City. My father, the poet and scholar Franklin d'Olier Reeve, was a graduate student at Columbia, working on a master's degree in Russian. My mother, Barbara Pitney Lamb, had been a student at Vassar, but just before they were married, in November 1951, she transferred to Barnard. At first they lived downtown on Prince Street, and my father would take the subway up to

59

Columbia every day, but soon they moved to a ground-floor apartment on East Eighty-eighth Street near the East River. Our building was near Gracie Mansion and a fireboat station. I rode a little fire truck around in the courtyard in the back, pushing the pedals and ringing the bell. I remember bumping along in my stroller as we headed off to Carl Schurz Park to watch the boats at the fire station.

My brother, Benjamin, was born on October 6, 1953, so we are only a year and eleven days apart. My father and his younger brother, Richard, had a similar separation in age, and similar problems: in both cases the older one usually got the first crack at everything and was often preferred. When we were very young our parents used to dress us alike. Later I often joked that the only way you could tell us apart was that I had the blue mittens and Ben had the red ones. I think today most parents are much more conscious of the need to allow each child to establish his own identity. But in the early fifties there was still a tendency to lump siblings together—particularly twins or children close in age. We were often referred to as Tophy and Beejy. I remember wanting to separate myself quite early on, and I think Ben did, too.

My parents' romance began during the Christmas holidays in 1950, when he was at Columbia and she was still at Vassar. They met because of an unusual family connection. Mahlon Pitney was my mother's uncle, and he married my father's mother, Anne d'Olier Reeve, after her divorce from Richard Reeve, Sr. My mother and her parents, Horace and Beatrice Lamb, were invited to Mahlon and Anne's house on a hilltop in

60

Basking Ridge, New Jersey. My mother had not been particularly interested in going until Horace told her that Anne had two sons, Franklin and Richard Reeve, Jr., who were both bright, handsome college students.

She was immediately taken with Franklin. As they were decorating the Christmas tree in the great family room, Franklin pulled a Styrofoam ball off a branch and teasingly threw it at my mother, who quickly grabbed another one and threw it back at him. A playful indoor snowball fight ensued. They spent most of the family holiday together, and no sooner had she returned to Vassar than my father called and asked to come visit her the following weekend. She was both excited and taken aback by the intensity of Franklin's interest in her. But this was a part of his character, which I think I inherited: the single-minded pursuit of a particular objective. My father was a real romantic in those days, prone to strong passions, whether in politics, ideals, or love. Whatever captured his interest became all consuming, at least for a time. He courted my mother ardently, driving up from Columbia almost every weekend. They took long walks by the Hudson and lingered in coffee shops near the campus. Soon her mailbox was filled with stories, poems, and love letters.

In the summer of 1951 my mother went to Europe with several of her college classmates. My father wanted very much to come along on this trip, but Horace and Beatrice strongly objected. I think they felt their daughter was too young for such an intense romance. So instead Franklin spent the summer working on the docks on the West Side waterfront, 'shaping up' every morning with the longshoremen, waiting to be chosen to unload banana boats. From this experience he developed an interest in the labor movement and socialism.

Franklin had come from a prominent Mainline Philadelphia family. His grandfather, Col. Richard d'Olier, was the CEO of the Prudential Insurance Company for more than twenty-five years. Money was never an issue; all his heirs attended the best prep schools and colleges in the East. On the other hand, Horace Lamb had come from a working-class family in Sandusky, Ohio, won a scholarship to Cornell, and eventually become the senior partner in one of New York's most prestigious law firms, with homes on Sutton Place and in New Canaan, Connecticut—virtually the definition of a self-made man. I think he resented the idea of my father, a rich young Princeton graduate, transforming himself into a 'workingman.'

In spite of the long hours on the docks, Franklin always found time to send passionate letters to various American Express offices in Europe, keeping up with my mother's itinerary. When her ship docked in New York in early September, my father greeted her on the pier with an engagement ring. Over my grandfather's objections they were married at the Presbyterian church in New Canaan on November 23, 1951. She was nineteen and Franklin was twenty-three.

But a widening gulf was developing between my parents when I was born. Franklin was beginning to turn away from his privileged background and to become more involved in his new interests—socialism and Russian language and literature. Coming from New Canaan, used to a privileged society, my mother still had a limited and rarefied

62

view of the world, and she lacked confidence in herself. When she was eighteen she had an old-fashioned coming out party in New York. But afterwards the phone did not ring and no eligible bachelors appeared at the door. I once asked her what that was like, and she said, 'Well, I came out, but I went right back in again.'

She was very pretty. In the pictures of her when she was young, she is a knockout. But when she was still in her early teens she was sent to an all-girls boarding school in Arizona because of her asthma. Then she came back east and graduated from Westover, another girls' school, in 1949. She had never had a boyfriend or even dated, so Franklin probably seemed too good to be true. He was extremely handsome, bright, funny, and charming. He was a scholar, a poet, an athlete (he set a record in the hammer throw at Princeton that lasted for decades). He was also something of an actor, having written and performed with the University Players.

Everything changed for my mother that Christmas of 1950, when she suddenly found herself in a whirlwind romance with an extraordinary young man. She got married less than a year later, became pregnant at nineteen and a half, had a baby at twenty, then gradually discovered that she was married to someone who was going off more and more in his own direction. His romantic interest in her was gradually being replaced by an equally romantic interest in his work and colleagues at Columbia. My mother was never an intellectual, and before long they had little to talk about. The atmosphere in our home became increasingly tense.

It must have been overwhelming for my mother to have to cope with two rambunctious boys at such a young age. Ben and I were usually going at each other, competing for attention and space. My father was devoted to both of us and enjoyed taking on much of our daily care. I think he even felt he could do a better job than my mother. But as my parents drifted apart, my mother had to take more responsibility. On some deep level I wished she were more confident and able to take control of us.

When she was a young mother, she loved us very much, but she let people push her around, including me. I'm more ashamed now of having taken advantage of her than I was at the time, but then I was always testing her. I wanted her to say, 'No, you can't get away with that.' I needed boundaries. Now I realize how young and frightened she must have been when her marriage to Franklin broke up.

My strongest memory of that New York apartment was the day we left it. A moving van pulled up in front of the building. This was a cause of great excitement for a three-year-old because the van was so huge. I remember running around inside it while they were loading the furniture, the clothes, and the bric-a-brac. I was only dimly aware that we were moving because the marriage was over.

We went to Princeton because my mother really didn't know where else to go. There she had friends from the days when she and Franklin were dating. We had half a house at 66 Wiggins Street and settled in on New Year's Eve 1955. Horace paid the bills. My brother and I went to the Nassau

Street School, just up the block. I was very happy there. We had to wear nice brown shoes every day. The minute I came home I would go upstairs to change so I wouldn't get them dirty playing.

At first Ben and I visited Franklin on a fairly regular basis, but gradually that tailed off. We were supposed to spend six weeks with him every summer, as well as alternate weekends and holidays, but it didn't work out that way. Within a year of the divorce the particulars of the court settlement became increasingly irrelevant.

In the early years he had changed our diapers, fed us, taken us for walks, and felt extremely proud of us. But when we ended up in Princeton, and especially when my mother married Tristam Johnson, a stockbroker and a Republican, Franklin had a harder time relating to us. After getting his Ph.D. in Russian, my father had applied for a teaching job at Princeton in order to be near us. But friends of my mother who had influence with the president of the university blocked the appointment, accusing him of being a Communist. This turned out to have a lasting impact on our relationship, because it meant he couldn't see us as much as he wanted to or be as involved in our development. In 1956 he married my stepmother, Helen Schmidinger, a fellow graduate student at Columbia, and in February of that year they had their first child, my half sister Alya (of the famous President Clinton phone call). Two sons, Brock and Mark, soon followed. After the rejection by Princeton, I think Franklin was bitter and disappointed. He realized that Tris would become a more prominent figure in our lives, and that he would be far less of an influence on Ben and me.

While the door was still open for visits, he turned his attention to his new wife and family.

I remember my father in the late fifties and early sixties as being both magnetic and unpredictable. Much of the time Ben and I basked in the glow of his interest and praise. He taught us to ski and played tennis with us patiently in the park. We used to lie down on gratings in the sidewalk and watch the subway trains roar by beneath us. I loved the trips back to Princeton in his red Volkswagen Beetle. It didn't have a gas gauge, so my father would write down the mileage at each fill-up, and we would take turns guessing how far we could go before the next one. He always turned off the engine when he went downhill to save gas and would never take the New Jersey Turnpike because he could save eighty-five cents by taking Route 1. When we stayed with him we bought root beer to have after our naps and often had a glass of ginger ale in the evening, joining the grown-ups for 'cocktails.'

But then there would be unexpected moments of remoteness or rejection, when it seemed impossible to figure out how to get back in good standing. Later, as my independence grew and I headed toward a life in the public eye that neither of my parents could control, our relationship became increasingly complex. Once during my freshman year at Cornell, I drove over to his house in Connecticut for the weekend. He was very distant, and I had to spend most of the time talking with my stepmother. Then, at one point, I abruptly asked him, 'Do you care? Do you care what happens to me?' And he said, 'Frankly, Toph, less and less.' It was a pretty honest thing to say, it was certainly what I was experiencing, but that's something you never forget.

But I adored my father, and he did have a strong influence on me. I think, for example, that this is one of the reasons I am not religious. I went to the Presbyterian church in Princeton, mainly because I liked to sing in the choir. (I was bothered by the hymns, though: so many lyrics are about God the Father Almighty and the vengeance of his terrible swift sword. The image of a vengeful father who sits in judgment was disturbing to me. But the pleasure of flirting with sopranos and altos made going to church quite enjoyable.) Franklin avoided churches and had no use for religion. When he drove us home or to the train station on a Sunday, he would make disparaging comments about the people coming out of services. He used to call them sheep, and of course I would instantly agree.

My father had a unique ability to give instruction in activities that he couldn't actually do himself, and that included riding. I was allergic to horses as a kid and couldn't get near one without wheezing. But I remember visits to a stable in Portland, Connecticut, and watching Alya and Brock take riding lessons. My father would stand at the ringside and quietly advise, 'heels down,' 'sit up straight,' 'hands together,' 'thumbs forward' as they passed by. He was not a rider himself, but he was born to teach.

Yet he could be so much fun. Pa was six feet four, with chiseled features and broad shoulders to climb on. And because he was so athletic and young, he could play with us like an older brother. He could make life really magical. Even routine activities could be joyful experiences. We used to burn our trash out in the backyard, all five of his children gathered around tossing egg cartons and papers into the fire, feeling it was a privilege to be with him. When Franklin's sun shone on you, the light was worth everything, and it wasn't only because it was in contrast to the dark.

He used to watch baseball with Mark after Brock and Alya were away at college. He was always against owning a television, but he finally dug up an old black-and-white one from someplace and put it in the attic, where it was usually freezing. This was his way of nearly *not* owning a television. He and Mark would go up there, wrap themselves in blankets, and watch baseball games together. And they would go fishing. That was their special activity. All the children had some unique relationship with him.

I had my moments in the sun, too. Often he would compliment me for a paper I'd written in school. I was singled out for a short story I wrote when I was twelve, about a kid who wanted to commit suicide. Franklin praised that story and my writing to the skies. Sometimes he would read my papers out loud at the dinner table. Later he would come to see me perform. When I was sixteen he saw me as Beliaev in Turgenev's *A Month in the Country* with the Harvard Repertory Company in Cambridge, and he was ecstatic about the performance. I was especially thrilled because the play was in his field of expertise, and I had expected him to be highly critical of the production. To my surprise, I was the man of the hour for an evening.

When I was about thirteen I started learning the guitar and soon joined a rock band, called, for some inexplicable reason, The Remnants. But we certainly didn't think of ourselves as leftovers; we thought we were extremely cool. We used to play at dancing school and at parties—fifty bucks for the evening, split among four of us. It was great fun; our standards were songs by the Beatles, the Rolling Stones, the Lovin' Spoonful, even the Turtles. I began by learning folk songs like 'Kumbayah,' 'Michael Row the Boat Ashore,' and 'This Land Is Your Land.' One night I gave a little concert for Franklin. I played all my songs, and once again he was full of praise. He could hardly carry a tune himself, but he always liked my voice.

One summer when I was nine and we were visiting him at my grandmother's house in the Poconos, Pa asked me to row across the lake all by myself to go to the general store and get tobacco for his pipe. All the other children were there. The honor of being chosen for this mission was tremendous. I had money in my pocket and would get to row our fairly big rowboat more than a mile across Pocono Lake. Another moment in the sun.

But the next night there was a square dance. I spotted a girl in a yellow dress. She was my first crush; I took a big shine to her and tried to be near her the whole evening. But Franklin teased me in front of the others about my attraction to her. With my father you could go from one extreme to the other very rapidly.

Meanwhile in Princeton my mother did her best to cope with my brother and me as we became more of a handful. If I did something that disappointed her, she would burst into tears and say, 'Oh, you beastly, beastly boy! Oh, you beastly, beastly boy!'—at which point I would calmly and rather arrogantly explain to her that I was *not* a beastly boy, which would make her cry even harder. It was cruel, I know.

But much of my time and energy went into trying to be as perfect as possible. I thought this would set me apart from all the half brothers and stepbrothers who became a part of my life when my mother and father both remarried. My school shoes were always placed neatly in the closet. I used to hang up all my clothes and always made my bed, trying to do everything right.

On the other hand, I took secret risks to see how much I could get away with: one of my favorites at age twelve was taking the family Rambler out for a spin when my mother and stepfather were away.

We spent part of each summer at the New Jersey shore, in an old house at Bay Head that had been in my stepfather's family for four generations. One time—I think it was the summer I was thirteen—I sneaked over to a neighbors' house on a dare and took a bottle of vodka from their liquor cabinet. My friends and I mixed it with 7UP and chugged away. I got absolutely clobbered and ended up passed out on the beach, right at the edge of the water. I woke up at about ten-thirty as the tide was coming in—I was being gently rolled from side to side by the waves. I staggered back to the house feeling absolutely awful, crept up the back steps, and almost made it to the second-floor bathroom before I heaved everywhere.

I crawled into bed, but the next morning I was supposed to sail in a very important Blue Jay regatta for the championship of the season. Somehow I got up on time and made it downstairs by 8:30. My mother was at the stove cooking bacon,

70

a terrible look on her face. Oh God, the smell of that bacon. I knew that this time I'd been caught. There was an excruciating silence as I tried to steady myself and make a piece of toast. Finally she said, 'I've been thinking about how to punish you. First of all, you're going to go next door to the Browns and apologize and pay them back. Then you go straight to the boat and race.' Feeling the way I did, getting in that Blue Jay was the last thing I wanted to do. But I did it. I made it there and did it. I certainly didn't win, but I almost appreciated my mother's punishment as an exception to the rule.

Later in life I gained real respect for my mother. She stopped letting people take advantage of her and began to come into her own. She always had an interest in writing and finally did something about it, eventually becoming associate editor of *Town Topics*, the local paper in Princeton. She bought her own house and at the age of sixty took up rowing despite a lifelong history of asthma. Today she is a serious competitor. In the winter she trains on an ergometer; in the spring and fall she can be found rowing the Head of the Charles, or out on the Schuylkill, often coming back with a trophy. She takes it as seriously as I took flying an airplane, sailing a boat, or competing on horses.

But as I grew up I felt torn between my parents' quite different and opposed worlds. My father's house was filled with books and visiting intellectuals and stimulating conversation; my mother and stepfather's comfortable house often seemed dull by comparison. I began to spend more time with other families who lived in the neighborhood.

71

Fortunately for me, I always loved school. I learned to read very quickly, and from the age of five I remember wanting to be bigger and older and more advanced. I used to beg Miss Griffith, the first-grade teacher, for homework to do because big kids had homework. I wanted to come home and say that I had to do my homework and go upstairs and have busy things to attend to. Ben was a lot brighter than me, and I guess I was trying to stay ahead of him. I had a strong compulsion to meet all my responsibilities, both real and imagined.

My mother's relationship with Tris Johnson had begun late in 1958. He had grown up in Princeton and worked for Laidlaw & Company, a local investment firm. (My father once explained to me that it was acceptable to be paid wages for a day's work but to profit from the stock market was morally wrong.) Tris had four children of his own and was divorced. Those children—Tristam Jr. (known as Johnny), Tommy, Beth, and Kate—lived in Utah with their mother, Bunny Miller. Tris started to visit my mother from time to time. He had a part interest in the family house in Bay Head and had spent summers there himself as a kid. We all began to go there after my mother and Tris were married in June 1959.

Tris was generous and relaxed, a kind man who always wanted the best for us. He thought it would be better for Ben and me to go to the private school of his childhood—Princeton Country Day, down near Carnegie Lake behind the playing fields of the university. In the fall of 1961 I started in first form, the equivalent of fourth grade. I loved it. On Monday nights we went to father-son carpentry

72

workshops, where we'd build little birdhouses together. Tris came to watch my soccer and hockey games. I developed a great affection for him. Yet this was complicated by the fact that what I wanted most was my father's approval.

Through Tris came a lot of fun things for a kid— peewee hockey, summers at Bay Head, a little duck boat to learn to sail. Franklin would have coached us, drawn diagrams about wind direction and sail trim, would have shown us how to coil ropes properly. Tris let us go out on our own, crash into docks, flip the boat over, run aground, and gradually get the hang of it. By the time I was twelve I had graduated to Blue Jays and was on the match-racing team for the Bay Head Yacht Club. My desire to win turned me into something of a tyrant, however; I could never restrain myself from screaming at my crew out on the racecourse. After one particularly successful season, I was awarded the coveted Seamanship/Sportsmanship Award, which is given to the outstanding junior skipper of the year. Obviously the officers of the club didn't know what really went on in my boat. But the other kids did. I went up to accept the prize at the Labor Day Ceremonies and received only a polite smattering of applause. I remember turning beet red and breaking into a sweat as I suddenly realized I didn't deserve this recognition. I never raced a sailboat again.

At school I was one of the few kids who were successful in both academics and sports. Often you're in one camp or the other, but I was on the honor roll and I could play soccer, baseball, tennis, and hockey. The sports made me popular with the 'cool' kids, whose respect I really sought, but I also

73

wanted to be academically on top so my father wouldn't be disappointed in me.

So I put a lot of pressure on myself. My mother would say later that I was always straining to be older than I was. It was as if I were trying to race through my childhood, to get it over with. I remember this desire from as far back as the age of six, wanting to read more difficult books, not only because the older kids did but because my father was always surrounded by books, always studying, always writing. Later on the scholar's image became problematic because I wasn't very good in math. But for many years I excelled academically, and that gave me a certain standing with my father, which I needed.

Ben started PCD a year after I did, and we entered one of the best periods of our relationship. We both played baseball for the Hulit's Shoe Store Yankees; we skied together on a little hill with a rope tow just outside of town; we rigged up an intercom between our two bedrooms and checked in with each other day and night. One summer we went to a day camp, where we both loved archery and building mud forts down by the stream.

This was also about the time we had some goldfish. But Ben and I decided it was wrong to keep them in captivity, and we should set them free. So we carried these goldfish in their bowl a couple of miles down to Carnegie Lake. We stood on the bridge on Washington Street and had a little ceremony. We told the fish, 'Go. Be free. Swim. Live. Enjoy your life. Good-bye.' Then we turned the bowl upside down, sending the fish to an instant death. Their little bodies floated on the water. We were so confused.

We rode our bikes to school every day through the town. That was both exciting and dangerous; we rode without helmets right out on Route 206. I nearly got killed by a truck riding home from school one day. I had to fall over onto the side of the road to avoid being hit. I came home with my arms and legs all banged up and scraped from landing hard on the pavement. Still, we were allowed to ride to school by ourselves. My friends and I used to race each other through the university campus down to Princeton Country Day. I savored the independence, the fact that we were given so much freedom.

I loved peewee hockey on Saturday mornings, and then going over to Deebs Young's house to skate on his pond. I remember one day in February 1964—I would've been in seventh grade—going to his house to have breakfast and skate, and seeing on the front page of the paper four really weird-looking guys with strange haircuts coming down the steps of an airplane. The Beatles were arriving for *The Ed Sullivan Show*. We thought, What freaks! We all had crew cuts in those days. We went to a barber named Bob Chaty down in Palmer Square, and if Ben and I didn't get our hair cut short enough, my mother would send us back. But I always had my hair cut exactly the way I was told to.

My mission was never to give anybody cause for complaint. When I was in fourth grade at PCD, our reading teacher, Wesley McCaughn, taught us to love stories. He would record them in a sonorous, Walt Disneyish voice, then play the tapes in class. We would sit there enthralled by the way he told a story. Later that love of storytelling informed my love of acting. On one of my report cards he wrote, 'Would they were all cut from the same cloth.' I cherished his words, because they validated all my efforts to excel.

Then one day in the spring of 1962, when I was nine, somebody came over to PCD from the Princeton Savoyards, an amateur group that put on Gilbert and Sullivan operettas once or twice a year. She asked if any of us could sing and would like to try out for a production of *The Yeomen of the Guard*. I shot up my hand and went for the tryout. I was cast with grown-ups over at McCarter Theater, the big thousand-seat theater that had been built in the twenties to house productions of the Princeton Triangle Club. I was given the small part of a townsperson. It was my first time onstage, and it was intoxicating.

It was one thing to be a good student-athlete, but acting was even better. I even got to miss school for rehearsals. McCarter had a state-sponsored program of student matinees, usually at 10:30 in the morning or 2:30 in the afternoon. I would get to pack up my books and walk out of the classroom for a performance. I was special.

Then I started to act at PCD. When I was eleven or twelve, we put on a production of Agatha Christie's *Witness for the Prosecution*, and, of course, all the parts were played by boys. I was cast as Janet Mackenzie, the sixty-five-year-old housekeeper in the mansion where the murders take place. I was outfitted with a gray wig and a dowdy Scottish tweed housekeeper's suit. At one point in the play, Janet Mackenzie fiercely defends her actions, insisting that she's not guilty. On opening night, as I was finishing a heated exchange

76

from the witness box, I got applause from the audience. Right in the middle of the first act. It went straight to my head, and I thought, This is wonderful.

I found every excuse I could to get down to the theater. Even before they started casting me in plays, I went down and wired dressing-room speakers for sound and worked on the light board. It was an old-fashioned one—sometimes you had to reach out with your foot to get one handle and stretch out an arm to get another one, and I was tall enough to do it. I would ride the curtain, too, and I loved that. Groups like the Joffrey or the Pennsylvania Ballet would come through, and I often had my eye on some ballerina. The quickest way to make an impression was to ride the curtain. I pulled the curtain down, then, in order to get it started the other way, I rode the rope that pulled it up as soon as the curtain hit the floor. I'd sail fifteen, twenty feet into the air, and then my body weight would start it down again. The girls in the corps de ballet often looked over to watch my acrobatics. After that it was easy to start a conversation.

Before long I was cast in small parts with the professional repertory company at McCarter. It felt like a family. I was part of a group of people who worked together every day on projects they believed in. All the horses were pulling the wagon in the same direction, toward opening night. And during the rehearsal process the excitement grew as a play started to jell. I loved the whole atmosphere. No strife, no tension here, at least none that I could see. I behaved myself and tried hard, and the adults liked me. Right there was the beginning of a way to escape the conflicting feelings I had about my two families. I'm sure that's why I became an actor.

That early success set me up for life. I didn't know what I was doing at first, didn't have a clue. As a result I did quite well; I just instinctively responded to the material and did what I was told by the director. They began to use me more and more at McCarter Theater, and by my senior year in high school I was playing some good parts.

The actors there were a wonderfully eccentric group. They were tolerant and kind—unless you missed an entrance or really screwed up in the work. But even then the consequences weren't too serious. I remember a time when John Lithgow, Tom Tarpey, Jim LaFerla, John Braden, and I were in a not-too-terrific production of *Troilus and Cressida*. During one Sunday matinee we were all down in the greenroom watching the NBA play-offs. A real cliffhanger was in progress: the Knicks against the Celtics in double overtime. We were listening to the play on the monitor, but we couldn't drag ourselves away from the game. We all missed our entrance. I think it was a council scene or a camp meeting where the Greeks are making plans against the Trojans. Unfortunately, the scene just didn't happen. The lights came up, and gradually six actors wandered on. Only the fact that so many of us were involved made it look like it might have been done on purpose.

While I was developing my interest in theater and working at McCarter, Ben's natural talent for things mechanical and mathematical took him down to the engineering quadrangle at Princeton. At the age of twelve or thirteen, he was working on computers with a lot of the 'brains' at the university, often staying out until one or two in the morning. He helped write a computer language that was taught at Princeton for many years.

Ben also had access to the university radio station, WPRB. He had permission to use their spare studios in the bottom of Nassau Hall. I would be the DJ, he'd be the engineer, and we'd pretend to do a show, cuing up songs and commercials and imitating Walter Cronkite reading the news.

These moments of collaboration and friendship were wonderful, but as we became teenagers there were not nearly enough of them. Too often we would push each other's buttons and one of us would get fed up and walk away. I remember when I was about thirteen, coming home from a visit to Franklin's house in Higganum, Connecticut. By then my father was teaching at Wesleyan and my stepmother at Connecticut College. I came into Ben's room and found him smoking a cigarette, listening to a Janis Joplin record. I tried to talk to him about what was going on up at Franklin's, that they had just moved to an old Victorian farmhouse (where my stepmother still lives today). Ben just clamped down. I felt that he wanted to know, he wanted to be included, but he didn't want to appear too interested. Perhaps he resented the fact that I'd been there by myself.

I wrote a short story about that episode for English class. It ended with the main character walking down the hall to his room saying, 'Oh well, we'll have to try again. There can be more attempts, but it's getting late. I had thought that physical distance might have solved the problems of distance brought on by being in the same place.'

Ben and I lived in the same house but usually felt miles apart. We kept trying to connect. Whenever we lost touch we missed each other and looked forward to reconnecting. But somehow we were never able to develop the real closeness that would have made our growing up easier for both of us.

Both Ben and I misbehaved fairly frequently in our new house at 25 Campbelton Circle, and by 1963 there were two new half siblings, Jeff and Kevin, who provided plenty of distraction. My brother would often stay out late or not even come home some nights. I used to take the family car and go down to Bay Head in the middle of the night, and there was the episode of raiding the Browns' liquor cabinet. I also liked to hang out with my older step-brother Johnny and his friends, especially during the summer after his senior year in high school. Once I went out on Barnegat Bay in somebody's motorboat and at one point found myself sitting in the cabin with a Marlboro in one hand, a Budweiser in the other, and a seventeen-year-old blonde in my lap. Obviously, my mother was right: I *was* in a hurry to grow up.

But somehow I almost never got into trouble, perhaps because no one suspected that someone of my apparently upstanding nature would do these kinds of things. But I did, and almost always got away with it. Ben did not.

He and my father couldn't seem to get along. Alya, Brock, Mark, and I all had ways of getting Franklin's approval, but I think it was much more difficult for Ben because it wasn't in his nature to go out of his way to placate anyone. Franklin's love for his children always seemed tied to performance. Perhaps my father was even a little afraid of Ben because he was so intelligent and wouldn't submit to his will. The rest of us were more pliable and had a much easier time. Over the years Ben and Franklin saw less of each other, until their relationship broke down completely.

For years Franklin talked as though our relationship with him had been decided by the divorce proceedings. He lost custody of us, then had to watch as Tris Johnson became the dominant figure in our lives. I think he felt that if we'd spent more time with him, if he had been given the teaching position at Princeton, if he'd been able to have a greater influence on us, we would have turned out better. Often when he heard what Ben was up to, he would just shrug his shoulders and say, 'What can we do? We saw this coming years ago.' Fortunately, his fears were unfounded. Ben graduated from Princeton and got a law degree from Northeastern. Today he does consulting work and is writing a book on systems and structures in politics and the law. His research into all aspects of spinal cord injury has been a tremendous help to me since my accident, and he has often given speeches on my behalf. Alya is a neuropsychiatrist; Mark is an environmental lawyer; Brock got an MBA from Harvard and works as a management consultant. I became a successful actor, although probably too much in the mainstream for my father's liking. Nevertheless, I did not end up a taxi driver or a waiter still hoping to make it at age forty-five.

Franklin himself had a difficult upbringing. Lives repeat themselves in succeeding generations, often in the worst ways, and patterns of behavior can be difficult to break. Like Ben and me, Franklin and

81

his brother, Dickie, are about a year apart. Dickie literally tried to kill Franklin a couple of times, once with a shotgun, once with a bow and arrow. They also had a complex relationship with a father who became a distant figure in their lives.

I only saw my grandfather Big Dick Reeve a couple of times in my life. When I was thirteen, in the spring of 1966, he flew my mother and Ben and me out to his place in Arizona. It was a big adventure. We were picked up in Tucson and driven out to his ranch, a spread of 400,000 acres where he raised cattle and trained Labrador retrievers. I think he loved those dogs more than any offspring he produced.

One day he invited my brother and me to hunt coyotes with him. We were to meet him by the fireplace in the main house—we were staying out in the guest lodge—at 5:30 in the morning. Typical teenagers, we overslept. I was mortified because I'd made a mistake. Whenever I made a mistake I'd go to pieces with embarrassment.

I woke Ben up, and we appeared in the main lodge forty minutes late to find our grandfather staring into the fireplace with his back to us. In we came, apologizing profusely. And he said, 'Well, all right, we'll go out there, but it's too late.' We went off in his Jeep, riding in silence to one of the more remote parts of the ranch. We waited, looked around for a while. No signs of anything except a beautiful sunrise. Our grandfather was taciturn, his face set in stone. Suddenly he announced that he had business with his foreman. Before we knew it he'd disappeared. He'd driven off in the Jeep, leaving us out there on a dirt road, both with loaded guns.

The mood was grim. Ben and I were pissed at each other because we'd both screwed up. I remember being very frightened. Walking back, I made sure Ben stayed in front—it was not impossible that one of us might take a shot. Further proof that Tophy and Beejy were not very different from Franklin and Dickie.

I didn't see my grandfather again until the summer of 1976, when I flew out in my first airplane, a little Cherokee 140 I had bought secondhand. After that I didn't see him until the summer of 1985, when he knew he was dying of cancer and made a trip east. He went around and touched base with everybody in the family. Franklin probably hadn't seen his father in thirty-five years, but now there was a reconciliation. They spent time together in Vermont. Franklin told me what a great old man Richard was, how much he respected him. It was a complete turnaround.

I was renting a house on Martha's Vineyard with Gae and the children. My grandfather chartered a boat out of Newport and came over to visit. I had my Swan 40, *Chandelle,* and we sailed in tandem from Menemsha over to the Sakonnet River, just east of Newport. We anchored for the night and had dinner, talking and catching up on missing years. I was astonished to learn that this formidable outdoorsman, veteran of Iwo Jima and Guadalcanal, had driven twenty miles down from his ranch into Tucson to see *Superman* and loved it. He couldn't have been nicer—he thoroughly charmed Gae, who thought he was wonderful. The next morning we sailed back, and that was the last time I ever saw him. He died the next year.

In 1988 my relationship with Franklin broke

down completely. I had recently returned from Chile and was working with the novelist and playwright Ariel Dorfman on a screenplay based on my experience there, trying to save the lives of seventy-seven actors who had been threatened with execution by the Pinochet regime. I showed Franklin the outline for the film and asked for suggestions, but he strenuously objected to being 'used' in this way and stormed out of the house. Two days later I received a letter saying he didn't want to see me anymore or have anything to do with me.

I was stunned. I had thought that sharing my ideas for the film would be received as an invitation for us to become collaborators. I certainly didn't think I was taking advantage of his talent as a writer for my personal gain. I remember wondering if we were going to play out the same scenario as Franklin and his father. After we hadn't seen each other for almost four years, I asked myself: Are we going to have a reconciliation scene when he's an old man? Or when he's in the hospital, completely defenseless, and needs visitors? What are we going to say to each other then? Of course, I didn't anticipate my accident and the irony of that speculation.

I kept trying to put an end to it, kept trying to break the cycle. Once during the years we didn't speak, I was on a train that had stopped on the bridge over the Connecticut River. I looked out the window and remembered how we used to circle around in his little sailboat, the *Sanderling,* waiting for the bridge to open. I wrote him a note recalling those fond memories, but he wrote back accusing me of cheap sentimentality.

Much to my surprise, he came to my wedding in 1992, but there were at least sixty people there, and we never found a moment to talk. In August 1994 he watched me compete on my horse Denver at a combined training event up in Vermont. We shared a tailgate picnic, and he seemed to enjoy watching our two-year-old Will run around. But nothing really substantial came of our relationship until my accident. Since then I have felt a new reaching out on both sides. My father has gone out of his way to visit me and has been constantly in touch. Every time I have a minor medical setback, he is terribly concerned. We have had long, satisfying talks in hospital rooms. Out of this disaster has come a new beginning.

But in my boyhood and teenage years, Princeton and Tris Johnson and McCarter Theater were my home base, the place where I felt most secure. I had great admiration for Tris, which I felt I had to conceal. There was even a time when I wanted to change my name to Christopher Johnson, to commit to the Johnsons as my real family. It would be Tris, Barbara, me, Jeff, Kevin, and Ben, all fitting in as best we could. I admired Tris's ability to give without expecting much back. He wanted to see all his children find their own way without imposing his values on them.

I thrived on Tris's generosity. He put me through Princeton Day School and Cornell and the Drama Division at Juilliard. He had been the lighting designer for the drama club when he was a student at Yale, so we had that in common: he liked the theater. In tenth grade I was Hal in William Inge's *Picnic*. It was a big success. After my performances we would always come home, make chocolate milkshakes in the blender, and sit around and talk about the play.

Once I went with Tris to see Johnny at Berkshire Academy in Sheffield, Massachusetts, and he let me drive the car up the Taconic by sitting right next to him and steering. He thought it would be good practice. Of course he had no idea that I'd previously 'borrowed' the car and sneaked off to the shore with it.

We used to have a little applesauce industry going at the house. We would turn on the radio to listen to the Princeton football games and climb our big apple tree next to the driveway at Campbelton Circle. We'd go way up in the tree, pick apples, and lower them down in a bucket while my mom would be making applesauce in the kitchen. I loved it. I loved the family dinners.

And then sometimes Tris wouldn't come home. The table would be set, and he wouldn't show up. He would disappear for a couple of days at a time without any explanation, without even saying that he owed us an explanation. Just that he was on business, just doing what he was doing. I had such high hopes that this little family would take hold, particularly when my half brothers, Jeff and Kevin, came along. But it didn't work; it wouldn't jell. We weren't able to come together under one roof. My mother convinced Tris that we should move to a much larger house over on Cleveland Lane, under the assumption that things would improve if we had more space. But in fact this created greater isolation in the household. Jeff and Kevin kept to themselves up on the third floor; Ben and I were separated by a long hallway as well as our natural jealousy of each other; my mother and Tris were experiencing the beginning of the end.

From my childhood I developed the belief that a few isolated moments of contentment or happiness were the best you could hope for in relationships—and they probably wouldn't last. Everything seemed to be built on shifting sand. Even in the theater, a play, a season, was a moment. Inevitably it would be over and everybody would move on. New friendships, new alliances would have to be built. I developed a tendency to stick to myself and not get too close to anybody. I didn't want to risk too much, to get too involved, because I was certain that loss and disappointment would inevitably follow.

I found relief from all this uncertainty in playing characters. I liked knowing the entire story line—beginning, middle, and end. At the same time I loved taking risks. Whether onstage or as goalie on the hockey team, I kept putting myself on the line.

Those years at Campbelton Circle—the coziness of that house, picking apples in the fall, playing soccer in the front yard, the kids on Allison Road, going to Bay Head in the summer—also lacked a solid foundation. Two things were going on at once, and they opposed each other: my dream house and the real house. By the time Jeff and Kevin were in grade school, it was all starting to fall apart. Tris was leaving my mother at loose ends. I didn't know the kind of distress she was in.

Both households were troubled. I remember asking my father why he left my stepmother, Helen, in his midfifties. He had always described the two of them as joined at the hip, 'so close that we're like one person. We share everything. This is what a family is.' And I thought, of course it is—this cozy

87

Victorian farmhouse in Higganum. Brock, Mark, and Alya were such adorable, brilliant children— the makings of a perfect family. When he did separate from Helen in the late 1970s, I asked Franklin when he first knew that the marriage wasn't working. And he said, 'In Paris, in 1956.' I was stunned. More shifting sand, more illusions.

Looking back now at Princeton and Higganum, I still wonder why such wonderful, extraordinary people couldn't build relationships that lasted. I came to believe that marriage was merely a set of obligations undertaken under false pretenses. It wasn't until I met Dana and knew I was falling seriously in love with her that all that changed. But it took time, and therapy, and Dana's patience with me to overcome that disrespect, that fear of marriage.

I saw marriage as a loss rather than a gain. All my life I had heard people say that they loved each other and that they would be together forever, to have and to hold from this day forward, and so forth, and then it would turn out not to be true. Or irreconcilable differences would emerge. My father was an intellectual, my mother was not. My stepfather was a staunch Republican, a Nixon supporter, while she was a romantic about Kennedy and very liberal. Eventually they, too, had little to say to each other. I witnessed a gradual loss of respect. My father had an affair. My stepfather often would not come home. When I was old enough to understand what was happening, I concluded that in most cases marriage is a sham.

Even the family that Gae and I created years later with Matthew and Alexandra wasn't completely genuine, because I still couldn't see the point of marriage. When we met there was a period of intense romance, but I think ultimately we should have been friends rather than lovers. I know that in many ways I was holding back. In fact we *were* friends, which is why when we separated in 1987 we did it amicably and were able to work things out well between us. We have joint custody of the children and discuss every aspect of their upbringing. Over the past ten years there have been no serious disagreements, no rancor or bad feelings. It was exactly the opposite of what happened when my mother and father divorced. But after we separated I didn't think I had much of a future as far as love and family were concerned. A good marriage seemed more improbable than ever.

And then there was Dana. She rescued me when I was lying in Virginia with a broken body, but that was really the second time. The first time she rescued me was the night we met.

After my first tries at acting at McCarter, I was accepted at the Williamstown Theatre Festival in Massachusetts. I began as an apprentice when I was fifteen and ultimately performed there for fourteen seasons. Even at the height of my film career, I tried to keep my summers free to rejoin the Williamstown family.

There is a cabaret attached to the festival, where many of the actors perform in a local inn after the shows. Some of us, myself included, really have no business singing, but admission is cheap and the theater audiences love to hear us perform everything from '50s doo-wop to Irving Berlin and Cole Porter. It's one of the delights of the festival.

Fortunately for the audience, a group of four or

five real singers known as the Cabaret Corps holds the evening together. In the summer of 1987 Dana was one of the corps, and I was appearing in Aphra Behn's *The Rover*. I'd been separated from Gae for five months. I had finished filming *Switching Channels* out in Chicago and came back to Williamstown determined to be alone, to mind my own business, to focus on the work and fixing up the house I'd bought just outside of town. It was set in the middle of forty acres on a hillside with one of the most spectacular views in the Berkshires. My plan was to have a quiet and reflective summer. I was certainly not looking for a relationship. But I went to the cabaret one night, and Dana Morosini stepped out onstage to sing.

She wore an off-the-shoulder dress and sang 'The Music That Makes Me Dance.' Oh, my God. Right then I went down, hook, line, and sinker. All my friends who were there saw it happen. Afterwards I went backstage. This was difficult, because whenever I'm really attracted to someone, really knocked out, I can be very clumsy. At the time I was a successful film actor and pretty established. You wouldn't think I'd have a problem with a simple conversation trying to meet a woman, but I could become very awkward. Playing Clark Kent was no stretch for me.

I went backstage and introduced myself, complimented her on her song, then offered her a ride over to a party at a place called The Zoo. It was located in one of the Williams College dormitories, very much an anything-goes kind of place, which is how it got its name. But when I offered her a ride, she said, 'No thanks, I have my own car.' All I could think to say was, 'Oh.' Then she was caught up in the swirl of her friends, and gone. I dragged myself out to the parking lot and sat for a while in my old pickup truck, trying to plan my next move. Later she told me that a couple of her friends had said, 'You idiot, why don't you go with him? We'll drive your car. Go for it!'

We both ended up at The Zoo, and I tried again. I wandered over and opened up a conversation. I have no idea what we talked about, but people who were there said we didn't sit down, we didn't get a drink, we didn't move. We stood in the middle of The Zoo and talked for a solid hour. Everything evaporated around us. And then I thought to myself, I don't want to make a mistake here and ruin this. I'm not going to try to rush things tonight. Much to my surprise, I found myself saying, 'Well, it was very nice to meet you.' Then I hopped in my truck and drove home.

We started dating in a very old-fashioned way. One day I found myself riding my bike along Route 7 toward Pittsfield, and on an impulse I stopped and went out in a field and picked wildflowers. I didn't want to be riding toward Pittsfield, I wanted to go back to the theater, where I knew Dana was rehearsing another cabaret number. I had the bunch of wildflowers in my hand, but as I cycled back I became more and more shy about actually giving them to her. Outside the rehearsal hall I lost my nerve. I found a girl passing by and said, 'Would you go in there and give Dana Morosini these flowers? Tell her they're from me, but don't make a big deal out of it.' She was happy to be a messenger for me and went right in. Dana was surprised and pleased, and she came out of the rehearsal to say thank you. But I'd left, thinking

91

that was a stupid thing to do.

Dana and I went slowly because I was concerned about Matthew and Alexandra, who were with me for the summer. I didn't want the children, who were only seven and three at the time, to come into the bedroom in the morning and find a strange woman in bed with me. It was a delicate matter to handle. So for most of the summer Dana and I just dated. One night I suggested we go swimming in a nearby pond after the cabaret but quickly offered to drive her back to pick up a bathing suit. Later she told me this had pleasantly surprised her and made the evening even more romantic.

Dana's parents made frequent trips up to Williamstown to see her perform in the cabaret. As I got to know Chuck and Helen Morosini, we developed an easy rapport. I remember telling Chuck how much I was enjoying dating Dana. I also told him about the additions I was making to my house, and that one of the best features was the huge master bedroom shaped like an octagon, with spectacular views in all directions and an especially comfortable California king-size bed in the middle of the room. He was polite enough not to make any comment. But at the rehearsal dinner the night before our wedding in April 1992, he recalled this story as he toasted us, and remembered thinking that his daughter was dating 'the ultimate bozo.'

Often Dana and I would take my truck up to a hill overlooking Williamstown and park in the middle of a field. We would make out like teenagers, then I'd take her back to the dorm. There was a big green Dumpster in front of it where all the festival trash went, and of course it took us a long time to say good night. For some reason we always parked right in front of the Dumpster. Friends walked by and said, There's Chris Reeve and Dana Morosini parked by the Dumpster. Very strange. But it was as close as I could get to the dorm. I never went up to her room, and she didn't stay over at my house until much later in the summer. She would come for dinner and start getting to know the kids, or we would go down to a little place near Pittsfield to play miniature golf, which they loved. They both took an incredible shine to her and she to them. She was instantly comfortable with them, which was wonderful to see. It filled me with joy.

When I saw Dana's natural ability and ease with the kids, and her sense of fun, I was relieved and thrilled that something that worked for me also worked for them. It all just fell into place. Late in the summer, after Gae had taken Alexandra back to England, Dana and I went sailing in Maine with Matthew and my half brother Kevin. Matthew and Kevin each had a single berth in the main salon, but Dana and I were in the double berth up forward. I worried about what Matthew would think when he saw us together in the morning, but he came right in and climbed up between us. Soon we were wrestling and pillow-fighting and playing mountain. I thought, This is going to be okay.

When the children came over again to be with us in Williamstown during the Christmas holidays, I felt Alexandra was ready to see us together as well. She and Matthew began a morning ritual. They would quietly sneak down the back stairs and make their way to the circular staircase that led to our bedroom. Then they would climb up on top of the dresser right behind our bed and jump on us with

93

shrieks of delight. Dana and I usually had a favorite blue blanket over us, and the kids decided that our bed was a swimming pool. They took turns diving off the dresser into the pool and swimming around all over us, sometimes pretending they were alligators. Occasionally we would hear creaking steps and suppressed giggles as they tried to sneak up on us, but most of the time we were dead to the world after a long day of rehearsals, performances, and the cabaret. So it was quite a shock when they landed on us at 6:30 in the morning.

In spite of that joyful summer, I was still carrying all my emotional baggage around with me. I was proceeding with caution—terror, actually. It took a long time for me to make the commitment that we finally realized in April 1992. Dana shared an apartment in the city with her sister, and I was over on West Seventy-eighth Street, but we were really at my place most of the time. We took it step by step while we pursued our separate careers. In January 1988 I went to Los Angeles for *Summer and Smoke* with Christine Lahti at the Ahmanson, and Dana stayed behind to audition for jobs in New York. Out in Los Angeles I found I was happy to concentrate on my work. I spent a lot of time playing tennis with friends, working on a screenplay, and missing Dana.

At one point I decided to throw a party for the cast and crew at Tommy Tang's, a Thai restaurant on Melrose. That same day Dana decided to hop on a plane to come out and surprise me. A close friend of mine heard about it and told her, 'I don't think that's a good idea. Don't surprise him; surprises aren't good.' He'd been one of my partners in crime throughout the early '80s. But

94

Dana said, 'Well, if I'm going to go out there and find him with someone else, it might as well be now.' So she flew out, and there we were at Tommy Tang's, the whole cast and crew. She walked into the room to find me talking to one of the electricians. We were thrilled to see each other, and I think so relieved that neither of us had strayed.

We knew that the relationship was growing. She stayed with me for a while in a house I'd rented on Tiana Road, and we had a lovely time together in Los Angeles. She came to the play about five times, because she enjoyed watching the production evolve. I had played Dr. Johnny once before at Juilliard, and once again at Williamstown, but she helped me find new layers in the role. After the run was over in April, I went to Yugoslavia to film *The Great Escape II*, and Dana joined me for most of the shoot. We loved being on location together. I particularly enjoyed riding together out in the countryside, often stopping for lunch in a fourteenth-century castle in the town of Mokrice.

We both went to Williamstown again that summer, and this time Dana was hired as an actress. We lived together at my house, which we began to think of as our house because the additions were made after I separated from Gae. It felt like a clean slate.

When the kids came over that summer, we felt like a little family. But not having a firm commitment from the man she was giving so much time and attention to, and having to function as the step-mother of his children, was making the situation difficult for Dana. It wouldn't become a crisis until later.

Dana and I shared wonderful times together and with friends, cruising the coast of Maine in *Chandelle*. At first she wasn't much of a sailor. In fact, her father often told me about his frustrating attempts to teach his three daughters to sail on Long Island Sound when they were kids. Dana usually felt fine on deck and soon learned to steer extremely well, but two minutes below in any kind of a sea would make her absolutely miserable. But she never complained and was always game for another trip because she knew how much I loved it.

Once she and Kevin and I sailed nonstop from Portland, Maine, to Shelburne, Nova Scotia. In the middle of the second night we were becalmed in dense fog off Cape Sable, not far from Blonde Rock, a navigational hazard that I had circled on my chart with three exclamation points, to be avoided at all costs. Of course at that moment our normally reliable diesel engine decided not to start. I had no choice but to call the Canadian Coast Guard at Clarke Harbour and hope they could get to us before we drifted into serious trouble. A forty-foot cutter arrived within an hour and towed us back to shore at such a high speed that I thought we would turn into a submarine at any moment. The next morning we met just about everybody in town, and Dana served coffee and breakfast to the Coast Guard crew who had helped us out.

This adventure didn't put her off in the least, so in 1989 we sold our beloved *Chandelle* and bought a Cambria 46, which we named the *Sea Angel*. She was built from scratch especially for us by David Walters in Portsmouth, Rhode Island. We would spread out blueprints on the dining-room table and talk about the shape of the galley or the main salon. At least once a week we flew up to Portsmouth to go over details with David and watch 'our baby' being built.

Finally she was launched in July of that year. Dana presented me with a photo album titled 'The Birth of a Sea Angel,' which showed every stage of the process from the first design meeting to the champagne celebration after our sea trial. Creating this boat with Dana was a complete joy and a new kind of experience for me. I was feeling more and more that we were meant to be together.

By 1990 we were living together on Seventy-eighth Street, but it was a place I had shared with Gae. Dana felt that we ought to start our own life in our own place, but I wasn't quite ready to do that. I still couldn't get past the issue of marriage. Our relationship nearly went on the rocks in '91, when I was shooting a movie called *Morning Glory* in Vancouver. It was a summer of many phone calls back and forth. Dana finally said that she'd had enough, that there was no future for us.

We had planned a weekend on Galiano Island, a few miles off the mainland. We were going to charter a boat and sail out there, then stay at the Galiano Inn, one of the most romantic spots in the world. Even though Dana had decided it was over, she ended up coming out for the weekend. We were supposed to be breaking up, yet we couldn't keep our hands off each other. It was the most agonizingly bittersweet time. After that weekend we realized that we couldn't be without each other, but something had to change. So I agreed to go into therapy as soon as I got home. During the fall of 1991 and for most of 1992, I finally talked through everything I had always feared about

97

marriage.

Suddenly it spilled. And in very short order, I realized that I would be a fool to lose this woman, this relationship. We had moved down to East Twenty-second Street by this time, to an apartment without ghosts and memories. I'd always liked living on the Upper West Side near the park, but Dana is nine years younger than I am, and she wanted to be a part of the downtown New York scene. So we found a wonderful apartment near the Flatiron Building. It was fun—a beautiful atrium upstairs, great restaurants, and the farmers' market at Union Square on weekends.

And then one night we were having dinner, and about halfway through the meal I just put down my fork and asked her to marry me. We didn't finish dinner, we went straight to the bedroom. I have never been happier, never. It was tremendously exciting to say those words. We hadn't planned it; it was a moment whose time had come. I have never looked back.

We were married in Williamstown in April 1992, although I still think of our real anniversary as June 30, the night I first saw Dana at the cabaret. I still feel that I met her yesterday. A crisis like my accident doesn't change a marriage; it brings out what is truly there. It intensifies but does not transform it. We had become a family. When Dana looked at me in the UVA hospital room and said, 'You're still you,' it also meant that we're still us. We are. We made a bargain for life. I got the better part of the deal.

CHAPTER FOUR

On June 28 I was taken to Kessler to begin the long process of preparing to go home. I no longer needed to be in intensive care, but I still required a great deal of help and attention. I had an infection in my lungs and had lost a lot of weight because I couldn't eat. At UVA a tube had been inserted into my stomach, and though I absorbed 2,000 calories from a gastrostomy tube every night, it was not enough to keep me from looking gaunt.

My body, devastated by the injury, was still very fragile. I learned that I had never fully recovered from the malaria I'd contracted in Kenya in 1993. My hemoglobin, normally at 13 or 14, was down to 9, which is alarmingly low. My protein levels were also low, about 2.7 rather than the normal 4.0. I was given several blood transfusions during the first few weeks, yet there were no signs of improvement. My blood seemed to be disappearing, and Dr. Green was concerned because he couldn't understand where it was going. There was a possibility that my bone marrow was not producing red blood cells, and this required a further series of tests. I also needed chest X rays almost daily because there was still fluid in both lungs, and I was in danger of developing pneumonia. The process of rehabilitation had to be delayed until all these problems could be resolved.

I was emotionally fragile as well. Kessler is a first-rate institution—light, open, and spread out among lawns and trees—but it is still a place for the ill, and it bears the inner harshness of all such places. I looked around and saw nothing but green walls, linoleum floors, and damaged people. I had a hard time realizing that I was going to spend quite a long time in an institution devoted to the disabled. I couldn't accept myself as one of them.

It seemed surreal, even though I instantly took to many of the people assigned to my care—particular nurses, certain aides—and even though I was in one of the nicest rooms in the hospital. I had a single room, while many others were in rooms of four to six people. They had no privacy; they could hear everybody. At least in the beginning I'm not sure I would have been able to stand that.

I'm fairly sure I was given a private room because I was a celebrity. The staff went way over the top in their efforts to protect me. It was almost funny. I was assigned security guards who dressed like Secret Service agents; they sat outside my room and made detailed entries in a logbook of everyone who came and went. They followed me everywhere, although they never lifted a finger to help.

Once I was in my room when my breathing tube popped off. I couldn't take a breath. It was nearly midnight, the alarm on my vent was screaming, and I was making clicking noises—*clk-clk-clk-clk-clk*—always a signal for 'I need air.' The security guard came in and asked, 'Are you all right, Mr. Reeve?' He could have turned on the light and tried to find the source of the disconnect, but rather than get involved he went down the hall to look for a nurse. By then I was starting to pass out.

Being suddenly cut off from my life support this way was even more terrifying at Kessler than it had been at UVA. As the air left my body, I would feel

100

a tingling first in my knees and then in my chest. And then, terrified that no one would come, I would lose even more air by thrashing around as panic took hold of me. In Virginia the nurses were nearby, and it was never more than about ten seconds before one of them would come in and reconnect the tubing. But when you go to rehab, you lose the safety net of the ICU as you become part of a general population of patients. It was a difficult adjustment to become one among many after a month of being the only vent-dependent patient at UVA.

I was given many special privileges in rehab, although this soon led to a kind of glorified isolation. This treatment was encouraged by Dr. Sipski, who had me as her only patient. It was all well-intentioned, but I was cut off from the other patients, which was not a good thing. Also, many of the nurses may have been more intimidated than I realized. I don't think of myself as intimidating or frightening, but to the staff at Kessler, I was unique. I came from the world of the quoted and the photographed.

The nurses' station was about sixty feet from my room, and they had many patients to attend to. Kessler is a busy place at all hours of the day and night. Spinal cord patients are situated in the west wing, and when I was there five or six of us were on ventilators. Until about 1992 they had never had vent patients, and their spinal cord handbook says nothing about injuries above C4. When I read through it I felt a little freakish, because there was nothing in it that specifically addressed my condition. I felt I was in unexplored territory. Even after I had been at Kessler for weeks, I still panicked about the pop-offs: What if nobody at the station was paying attention? The security guard outside my door either couldn't or wouldn't help me. I joked that I always checked the footwear of the nurses on duty to make sure they were wearing sneakers. I wanted them to be able to race down the hall without slipping.

Of course, the joke was halfhearted, a device. When I couldn't breathe I felt like a fish that finds itself on the deck of a boat, flopping around with the hook still in its mouth. My imagination flailed too: I can't breathe, I don't know if anybody's coming, it's the middle of the night. If they do come, will they turn the light on? Will they be able to find the disconnect? The break could be at my throat, could be down near the floor, could be at the vent. I'll lose more time as they try to find it. I can't breathe, there's no more air, I can't make it, can't do this. I'm chained, hooked, tied to this damn thing. And I'm totally dependent on other people.

This panic was a reflection of my general state of mind. In fact, the nurses are always alert to pop-offs with vent patients. When one occurs they come charging down the halls. I will always remember Janet, one of the senior nurses and definitely the one you'd want in a crisis, if you're having what's called a code. Janet is very skilled in emergency procedures, but she's a rather large woman. I remember her running down the hall and into my room. As she burst in to come to my rescue, her shoulders and arms would often bump against the walls, and most of the pictures, papers, and notes on the bulletin board would bite the dust. The next morning someone would have to help me put the room back together again. But Janet always went right to the source of the problem.

One night a different nurse came in, and she had trouble finding the light switch. Then she couldn't locate the disconnect. I knew where it was, but I couldn't speak. I tried to point with my head. She grabbed the ambu bag on the wall and squeezed breath into me by hand while she called for help. Two more nurses arrived, found where the pop-off was, and put me back on the vent. These episodes intensified my feelings of utter helplessness.

Over the months I grew accustomed to the pop-offs, and they became fairly routine. I began to think of them as a metaphor for the entire experience of rehab: you start to realize that you are becoming physically and emotionally stronger and can get through more situations than you had thought you could. It gets easier to make it through the night. You become more comfortable with your surroundings. You develop friendships with the nurses.

I have great memories of the staff at Kessler and feel a deep fondness for many of them. The nurses and aides are really psychologists as well. They're the ones who can help you face reality. You may see a professional psychologist once or twice a week, but you rely much more on the staff you work with every day.

There was Patty, who became like a younger sister. There was Meredith, also in her twenties; I called her Ruthie because one of her elderly patients always confused her with her only daughter. She was the morning nurse and often helped me make the transition back to reality after a night of vivid dreams—she would tell me all about her progress in getting her boyfriend, Joe, to put a ring on her finger. Then there was Janet; and Sylvia, who was a sweet and soothing presence on the mornings when Meredith was off; and a wonderful Jamaican aide called Juice, whose real name is Glenn Miller. When I gave a speech at the Pierre Hotel my first time out of Kessler, Juice wheeled me onto the stage, and I introduced him to the audience: 'This is my good friend Glenn Miller. He used to be a bandleader, but he gave it up to be a physical therapist.'

We called him Juice because he made fabulous concoctions in a blender. I don't know what he put in there, but those drinks were delicious. It was just an extra bit of thoughtfulness. He's a big man, about six feet tall, with strong arms and huge hands. He wears steel-rimmed glasses that he is always losing, and he has the biggest smile I've ever seen. He was always talking a mile a minute and would enter the room as though shot from a cannon. We became very close. He has been in this country about nineteen years, but he sounds as if he just arrived from the island yesterday. I would ask him, 'What happened? Why is your accent still so strong?' He always answered, 'Cause I don't want to lose my roots.'

Juice is very religious, and he believes that I survived for a reason and was in Kessler for a purpose. Every day he came in with such great energy and optimism, and so much giving. He; Patty; Meredith; my physical therapist, Erica Druin; and my new physiatrist, Dr. Steven Kirshblum—the director of the Spinal Cord Unit, who replaced Dr. Sipski as my principal doctor— were the guides who helped me begin to accept my new life.

When Dr. Kirshblum took over the responsibility for my care, it was a tremendous psychological boost. I had not hit it off with Dr. Sipski and often had a sinking feeling when she came into my room. Dr. Kirshblum and I had an instant rapport. He is funny, irreverent, and deeply committed to his patients.

When I was in Northern Westchester Hospital for treatment of a blood clot in February 1996, long after my discharge from Kessler, he suddenly appeared in my room, saying he was in the neighborhood anyway and decided to drop in. I'm certain he had no reason to be 'in the neighborhood'; he had obviously cleared his schedule at Kessler and driven more than two hours from New Jersey to confer with the local doctors about my condition.

Many times at Kessler we would be in the middle of a conversation on a Friday and I would have to remind him what time it was, because he is an Orthodox Jew and has to be home by sundown. His house was seven minutes away if he sprinted, and he always left with only seconds to spare.

As we got to know each other, I felt comfortable enough to tease him about his posture; although he is only in his midthirties, he has the slouching shoulders of a much older man. I told him that on behalf of those of us who can't walk, he had to stand up straight. Whenever we passed each other in the hallway, he would remember to hold himself upright, or I would play drill sergeant and order him to comply with the regulations. Of all the doctors who have come into my life—many more than I would ever have imagined—Steve Kirshblum

105

sets the standard for his skill, compassion, and generosity.

Little by little, as I became more comfortable at Kessler, I began to emerge from my isolation. I started to visit the other patients, and soon they came to visit me. At first I felt that this was an imposition; I didn't necessarily want to see them. Gradually I discovered that it was fulfilling to share experiences and feelings, and I started to leave my door open. I never knew who would wheel in or what kind of a conversation we'd have. I found myself talking in depth with people I wouldn't ordinarily have met. Each person had something to offer. Before the accident I think that I tended to pigeon-hole: This is the guy behind the counter at the gas station, I pay him with my credit card and maybe he says, 'Have a nice day,' and I say, 'Thanks.' Or this is someone in a deli who makes me a sandwich, but I don't really care about him. I don't think of him as a person with individual characteristics and a history of his own. It's so easy not to really see people.

In Kessler I met people from every walk of life, of many nationalities and ages: a fourteen-year-old boy who'd been flipped on his head by his brother when they were wrestling; a sixty-year-old stagehand at Radio City who had stepped backwards off some scaffolding and fallen thirty feet to the stage below; a guy my age who'd been dumped into the sand by a wave when he was bodysurfing; people who were gradually losing their body functions to multiple sclerosis or who had suffered strokes. And I found myself connecting with many of them in ways that I would never have thought possible. I had been separated from the other patients by a wall of security that somebody thought I needed because of my celebrity status, until one day I said, 'This is ridiculous. I don't need these guards.' I started interacting with the other patients. I was becoming less resistant to being one of them.

Acceptance of your condition is an essential first step in rehab. Ordinary functions are now completely different. For example, every couple of nights you need to take a shower. The prospect absolutely terrified me: What if something happened to the vent in the shower? What if water got into the trach or the tube from the ventilator to the opening in my throat? They put a special stretcher under the bed, rolled the bed away, and placed me in a kind of net. Once again, I felt: I can't do this. There is no way. The idea of immersing myself in water petrified me. I kept putting it off, saying, 'Just give me a sponge bath. I can't face a shower.'

Janet and Juice were very patient. They didn't ridicule me or make me feel stupid. Juice kept saying, 'You're gonna feel so good, man. You're gonna want a shower every night.' But I couldn't believe it. I was afraid of the transfer, afraid of being rolled down the hall, afraid of the water. It seems utterly ridiculous now, but it didn't then, not to me.

Finally one night after stalling for a week or two, I agreed to try it. Dana was with me, and she literally had to walk into the shower with me and stay there, just so I could see her and talk to her. I'm not sure what my deepest fear actually was, but my condition made me feel open to every imaginable terror. Each step was a huge and horrific adventure.

Juice got me through it. Without him I wouldn't have been able to face any of these ordeals. He was able to 'stand-pivot' me out of a chair by himself, squatting like a weight lifter about to do an overhead press, then lifting me up. When he would grip me, as I leaned forward on his shoulder and he prepared to transfer me out of the chair, I always knew that everything was okay. I felt the way a child must feel when a father picks him up and carries him off to bed—both safe and small.

My first time in the shower, as I lay on the stretcher still very frightened, Juice told me a story: 'You think you got it bad? One time we had a lady here who had a spinal cord injury, and the way she got it was, she was on the porch of her house and her dog, who was old, went into cardiac arrest. So she started to give mouth-to-mouth to the dog. She closed the dog's mouth and was breathing into his nose. She was so worried about the dog, and she was struggling so hard with the dog to help the dog that she forgot where she was. She fell off the porch and broke her neck. Then the dog died anyway.'

I laughed so hard that tears were streaming down my face. All sense of propriety and any compassion for this poor woman went out the window. The worst part was that the story was true, yet I could only find it so ridiculous that I nearly went into convulsions from laughter. Probably my reaction was fueled by my state of anxiety as I lay in the shower on a net, scared of coughing or breathing. The lady and her dog became a running joke between us. I felt guilty for laughing at it over and over again, but somehow I think it helped me

108

accept the idea that life is more unpredictable—and even more absurd—than any of us can imagine.

At one point I said to Juice, 'When I leave here, I wish you could come work with me.' But he said, 'No. By the time you leave, you're gonna be okay. And my job is, I gotta help. I gotta help a lot of people.' That's his mission. That's why he's been there for fourteen years, earning eight dollars an hour. It's his service, his giving, his gift.

He always pushed me to do a little more. After he helped me work up the courage to go into the shower, he helped me work up the courage to sit in a wheelchair. Even that was a frightening prospect.

They brought in a chair very much like the one I have now. It has six areas of command. To go forward or back, to go to the left or to the right, to go quickly or slowly in this kind of chair, I sip air from a plastic straw or blow into it at various strengths. It took me quite a while to learn to drive it, and I had a number of mishaps in the process.

I remember practicing one Friday afternoon in the rotunda at Kessler, a large area where I didn't have to negotiate corners or hall-ways. On one side of this practice area a very pleasant old lady was seated at an upright piano on wheels, playing show tunes for a small group of patients, which was a Friday ritual. As she played selections from *The Sound of Music*, *South Pacific*, and *The King and I*, I did 360s and worked on speed control on the other side. Then I decided to head back to my room, feeling quite confident that I could go in a straight line without much difficulty. As I passed by the piano, I must have blown a little too hard; suddenly I swerved to the right, and as she continued to play

'Getting to Know You,' I hit the piano at full speed and pushed it backwards about five feet. The intrepid pianist didn't even miss a beat. She simply stood up and played on as I apologized profusely and tried to shift my chair into reverse. No one in her audience even raised an eyebrow. Obviously this was a regular occurrence. I succeeded in backing away and went a little more cautiously down the hallway to the west wing. After a few weeks I learned to drive much more responsibly.

I'm so accustomed to the chair now it's like a part of my body. But in the beginning it, too, held terrors. To be put in the wheelchair, I would have to be lifted out of the bed and then lowered into the chair in a three-man lift. Three aides would disconnect my vent from the bed, carry me lying straight out, put me in the chair, then reconnect me to the vent on the chair. This meant not breathing for four or five seconds. (I didn't realize at the time that the purpose of this technique is to introduce the patient to the experience of breathing on his own.) I was frightened more than I can say: I was totally dependent on the three aides. What if they didn't reconnect me in time? What if the vent didn't work? Again, my mind would teem with all the possibilities of what could go wrong.

Not all the aides were as patient or compassionate as Juice. They would give me a look that seemed to say, 'What *his* problem?' And I felt angry at myself, and frustrated because I couldn't control my fear. I'd lie on the bed looking at the chair, and I'd think, What *is* my problem? But the chair seemed so far away. I didn't want to do it, I didn't think I'd be able to go there.

My first time in the chair, I had a full-blown

anxiety attack. I was sitting back, and I panicked: I can't be here, can't do this. Get me out. I can't, I can't. I can't sit back in this chair, I don't trust it, I'm scared. Dana was with me at the time, and she said she had never seen me in such a state. But I was unable to stop it. Sitting back in the chair made me feel confined. I saw the straps pinning my arms to the rests, the seat belt, my legs strapped onto the foot pedals. I felt as if I were being put into an electric chair.

There were six or seven people around me, and I was yelling, 'No, no, I can't. Don't do this to me. I can't sit here, I don't feel safe. This thing's going to tip over.' I was totally out of control. I was afraid I wouldn't be able to breathe. I thought if I sat back I wouldn't get enough air. I didn't trust the vent on the chair. I was really frantic.

These episodes of panic were not entirely baseless. One reason my fears were so great was that I had nearly died a week after I arrived at Kessler, on the night of July 5. I may still have been reacting to the terror of that night.

It began with a drug called Sygen, which many people who are spinal cord injured have been taking, although it hasn't been approved by the FDA. You need to have it flown over from Italy or Switzerland, and it's very expensive. But there is a theory that Sygen helps reduce damage to the spinal cord. Some people who have tried it think it has helped them tremendously, while others say it's done nothing. There is no conclusive proof.

But I was willing to try anything. My family ordered it, and a month's supply arrived from Italy. On the afternoon of July 5, I received my first injection of about 400 milligrams.

At about six-thirty that evening, I was in bed. Patty was in the room. I began to feel constriction in my lungs, wheezing, and difficulty breathing. It quickly got worse, and breathing became even harder. Patty went to get Dr. Kirshblum, Dr. Green, and a few more nurses. Before long emergency medical teams from two towns had arrived. I was in anaphylactic shock, and my lungs had shut down. I couldn't breathe at all.

I realized this was happening, although I could do nothing about it. My heart rate went way up, while my blood pressure dropped to about 40 over 20. I had never experienced anything like it. They boosted the oxygen supply to 100 percent, but I still couldn't take in any air. I was struggling, the doctors were shouting. It was pandemonium.

Everything was closing down. Things seemed more and more surreal as I fought for air. I felt like I was going to drown, the way you feel if you're diving and are down too deep, and you need to make it to the surface but you know you can't. Everything around me went gray. I could still hear the people in the room; they were giving me various drugs, arguing about whether they should speed me up or slow me down. They were worrying about a histamine condition I have, known as mastocytosis. Dr. Kirshblum took over.

Then I had one of the eeriest experiences of my life. I had often heard about near-death and out-of-body experiences but had always discounted them. I'd never given any credence to seeing the white light and the tunnel and all those kinds of things. But now something very strange happened to me. I struggled and struggled, fighting for air. Then, after a while, I couldn't fight anymore. And I clearly

112

recall thinking or perhaps even saying aloud, 'I'm sorry, but I have to go now.' I remember the words very specifically. Again, I had that feeling of embarrassment, that I had to apologize because I'd failed. I had fought as hard as I could but hadn't made it.

And then I left my body. I was up on the ceiling. There was no white light, but I looked down and saw my body stretched out on the bed, not moving, while everybody—there were fifteen or twenty people, the doctors, the EMTs, the nurses—was working on me. The noise and commotion grew quieter as though someone were gradually turning down the volume. I watched myself lying still and saw everyone swirling around with blood pressure cuffs, stethoscopes, and needles.

There was a crash cart because they had called a code. A decision was made to give me a massive dose of epinephrine. It jump-started my heart, and my pulse shot up to some astoundingly high number, maybe 175. And then, with a jolt, I was down from the ceiling and back in my body. I felt my heart racing, my face turning crimson, my whole body pounding as though my pulse was everywhere.

Air started to come back, and I gulped it in. My blood pressure began to rise, and my mind cleared. I was seeing things again from my normal perspective, from within my body. Sounds were incredibly loud, and everything was chaotic. The epinephrine had gotten me going again. I was back.

They put me on a stretcher, and my friend Juice carried my vent so I wouldn't have to be switched to another one, because he knew how that always terrified me. They wheeled me out the door and into an ambulance, and Juice sat with me, still holding the vent. We arrived at the nearest hospital, St. Barnabas in Livingston. They wanted to put me on one of their vents, but Juice said, 'No, you're not taking him off this one.' He was almost in tears. He stayed with me until midnight just to be sure I was all right.

They ran some tests, injecting me with a dye that diffuses throughout the body in preparation for an MRI. By about seven-thirty or eight o'clock I was stabilized and feeling better. They gave me tranquilizers, and I was admitted to the hospital.

Dana and Will knew nothing about all this. They had left Kessler just before 6:30 to have dinner at a nearby diner. As Will was eating his spaghetti, he said, 'Look, ambulance. Look!' He had always been fascinated by flashing lights and ambulances. Neither of them suspected that I was inside this one. An hour later word reached Dana back at Kessler, and she came over and stayed with me.

I spent the next three days in intensive care. On the second day I asked to try the Sygen again. I felt that if this was a drug that might actually help me, but if I was unable to use it, it would be a terrible loss. Nobody had ever had an allergic reaction to Sygen before. I wanted to be sure. With all the doctors and nurses around me, they introduced the drug again. But when I started to feel the wheezing and the clamping down in my chest, I had to tell them to stop because I was having the same allergic reaction. They gave me a shot of epinephrine right away, and that was my last experiment with Sygen.

My confidence was shaken by this episode, yet I also felt strengthened by it. Once again, I had survived. The experiences with the shower and the

114

wheelchair had a similar effect. I began to believe that I was safe and that I was improving. Whenever he walked into the room, Juice would point out something new that I had done, something that was better than the day before. And when Dana would arrive he'd say, 'Here comes your medication, mon.' Juice took real joy in seeing the healing effect my family had on me. His lightness of spirit raised ours.

Kessler has an intercom system wired into every room. Often the aides would be paged for a lift or some other assistance. I was in Room 118, and Juice and I would hear, 'Juice, you're needed in Twenty-eight.' He'd always respond, 'I can't, mon, I'm on the bobsled.' This routine started because one night we watched the video of *Cool Runnings*, about the Jamaican bobsled team in the 1988 Olympics. We started joking about it.

Juice said that sometime for fun we'd put ourselves on a bobsled: the two of us plus Charles, another favorite aide, with Patty in the back. Together we'd go flying down the bobsled run. So whenever Juice was with me we played at being on the bobsled. We were speeding down and couldn't get off until we reached the bottom. Whenever he was paged, he was 'on the bobsled.' It was his way of saying that he was busy and wasn't going to leave me to take care of somebody else. When it was my turn he would focus on me completely, then he'd do the same for the next person. It was a simple little joke, but I clung to it. The picture of the four of us zooming down at eighty-five miles an hour was such a lovely image of togetherness, excitement, possibility, absurdity. And freedom.

Juice often said that he had liked me as an actor

but that now I would become a great director. He said, 'You're gonna direct the next bobsled movie. You'll do *Bobsled Two*.' Then he'd laugh—he always cracked himself up. He would shake both his hands so that the fingers would snap against each other, and he would laugh so hard that he doubled over. We could always find something to laugh about. His face would crease up so much that his eyes would almost disappear.

I had to go to bed at 6:30 every evening because I was only allowed to sit up for a limited number of hours. A decubitus ulcer had developed on my sacral area, where pressure had caused my skin to break down. So I couldn't sit for too long. The wound eventually penetrated to the bone; it was so big that you could put a hand inside it. The doctors wanted to operate, which would require taking skin from my hip and grafting it over the wound. I hated the thought of one more invasion of my body, one more manifestation of helplessness. I said, 'No, you've got to let me try to heal it. What do I need to do?' I had to increase my protein intake and stay in bed for eight days.

I didn't think I could stand eight days in bed. But Dr. Kirshblum made it clear that if I wanted to avoid an operation, I had to stay off my backside. So I lay on my side, which was extremely uncomfortable; this position compresses your shoulders and contracts your lungs, so you take in less air. My SATs dropped, provoking more anxiety attacks. I hated being turned on my side, but I knew it had to be.

Even in my nice private room, the view from the window was of a brick wall. But the wall wasn't very high because Kessler is a one-story building, so I'd

116

look at the roof, and the clear blue sky and clouds above it. I daydreamed about climbing that wall, then going up on the roof, then with a running start, getting away, a prisoner escaping.

As the summer wore on I would sometimes sit outside. I couldn't be left unattended in case of a pop-off, and I was still on oxygen, so a nurse and an O_2 tank went with me everywhere. I would stay out in the late afternoon, about four-thirty or five o'clock, when the day started to cool down. Out on the terrace, gazing at clouds for hours at a time, I felt very peaceful.

But on other days I couldn't bear to go out and look at those clouds. It was too painful; I wanted to be up there in my sailplane, gliding underneath them the way I used to. One day the clouds could be a wonderful source of serenity and reassurance; another day, a source of bitter resentment.

I felt the same way about Kessler. Some days it was a warm and friendly place of safety, a place where I would get better. Other days it felt like a prison where I had been condemned to spend an indefinite amount of time. And I would think: How do I get out? Anything to get out. I'd joke with Juice about a jailbreak.

I received a surprisingly large number of letters from faith healers, psychics, experts in alternative medicine, and assorted crackpots. It was hard to tell them apart. One man was especially persistent. He described himself as a healer who had a large practice in his native Ireland and believed that merely by the laying on of hands he could cause me to regain both sensation and motor function. At first I placed his letters in the crackpot pile. Then he began calling Kessler on a daily basis. He was so insistent, even desperate, to help me that my resistance wore down. When he offered to come over at his own expense and not charge for his services, my curiosity got the better of me, and I agreed to give him a chance. Perhaps this was a sign of my own desperation.

The very next day he arrived. He was about five feet three and wore a bright green jacket. I couldn't help thinking that a leprechaun had materialized to save me. It had been agreed that he would only be allowed to work on me with Dr. Kirshblum and one of the nurses present. Off came the green jacket, he rolled up his sleeves, and with nonstop commentary about his past successes he went to work. He explained to the curious onlookers gathered in the room that he would locate points of pain or 'distress' in the body and apply intense pressure to them with his hands. Endorphins would then rush to those locations, causing the pain to subside. I explained to him that I felt no pain whatsoever. Undeterred, he began to work on my upper body and arms. He pressed and asked if I felt the pain. I replied, 'Not at all.' He tried other locations, always with the same response. All of a sudden, my right arm spontaneously moved as he was putting pressure near my elbow. 'There we go!' he proclaimed. 'The energy fields have been restored, allowing him to move.'

With this statement his credibility was obliterated. I had simply had a routine spasm, caused by his hand gripping my arm. In an able-bodied person the brain directs an appropriate reaction to any kind of stimulation. If a fly lands on your leg, the brain processes the information and tells it not to react with wild, uncontrollable

118

movement. Because this connection to the brain is missing in a person with a spinal cord injury, there is nothing to stop the body from overreacting. Spasms can also be caused by fatigue, infection, or tension in the body.

The leprechaun was the only one in the room who didn't understand what had happened. 'That's enough for today,' he announced decisively. Dr. Kirshblum and I shared a glance. The next morning he was on a plane back to Ireland.

Episodes like that were ultimately very depressing. Fortunately, my down moods didn't last very long. I'd descend into a place of real gloom, then climb back up again. Sometimes the sight of Dana walking into the room would save me. Or Juice coming in and doing something silly. Sometimes I'd go down the hall and visit my friend Kirk, who had been a minister. I would talk to him about my struggle with religion and with belief in God. He never lectured me or tried to change my point of view, which I greatly appreciated. It was a tremendous relief when he would say something as simple as, 'God is in the way you look at your son.'

Sometimes when Dana and Will were visiting, we would go out into the courtyard, where there was a little tree. It was only about ten feet high, but Will would delight in climbing it, and delight in us watching him. That helped to get my attention off myself.

Patty was instrumental in preparing me to go back into the world. She has more energy than three people put together. She's about five feet seven and slight, a Jersey girl with a Jersey accent. She says 'coo-ough' and 'joo-aw.' She'd wear her dark blond hair in a bun like a dancer and glide around the room in her colorful uniforms. One had brightly colored fish on it. She did everything with relentless efficiency. If you said, 'Gee, I'd love some ginger ale,' there'd be a six-pack of it in your icebox a moment later. She was always challenging me, too; that was her special gift.

Patty helped me break through my arrogance and denial. Juice approached me with evangelical zeal about my mission and my purpose; Kirk helped me to see that I was still a worthwhile person. But Patty made me confront my condition. Her attitude was, 'Let's face it.'

In the early days she would stay in my room. From 3:00 to 11:00 I was assigned 'one-on-one,' which meant that I was her only patient. And rather than spending her time at the nurses' station, Patty would push me further and further into looking at myself and my circumstance—into confronting being a quadriplegic. I'd been trying for a long time to avoid it.

Unlike many others she wasn't intimidated by me for a second. She would stand by my bed and hold up the manual about spinal cord injuries. It was the last thing I wanted to read: a book about my fearful present, my dismal future. But she made me read about bowels and sexuality and dysreflexia.

Dysreflexia is a condition that results from a clogged bowel or urinary tract or even something as simple as an ingrown toenail or a kink in the catheter. It often happens quite suddenly, causing high blood pressure, and in some cases a heart attack or a stroke. It is particularly dangerous because a patient may not become aware of it until it is too late. The worst situation is to have it

120

happen in a place where people know nothing about it. One day some of the rehab staff at Kessler took me to Newark Airport to learn how to board an airplane. We were sitting in the American Airlines Admirals Club, waiting to get on a plane that was between flights. I asked where the plane was going and learned that the destination was Dallas. I said, 'No, never mind. If it was going someplace exciting . . .' We were all laughing.

I was relaxing and drinking a ginger ale when suddenly I felt my heart pounding in my chest. It was really strange; my heart was just booming. I asked Sylvia, 'Could you take my pulse, my blood pressure?' My blood pressure was 140 over 100. Usually it's about 110 over 70. And my heart rate, usually about 68, was up to 135. Then I started to have an excruciating headache—like an ice cream headache but times five, and we knew I was experiencing my first bout of dysreflexia. We went into a little cubicle at the back of the club.

What frightened me most was that we were in a public place. We were stuck in Newark Airport without a catheter irrigation kit or any nitro paste to keep my blood pressure down. There was a kink in the catheter, and my bladder wasn't draining. If my blood pressure went too high, I would have a heart attack or a stroke.

But this time I actually remained fairly calm. Sylvia decided to call the airport EMTs. Although it was Saturday, not a busy day, it took them a half hour to arrive. My blood pressure climbed to 170 over 120, then 190 over 130, and finally 210 over 150. I could only sit there with my heart pounding, thinking, I'm really stuck. At last the EMTs showed up, Sylvia did a bladder irrigation with saline, and the flow was restored. In the space of five minutes, 1,100 cc's of urine came out. The average person starts looking for a bathroom at about 350. By 400 or 500 he is desperate: if he's on a bus, he's begging the driver to let him off.

The trouble is that if you are paralyzed you don't know when clogging is taking place. And many hospitals don't even recognize it when it happens. If you went to the emergency room of the average hospital with dysreflexia, they wouldn't know what you were talking about. That's why it is so important to know the details of your own care; you've got to know what is needed. That's why Patty made me read that manual.

This was hard for me, because there are many things about the body and its functions and problems that I had simply never been interested in. Until Memorial Day 1995, my body had never let me down. I thought I was pretty indestructible.

But now I had to be aware of my body all the time. I was forced to become a serious student of myself. Many times at Kessler when I would want to read or watch Monday night football, Patty would come in with that damn handbook and force me to confront its contents. At first I would read a few pages or a single chapter and say, 'I can't. I want to talk on the phone. I want to watch TV.' But she would make me come back to it, make me study it in detail.

Gradually I realized I had to learn to think of myself the way I used to think about a new hobby or a new sport. I had to be as disciplined about my body as I had been about learning to fly a plane, or sail a boat, or ride a horse. I had to understand exactly where I was now, and how I would be for the foreseeable future. How could I master my situation? Who would I become?

My days at Kessler began at about seven-thirty, when the morning nurse came in. She would turn off the G-tube, which had been pouring liquid nutrition directly into my stomach all night. Charles, the aide on our bobsled team, would come in to help. They would turn on the radio, then range my legs and arms in the bed, pulling and massaging them to maintain flexibility and good circulation. Charles and Meredith would dress me, and there was the ordeal of the old-lady T.E.D.s, the Ace bandages, the abdominal binder. These were all necessary to keep my blood pressure from dropping sharply when I was moved into the chair. Then sweatpants and, because it was summer, a T-shirt.

Putting on the T-shirt required special care. Anytime I was moved I had to wear a collar that went up under my chin and down to the bottom of my neck, so I couldn't turn one way or the other. The collar immobilized my neck and stabilized the bones that had been grafted from my hip and were still healing. I had to keep it on for the first eight weeks at Kessler, except when I was lying still at night.

When I was dressed and ready, I was put into the chair. By ten o'clock I was down at physical therapy being transferred onto a padded table, and my arms and legs would be ranged again.

The physical therapy gym at Kessler is huge, at least a hundred feet long, with high ceilings and fluorescent lights, filled with people dealing with their disabilities. It is a room of sweat and struggle and disappointment, where people are fighting for

123

their lives. It has a musty, stale smell, especially in the summer.

Everybody went to the same individual spot day after day. There were people with every imaginable disability—amputees, people trying to walk, people trying to learn to roll over, people trying to sit up for the first time. There were about fifteen physical therapists. I found it hard to go into that room.

Therapists shouted out instructions and encouragement; patients were urged to do another, try harder, not give up. 'C'mon, you can do it. Another five.' Sometimes you'd hear cheering and clapping when somebody made a little progress or had a breakthrough.

When I was on the mat, I'd have to be rolled on my side because of the decubitus wound. At first I could only make small movements with my head. Erica, my therapist, would very gently put pressure on one side of my head, and I would push against it, moving about an inch. That was it.

I tried to move my shoulders a little. I could coax some motion from the trapezius muscles in my right shoulder, but really nothing else. Even trying to move my trapezius muscle was a test of endurance. You could see a flicker of movement, a little bulge of the muscle right along the top of my shoulder. But this small movement was reason for hope, because it took place below the level of my injury. It was something to build on, although I couldn't see that at the time. I did it simply because I was told to. But it was important to persevere, because if you can get a muscle to start moving, sometimes you can get others next to it moving, too.

I was also taken to a room in the outpatient

124

department where I sat in my wheelchair in front of a biofeedback machine. Electrodes were placed on my shoulders, and a graph would record my responses on a screen as I moved my trapezius muscles. I could actually *see* the movement this way. This allowed the therapists to take advantage of my competitive personality, to increase my motivation. They would set a target level and throw numbers at me, shouting, 'You've got to beat that number.' It was a simple exercise, but it got me going. Each day I tried to beat the previous day's numbers.

At first it was a wholly new experience for me to try to move one muscle at a time. It took a while for my brain to make a connection with the muscle I wanted to move. I'd have to think: My brain to my right shoulder. Okay, I just want that trapezius muscle at the top of my right shoulder to move. All right, let's go. One, two, three, *go*. I would will it to move. Gradually, the numbers began to improve.

I couldn't give up, because additional recovery can occur after six months, a year, even eighteen months, two years. That motivated me to keep exercising. Nerves can find new pathways, new ways to stimulate the muscles. I heard about a man who was suddenly able to move his leg three years after his injury. By March 1996 I could move my scapula muscles just behind the shoulder blades, which was a significant improvement.

After about an hour with Erica I would be taken to Occupational Therapy, where they taught me about different kinds of wheelchairs and special computers. They would talk about what kind of chair I would have when I went home, or what kind of voice-operated computer—none of which I

125

wanted to hear.

From May until December I ate virtually nothing. I had developed an extremely keen sense of smell, a typical consequence of a spinal cord injury. Once I asked Dana to order Chinese food for us; we were going to eat and watch a movie together. But when our order arrived it made me nauseous. Dana had to eat at the nurses' station and give my portion away.

At lunchtime, while most of the other patients went to the cafeteria, I would go to the lounge and gaze out the window. At two o'clock it was back to physical therapy. I'd be lifted out of the chair again and placed on the mat. Erica would range me again, and try to get my head moving a little bit more. She was always very patient. At three it was back to Occupational Therapy. By four the sessions were over.

There were days when I didn't make any progress, or even regressed. The worst days were when Bill Carroll, the respiratory therapist, would come to take a vital capacity, a test to see how much air you can move on your own. The therapist takes a little meter, sticks it on the trach and closes it off. Then the hose from the vent is removed, and you try to take in as much air as you can by using your diaphragm, neck muscles, shoulder muscles, and by raising your head. In other words, 'any way you can get it.' As you exhale the meter shows how many cc's of air you've been able to take in with this maximum effort.

I couldn't stand it. Back in Virginia, Dr. Jane had predicted that with time I ought to be able to get off the respirator and breathe on my own. But here I was failing miserably. To even consider

126

weaning yourself off the ventilator, you need a vital capacity of about 750 cc's. But I could hardly move the needle above zero.

Bill did another test, called an NIF—negative inspiratory force—that measures the effort your muscles are making as you try to take in air. First you exhale completely. Then the trach is closed off again, and the therapist measures the effort your muscles make as they attempt to pull in air. But in this test you don't get a breath; it is strictly a measure of muscle strength. Again, I could hardly move the dial. I thought: What's going wrong? Why can't I do this? They lied to me in Virginia. They were only trying to cheer me up. This is impossible.

Whenever I saw Bill Carroll coming around with his instruments, I was filled with dread. Like almost everyone there, he was very well meaning, and he would try to cheerlead. He'd shout, 'Go, go, go, go, go.' But nothing happened. The dial didn't move. Finally I rebelled, out of sheer frustration. At the next team conference I said, 'I can't eat, so don't make me eat. I can't do this breathing, so don't make me breathe. I can't do any of it.' And they let me off the hook. They didn't make me do it anymore. The philosophy at Kessler is that you are the leader of your own team. And to a large extent your progress depends on how much motivation you bring to the work. If you want to just sit in bed and do nothing, you can. Nobody actually *makes* you do anything. This is not simply capitulation on their part; they are trying to get you to take responsibility for yourself.

At about this time I had to decide if I was well enough to attend the annual fund-raising dinner of The Creative Coalition, scheduled for the

127

seventeenth of October. As one of the founders and recent copresident, I felt a strong obligation to attend, especially because as far back as January I had asked my close friend Robin Williams to be one of the two honorees of the evening. The Creative Coalition was founded in 1989 by Ron Silver, Susan Sarandon, myself, and a number of other celebrities to bring certain issues before the public to try to effect change. We were in the unique position of having access to the media as well as to key players in Washington. Our focus was mainly on the National Endowment for the Arts, homelessness, the environment, and campaign finance reform. Robin was to be honored for his appearances on HBO with Billy Crystal and Whoopi Goldberg for Comic Relief, which had raised millions of dollars to help the homeless. After consulting with Dr. Kirshblum and making special arrangements for Patty and Juice to come with me, I told the board of TCC that I would attend and present Robin his award.

No sooner had I agreed than it dawned on me how challenging this short trip to the Hotel Pierre was going to be. It would be the first time I would be seen or heard in public. I wondered if I would be able to address the audience or if I would be too nervous to speak at all. Would I spasm? Would I have a pop-off? I also knew that getting in and out of the hotel would require well-coordinated security, because the press and photographers would be extremely aggressive in their efforts to get the first pictures of me since the accident.

Dana and I talked it over and decided that the psychological advantage of keeping a long-standing commitment outweighed the risks of just getting through the evening. Robin put his own security people at our disposal. We rented a van from a local company, Dana dusted off my tuxedo, and on the afternoon of the seventeenth I finished therapy early and braced myself to go out into the unknown.

I vividly remember the drive into the city. For nearly four months I had been cruising the halls of Kessler in my wheelchair at three miles per hour. Driving into the city at fifty-five mph was an overwhelming experience. All the other cars seemed so close. Everything was rushing by. As we hit the bumps and potholes on the way in, my neck froze with tension and my body spasmed uncontrollably while I sat strapped in the back of the van, able to see only taillights and license plates and the painted lines on the pavement below us. As we pulled up to the side entrance of the Pierre, Juice and Neil Stutzer, who we hired to help us with the logistics and accessibility, taped sheets over the windows to protect us from the photographers. There were hundreds of them, straining at the police barricades that had been set up to give us room to park. The block had been sealed off, and mounted police patrolled the street. A special canopy had been constructed that reached from the side door of the hotel to the roof of our van. Once that was in place I was lowered to the ground and quickly pushed into the building.

We made our way through the kitchen to the service elevator. As I went by, the kitchen workers stood respectfully against the wall and applauded. I was in something of a daze, but I managed to nod and thank them. Soon I found myself in a suite on the nineteenth floor, where I was transferred into a hospital bed to rest and get my bearings. I had made it this far, but the whole experience had been much more intense than I had anticipated, and the evening was still ahead of me.

Soon it was time to get back in the chair and make all the final adjustments before joining a special reception of friends and honored guests. I wheeled into the suite's living room to find my friends and colleagues from TCC as well as Barbara Walters and Mayor Giuliani, Robin and Marsha, and a sea of other faces, all waiting to greet me and wish me well. For a split second I wished a genie could make me disappear. Somehow I made it through the reception, occasionally doing weight shifts in my chair while Patty discreetly emptied my leg bag and checked my blood pressure. Finally the guests went down to dinner, and I was left alone with Dana to recover. She hugged me but didn't need to ask how I was doing; she could tell that even though I was white as a sheet, I was happy to be out in the world again.

We watched the evening's entertainment on a closed-circuit TV until it was time for me to prepare to go onstage. A special ramp had been built from near the kitchen entrance to the stage of the grand ballroom. Black drapes had been hung to shield me from the audience until it was time for me to go on. At last the moment came. I heard Susan Sarandon introducing me from the podium, and suddenly Juice was pushing me up the ramp and onto the stage. As I was turned into position, I looked out to see seven hundred people on their feet cheering. The ovation went on for more than five minutes. Once again I had mixed feelings—of gratitude, excitement, and the desire to disappear.

At last the applause died down, and the audience lapsed into an intense silence. A blind person walking into the room probably would not have been able to tell that anyone was there.

In a moment of panic I realized that I hadn't prepared any remarks. All my attention had been focused on the practicalities of the evening. Luckily, a thought popped into my head, and I went with it. I said, 'Thank you very much, ladies and gentlemen. I'll tell you the real reason I'm here tonight.' (A long pause, as I waited for the ventilator to give me my next breath.) 'When I was a senior at Princeton Day School (another pause for breath), my English teacher George Packard once asked a student, "Why weren't you here yesterday?"' (Another pause as I tried to form my thoughts.) 'And the student replied, "Sir, I wasn't feeling very well."' (Now I knew where I was going.) 'And George Packard replied, "The only excuse for nonattendance is quadruple amputation."' I could feel the audience holding their breath. '"In which case, they can still bring you in a basket."' So I thought I'd better show up.' A huge laugh and applause. I'd made it.

The rest was easy. I introduced Juice as Glenn Miller, talked about how much I'd missed everyone at TCC, talked about Robin and his accomplishments, then brought him up onstage. For the next twenty minutes he and I bounced off each other. He took the curse off the wheelchair, going around behind it and pretending to adjust all the controls, referring to my breathing tube as a stylish new necktie, and suggesting that I use the chair for a tractor pull. He told the audience that I had to be careful with the sip-and-puff control; if I

131

blew too hard into the tube, I might pop a wheelie and blast off into the audience. The evening was transformed into a celebration of friendship and endurance. A large group of people, many of whom were strangers, were suddenly drawn together into a unit that felt almost like family.

I had promised Dr. Kirshblum I would be back at Kessler by midnight. We joked about the van turning into a pumpkin as we said good night to everybody and hustled through the back hallways of the Pierre and out into the street. We managed once again to get past the paparazzi. (The few official photographs that had been taken of the evening were sold around the world the next morning for nearly $150,000, which we donated to the American Paralysis Association.) Now as we bounced along over the potholes and through the Lincoln Tunnel back to New Jersey, I hardly noticed the rough ride. Dana, Juice, Patty, and I were practically babbling with excitement about the evening. We pulled into the parking lot at Kessler and forced ourselves to be quiet as we rolled out of the elevator past all the sleeping patients and into the safety of my room. Dana had commandeered a nice bottle of Chardonnay from the suite at the Pierre. We found a corkscrew and some paper cups and drank a toast to this milestone in my rehabilitation.

*   *   *

Soon I realized that I'd have to leave Kessler at some point. A tentative date was set for sometime between Thanksgiving and mid-December. I thought: God, I've totally given up on breathing. So

132

what am I going to do, stay on a ventilator for the rest of my life?

There were other possibilities. One option was phrenic pacing, a drastic and dangerous procedure. Batteries are surgically inserted into your chest to stimulate the diaphragm. After the implantation you have to stay in intensive care for months of constant monitoring. The risks are enormous. Batteries fail. Phrenic nerves can be damaged by the constant electrical impulses. The procedure frees you from a ventilator, but the outcome can be fatal. Other techniques were suggested to me, but none of them worked very well. A mouthpiece could be rigged on my wheelchair. I would have to take a breath through the mouthpiece, then turn to the sip-and-puff on my chair and try to drive it. The idea was to gradually reduce dependence on the ventilator. But the breath control needed to operate the chair would have made this far too complicated and dangerous. I could just see myself driving along, then turning my head for a breath from the mouthpiece and losing control of the chair. So I dismissed that idea as well.

But my diaphragm had been doing nothing since May, and now it was the end of October. From my study of the spinal cord handbook, I was aware that if I allowed it to atrophy, I might never be able to use it. I decided I *had* to make another attempt to breathe on my own.

They brought in Dr. Thomas Finley from Kessler's research department. He wanted to place electrodes all over my chest to see if there was any muscle activity that would give some hope. But Dr. Kirshblum advised against it, because of the danger of puncturing a lung when the electrodes were

133

inserted.

I announced that on the first Monday of November, I was going to try again to breathe on my own. At 3:30 in the afternoon of November 2, Bill Carroll, Dr. Kirshblum, Dr. Finley, and Erica met me in the PT room. And I remember thinking: This is it. I've *got* to do something, I have simply *got* to. I don't know where it's going to come from, but I've *got* to produce some air from someplace.

Dr. Finley said, 'We're going to take you off the ventilator. I want you to try to take ten breaths. If you can only do three, then that's the way it is, but I want you to try for ten. And I'm going to measure how much air you move with each breath, and let's just see where you are. Okay?'

And I took ten breaths. I was lying on my back on the mat. My head moved up as I struggled to draw in air; I wasn't able to move my diaphragm at all, just my chest, neck, and shoulder muscles in an intense effort to bring some air into my lungs. I was only able to draw in an average of 50 cc's with each attempt. But at least it was something. I had moved the dial.

We came back the next day, and now I was really motivated. I prepared myself mentally by imagining my chest as a huge bellows that I could open and close at will. I told myself over and over again that I was going home soon and that I couldn't leave without making some real progress. Dr. Finley asked me to take another ten breaths for a comparison with yesterday's numbers. I took the ten breaths, and my average for each one was 450 cc's. They couldn't believe it. I thought to myself: All right. Now we're getting somewhere.

At 3:30 the next day I was in place and ready to

begin, but several members of the team were late. I thought: Come on, we're going to have discipline here, we've all got to get together if we're going to make this happen. Finally I was really taking charge. When Dr. Finley arrived once again he asked me to take ten breaths. This time the average was 560 cc's per breath. A cheer broke out in the room.

And the next day we met again. All along Dr. Finley had been telling me when to breathe. He'd say, 'Let it out. And breathe. And let it out, and breathe.' But now I suggested that I might do better if I just timed my own breaths when I felt the need for more air. So he took off the hose, and I started again. I was gasping, sucking for air, and my eyes were rolling up in my head. It was a maximum effort, psychologically and physically. But I breathed on my own for seven and a half minutes.

When I got up to the west wing near my room, Bill Carroll was beside himself. He said, 'I've never seen progress like that. You're going to wean. You're going to get off this thing.' For the first time I thought it might be possible.

After that Erica and I worked alone. Every day we would breathe. I went from seven minutes to twelve to fifteen. Just before I left Kessler on the thirteenth of December, I gave it everything I had, and I breathed for thirty minutes. I remember Dr. Kirshblum saying, 'I don't know how you're doing this, but then I don't know how you do a lot of what you do.' The previous summer, still adjusting to my new circumstances, I had given up. But by November I had the motivation to go forward.

Something else happened to me during those months, which was as therapeutic as any physical

135

progress. When I first came to Kessler, I wanted no part of the disabled population. Gradually I had come to see that not only was I part of it but I might be able to do something important for all of us. I began to think that I could be useful to the scientists who were searching for a cure for paralysis. I had begun to understand something about the special character of celebrity. Although I had made several more 'serious' movies, such as *The Remains of the Day*, it was clearly my portrayal of *Superman* that the public had taken to. I knew this role had a unique resonance and had won a great deal of affection for me, for which I had always been grateful. And it seemed that my injury, if anything, had created a new level of public support.

No one was specifically saying, 'You could lead the charge on spinal cord disorders,' but hearing from certain people helped me formulate the idea. I was visited by Dr. Wise Young of New York University—Bellevue Medical Center, one of the great pioneers in spinal cord research, and by Arthur Ullian, an activist who had been paralyzed from the waist down in a bicycle accident. Arthur has been lobbying Congress for years, and they were the first to impress upon me the unique role that I could play. At about the same time I was contacted by Henry Steifel, chairman of the American Paralysis Association, asking if I might find a celebrity host for their annual fund-raising dinner that November. I was able to enlist Paul Newman, and with his participation the dinner was a tremendous success.

Juice had often told me, 'You've been to the grave two times this year, brother. You're not going there again. You are here for a reason.' He thought my injury had meaning, had a purpose. I believed, and still do, that my injury was simply an accident. But maybe Juice and I are both right, because I have the opportunity now to make sense of this accident. I believe that it's what you do *after* a disaster that can give it meaning.

I began to face my new life. On Thanksgiving in 1995, I went home to Bedford to spend the day with my family. In the driveway, when I saw our home again, I wept. Dana held me. At the dinner table, when each of us in turn spoke a few words about what we were thankful for, Will said, 'Dad.'

CHAPTER FIVE

My original discharge date from Kessler was during the second week of November, but Dr Kirshblum had convinced my insurance company to let me stay another month in response to my initiative about breathing.

Getting permission to stay longer in rehab was a major victory in our ongoing battles about insurance. During most of my stay at Kessler, Dr Kirshblum, Dana, and I had to spend a tremendous amount of time writing passionate letters, fighting for reimbursement for medical necessities. The first major struggle was over nursing hours: the company wanted to pay for only forty-five days of home care, with a nurse on duty from 7:00 A.M. TO 3:00 p.m. Outside those hours they expected Dana to be responsible for my care. They also refused to pay for a backup ventilator. Their argument was that if the vent failed, I could be kept alive by a nurse or Dana using an ambu bag while another ventilator was brought over from the supplier's office in Hawthorne, half an hour away. But the person on call for such emergencies might live in another town, as far as an hour away. And of course if the vent failed while I was out of town on a speaking engagement (my major source of income), I would be left in an impossible situation because you can't talk while you are being 'bagged.' The company even claimed that it was unnecessary for me to travel.

But what angered me most about the insurance company's position was their refusal to pay for any exercise equipment. Countless researchers have emphasized the importance of preparing the body for new treatments and therapies. If the muscles are allowed to atrophy, or if there is a significant loss of bone density because of inactivity, if the diaphragm is not exercised, then the patient will not be able to benefit from the progress scientists are making. In my case the company would not pay for any physical therapy work below the shoulders.

Because I believe so strongly that a cure for paralysis is possible, I equipped our home with essential exercise equipment, some bought and some donated. Electrologic of America provided me with a bicycle, which allows me to maintain the strength and mass of my leg muscles while giving me a cardiovascular workout. First I put on a pair of shorts with special electrodes that attach to the muscles of the thighs and buttocks. Then I'm lifted onto the bike and strapped in. Electrical stimulation causes contractions in the muscles that drive the pedals of the bike. At first I could only manage to keep the machine going for about five minutes, but within a few weeks I could cycle for half an hour without stopping. The benefit of this bike is tremendous, and it should be available to anyone with a spinal cord injury. Unfortunately, the retail cost is $100,000.

I also have a StimMaster (which cost $30,000) and special pants with electrodes attached that work all the leg muscles. Thanks to this machine, made by Bioflex (a small company in Ohio), the dimensions of my thighs and calves are almost the same as before the injury. We also use the StimMaster to work the abdominal muscles and the arms, two areas that can easily atrophy.

And at least twice a week I try to find time for the tilt table (retail cost $15,000), a device that allows me to stand with my legs and feet supporting my full body weight. First I'm transferred from the chair onto the board in a flat position and securely strapped in at the knees, waist, and upper chest. Then the nurse or aide gradually turns the handle that elevates one end of the table. We proceed slowly because if I go up too fast, my blood pressure will drop dramatically and I'll pass out. That happened several times as we learned how to use the table properly. (Now we have a rule that I have to keep my eyes open to reassure everyone I'm still conscious.) Usually it takes about fifteen minutes to reach the top, an incline of about 70 degrees, and I generally remain upright for about an hour. Suddenly I'm six feet four again. Dana and Will often come in to stand with me on the table for a family hug. Will likes to pretend that he's a mountain climber, and when he reaches the summit he perches on my head. I always let him know when I plan to use the tilt table because I think it's important for him to see me standing up, free from the confines of a wheelchair.

One of the reasons that insurance companies deny essential equipment and care is because only 30 percent of patients and their families fight back. While this allows the insurers to save enormous amounts of money, they would save even more by providing patients with the things they need: in most cases patients would improve dramatically or even be cured and no longer require costly reimbursements.

In addition to wanting to work on my breathing, I felt I needed the extra time at Kessler to prepare for the transition to life at home. My one-day visit home on Thanksgiving had been very stressful and depressing. Although I had tried to cover up my feelings as best I could, I spent much of the day parked by the fireplace. Ordinarily I would have been hosting the gathering, carving the turkey, organizing a pickup soccer game out in our front yard. We had not yet adapted the house to accommodate my wheelchair, so every time I wanted to move from one room to another, ramps had to be put in place and I would have to ask Chuck or Dana for help. My appetite was just starting to come back, and I struggled to be cheerful, not to ruin everyone else's day, as Dana fed me a tiny portion of turkey and mashed potatoes.

I was still feeling a lot of anger toward my insurance company. My trip to Bedford had been approved only on the condition that I return no later than 8:00 P.M. The case manager maintained that if I could stay at home for a longer period, it meant that I didn't need to be in rehab anymore, and they would not pay for any additional time there. I would be forced to absorb the $1,300 per day cost myself or go home immediately.

So at 5:30 I was loaded into the van we had rented for the day and headed back to Kessler with Dana and a nurse and driver. Dana's parents stayed behind to look after Will and host the rest of the day. But the mood in the house had collapsed. We had tried our best, but everyone knew that this Thanksgiving was painfully different.

Over the next couple of weeks, Dana and I made arrangements with Tracy DeLuca, one of the owners of Care-More, a home care nursing agency. I would need twenty-four-hour-a-day nursing, plus a staff of aides to help lift me in and out of bed and do work around the house that I would ordinarily have done myself. I knew that some of them would be intimidated at first and that I would have to make an effort to put them at ease, regardless of how I was feeling on any given day.

I also had to come to terms with the fact that because of the danger of a pop-off or a sudden vent failure, I would never be able to be alone again, even in my own house. I had always cherished my independence, and while I often enjoyed other people's company, time alone was very important to me. One of my greatest pleasures was sailing long distances by myself aboard the *Sea Angel*. And I remembered fondly a solo trip across Canada in my Cherokee 140, landing in private fields and often sleeping under the wing. At our country house in the Berkshires, I enjoyed taking long walks and riding up in the hills. I always came back refreshed and ready to return phone calls or socialize.

I had many conversations with Dr. Kirshblum, who had become a good friend. I admitted to him that one of my fears about leaving the sanctuary of Kessler was that I would have to resume being a public figure. In addition to the attention I could expect from the media, soon I would have to respond to the challenge laid down by Wise Young and Arthur Ullian.

Steve Kirshblum very kindly advised me that I had no obligation to be the poster boy for spinal cord injury. I appreciated this, but I felt I needed to do something—not just for myself but for everyone else in the same condition. Even if I had wanted to (which I didn't), I would never be able to forget the other patients I had met at Kessler. I had seen too much of their struggles and pain. I couldn't go home, devote my life to myself and my family, and ignore the larger picture.

And I had spent a lot of time studying the research in depth. I knew what the possibilities were as well as the obstacles. I had met and spoken with the scientists who were working on nerve regeneration. I understood that there had recently been several exciting discoveries, but that without public interest and enthusiasm, without an influx of money, progress would be difficult if not impossible.

I had received many letters saying that with my spirit and determination, I could overcome my injury. I assumed that meant that I could conquer the emotional and psychological problems that lay ahead, because clearly spirit and determination cannot put nerves that have been torn apart back together again. The regeneration of nerves within the spinal cord, gene therapy, fetal cell transplants, and remyelination—all the fronts on which scientists are attacking the problem—require intensive research and experimentation. And money. If I had been around in the 1940s, I couldn't have assured someone with polio that with strength and determination he could overcome it. The cure for polio was the result of research and funding initiated by President Roosevelt. I knew that my ability to adjust to life in a wheelchair might depend on my spirit and determination, but my future would lie with medical science.

During most of my stay in Kessler, I was mainly concerned with my own health and learning to adapt to a new life. But after the visit from Wise Young and Arthur Ullian and the APA dinner in November, I began to read everything I could find about the science of my injury. I found it fascinating. Soon I wanted to learn as much as possible about the research in the field and to understand my own condition in much more detail. I even persuaded Dr. Kirshblum to let me have another MRI so that I could see what my spinal cord looked like six months after the injury. We spent hours studying the photos. They showed that the hemorrhage on the left side at the C2 level had turned to scar tissue, that the spinal cord had shrunk considerably, but that there was no evidence of new damage.

One of the reasons the search for a cure for paralysis had never captured the public interest is that it had always been considered impossible. Even the Egyptians wrote in hieroglyphics 2,500 years ago that a spinal cord injury is a condition 'not to be treated.' This belief became conventional wisdom. And, sadly, few victims of spinal cord injury survived long enough to attract much attention; most died of the pneumonia that inevitably sets in within days of the initial trauma.

Scientific interest was first sparked in the 1830s, when an anatomist named Theodor Schwann discovered evidence of cell regeneration below the cut nerve of a rabbit. This was very exciting because while the central nervous system seemed inexplicably unable to fix itself after an injury, the peripheral nerves apparently could. (Cells in the peripheral nervous system have been named Schwann cells in his honor.) What was preventing regeneration in the spinal cord?

For a long time it was assumed that the damaged nerves were simply, for some reason, incapable of regrowth. Then in 1890 Santiago Ramón y Cajal suggested that the central nervous system failed to regenerate because of an 'inhospitable environment.' In 1981 Alberto Aguaya, a researcher at McGill University in Montreal, posited that the spinal cord could not regenerate because some vital ingredient was missing from its environment, and this theory became widely accepted. Researchers began focusing on nerve growth factors (NGFs), first identified in 1951 by the Nobel Prize winner Rita Levi-Montalcini, which were found elsewhere in the body but not in the spinal cord.

Aguaya demonstrated that a nerve taken from an animal's leg and grafted into the central nervous system allowed the nerve cells to grow along the transplanted nerve. This seemed to confirm that the problem did not lie in the damaged nerves themselves. It appeared that something in the
144

central nervous system was impeding their growth.

Then, in 1988, there was a major finding: Martin Schwab, working on nerve regeneration at the University of Zurich, discovered two proteins that inhibit growth in a mammal's damaged spinal cord. This altered the assumption that the cord's inability to regenerate was due entirely to the absence of NGFs. Two years later Schwab was able to induce nerve regeneration in the spinal cord of a rat by blocking the inhibiting proteins with an antibody called IN-1. In 1994 Schwab achieved considerable regrowth of nerves in the partially severed spinal cords of rats after treating them with IN-1 and a growth-promoting factor called NT-3.

What excited me most about Schwab's work with antibodies and growth factors is that the regeneration he accomplished was through drug intervention, not surgery. In addition, he surprised scientists all over the world by demonstrating that as nerves regenerate they seem to have some kind of sense memory of where to go. Researchers had always feared that even if regeneration is possible, the new nerves might simply wander aimlessly or make inappropriate reconnections. You might end up thinking, 'Move my left toe,' but have your right elbow move instead. The question would become whether the brain could learn to overcome this problem, as it can with dyslexia, for example. (Some scientists think that would be possible because the brain has an incredible ability to reorganize itself.) Schwab achieved regeneration of about 3 to 4 millimeters in his rats in an absolutely straight line. This linear regeneration was astounding in and of itself, but even more impressive was that the nerves made appropriate reconnections.

In 1988, the year of Schwab's breakthrough discovery of the two proteins that inhibit nerve cell growth, Wise Young organized the first center for the study of animal spinal cord injury. Today every researcher in the field agrees that regeneration is not only possible but within our reach. This has created real excitement in the scientific community and brought in many new investigators.

I've always been a practical person, not one to waste time in the pursuit of unrealistic goals or dreams. By the end of 1995 I was firmly convinced that the push for a cure was based on reality and not on unfounded optimism. It also seemed clear to me that scientists like Martin Schwab and Wise Young needed solid financial support so that they could progress as quickly as possible. I remembered the old adage that in business 'time is money.' In scientific research money is time. On behalf of all of us with spinal cord injuries, I decided I wanted to do what I could to help keep the top researchers busy in their laboratories instead of having to waste valuable time begging the NIH or various foundations for more money.

My first step into raising public awareness and money for research had been asking Paul Newman to host the APA dinner. The event brought in close to a million dollars; previous benefits had raised only about $300,000. I was asked to give a speech that night. When I had the audience's attention, I began by saying, 'I want to tell you about the wall of my room at Kessler. A fascinating subject, don't you think?' (I could feel them wondering where this was leading.) 'But on it there was a poster, a picture of the space shuttle blasting off at night,

146

signed and sent to me by all the NASA astronauts currently in training. Written across the top was, "We found anything is possible." '

I reminded the audience that in 1961 President Kennedy had issued the challenge to land a man on the moon before the end of the decade. At the time scientists thought the goal was impossible; no one had yet envisioned a vehicle that could make a successful landing on the moon and then take off again. Many considered Kennedy's speech irresponsible because he had delivered it without consulting the experts. Yet the vision was so captivating, to both scientists and the American public, that it became a reality. It took the combined efforts of 400,000 workers at NASA and dozens of companies that made component parts, but in July 1969 Neil Armstrong took that giant step for mankind.

I reminded the audience of another extraordinary chapter in our history of missions to the moon. As the crippled *Apollo 13* craft was returning to earth, dangerous levels of carbon dioxide were building up inside the command module, and the astronauts had less than thirty minutes to live. At mission control engineers who were used to doing everything by the book had to rely on their experience and ingenuity to solve the problem. As Eugene Kranz, the flight director, states in Ron Howard's film *Apollo 13*: 'Failure is not an option.' The challenge, in effect, was to fit a round peg into a square hole. They improvised a solution with cardboard and socks. Instructions were relayed to the spacecraft, and the astronauts survived.

I suggested that it was time to propose a similar

challenge to medical science. This time the mission would be the conquest of *inner* space, the brain and central nervous system. I had no doubt that an all-out attack would produce dramatic results. To create a sense of urgency, and to give the quest a human face, I declared my intention to walk by my fiftieth birthday, only seven years away.

As I came offstage, I realized that I had just taken on a new responsibility. I would have to back up this speech with action. From my work with The Creative Coalition, I had access to Washington and friends like Senators Paul Simon, Jim Jeffords, Patrick Leahy, and John Kerry, who could help guide me. I even had a working relationship with President Clinton, having campaigned for him in 1992. I also knew it was important to reach out to the other side of the aisle, because any real progress would have to come from a bi-partisan effort.

Everyone at APA was delighted with the evening. A few weeks later I was elected chairman of the board.

The mission of the American Paralysis Association is to find a cure. Nothing less. One of its goals is to speed up the pace of research by convincing some of the world's leading investigators to work together. I learned that the APA funds scientists at the Miami Project to Cure Paralysis, Wise Young (now at Rutgers), Lars Olson in Sweden, and Martin Schwab in Zurich, as well as young researchers with innovative ideas who would probably not receive funding from the National Institutes of Health. This wide-reaching approach seemed sensible to me. Just as it took forty or fifty scientists working together to develop the polio vaccine, the hope for speedy progress in the search for a cure for paralysis lies in the pooling of scientific information and financial resources.

The Miami Project is a major center for research. Dr. Mary Bartlett Bunge, a cell biologist there, is working on the problem of getting an adequate amount of regeneration with enough length for fibers to reach their appropriate target. Bunge's group has focused on Schwann cells in the peripheral nervous system because they produce and secrete elements essential for nerve growth. Schwann cells can be cultured, so if Schwann cell transplants work, researchers will be able to create millions of cells that can be transplanted to an injured area without immune rejection. Only 10 percent of the cells need to 'catch' to achieve movement.

At the Weizmann Institute in Israel, Michal Schwartz has been working with compounds taken from fish brains. She came to visit me in Bedford not long after I got home from Kessler and has kept in touch. Her approach is to culture fish brain compounds and inject them into the injured site, bridging the gap across the scar tissue and making new connections.

In June 1996, just a few months after I'd returned home, a group of researchers working under Dr. Lars Olson at the Karolinska Institute in Stockholm succeeded for the first time in growing nerves across gaps in the spinal cords of rats. These cords had been completely severed, yet after a cell transplantation across a gap of about one-fifth of an inch, the rats started to flex their hind legs. A year after the surgery they could support their

149

weight and move their legs.

This experiment received a great amount of publicity. It was regarded as a milestone because it showed that something that had been regarded as impossible is possible. But I was very skeptical about its viability in humans. The nerves that had been grafted onto the rats' spinal cords were from the peripheral nervous system, which does regenerate, but they would probably be incompatible with the central nervous system in humans and thus unlikely to produce motor function. In addition, many of the rats did not survive the surgery. Also, they were originally injured at the thoracic level, where the spinal cord is relatively wide. An operation on a high-level injury in humans, where the spinal cord is very thin, would be extremely dangerous. And the rats in the experiment had their cords completely severed, which is almost never the case in an injury to humans. Building a bridge across a complete transection is a very different procedure from bridging a partial gap. It was hard to imagine that any neurosurgeon would be willing to completely sever a section of a human spinal cord in order to apply the Olson bridging technique. Even if the patient were to survive, I believe that would be a serious violation of the Hippocratic oath, which states, 'First do no harm.'

That fall, Wise Young came to visit. He brought me up to date on the work in his laboratory, then dropped a bombshell: the next day he was going to Brazil to see six patients who, without Olson's participation, had undergone the Olson procedure. A year earlier all six patients (who had suffered complete spinal cord injuries and/or transected cords) had peripheral nerves grafted into the sites of their lesions. But several weeks later Wise reported to me that there had been no recovery of function. The one improvement the patients experienced was decreased spasticity: their bodies no longer moved uncontrollably at unpredictable moments. I concluded that Lars Olson's work was not yet suitable for humans, but that it was a promising example of a radical approach, the sort of bold step that is needed if you want to go to the moon or to cure paralysis.

A few years ago researchers knew only that it was essential to preserve as many nerves as possible in the early stages of an injury. They believed that whatever nerves were lost were lost permanently. Ramón y Cajal had even won the Nobel Prize back in 1906 for 'proving' that nerves in the spinal cord cannot regenerate. When Paul Newman learned this, he said, 'If that guy were still alive, we'd have to find him and take the prize back.'

Today, with scientists convinced that regeneration is imminent, preserving nerves is only one aspect of spinal cord research. I've learned that it now centers on three approaches: preserving the intact nerves; restoring function in the surviving ones; and the most exciting possibility— regenerating nerves in the spinal cord.

To preserve intact neurons, researchers have to catch them before they decay. Stroke research has shown that chemicals flood in to kill nerve cells after a trauma. This is known as *apoptosis*, or programmed cell death. To a spinal cord victim, this can seem like a cruel joke of nature: not only do you suffer the original injury but healthy cells near the site seem to commit suicide anywhere from a month to six weeks after the initial trauma. A drug has been developed to block this process in stroke victims, and others are on the way. This may have a crossover benefit for spinal cord patients. Dennis Choi at Washington University in St. Louis specializes in programmed cell death. He claims, 'We have a good sense of the cascade that destroys nerves after impact, and there is a lot of commonality between the brain and the spinal cord in this respect. Many of the same approaches that work in the brain work in the spinal cord.'

In the second main area of research—getting damaged nerves to function again—researchers focus on restoring connections that are intact after an injury but for some reason no longer work. Research with animals has shown that a lack of myelin, a fatty substance found on healthy nerve fibers that allows conductivity, is significant in the loss of muscle control. Multiple sclerosis is a disorder in which immune cells strip spinal cord nerves of their myelin sheath. Decades ago researchers working on MS began testing 4-AP (4-aminopyridine), a derivative of coal tar, to help MS patients gain as much use of their existing nerves as possible. The drug works by temporarily acting as a myelin coating, allowing impulses to travel through the nerves. Paralyzed animals given intravenous 4-AP have shown improved muscle reflexes. Many scientists believe that 4-AP holds real promise for the future.

But to me the best news is that new researchers are entering the field. Dr. Dan Jay, a professor of molecular biology at Harvard, wrote me in April 1997 to say that he had changed his career to focus exclusively on spinal cord research. Today he is working with several of the leading experts around the world and is about to publish an article about a significant breakthrough in remyelination.

It is the third approach, the regeneration of nerves, that excites researchers and patients the most. Nerve growth factor is now being used in the spinal cord to encourage the growth of new axons, which conduct electrical impulses from the brain. Spinal-cord-injured rats given intravenous NGF have regained connections between the spinal cord and the brain. And there are other potentially useful substances, such as fibroblast growth factor (FGF), which aids in the healing of wounds, and gangliosides, which may also protect and promote the growth of axons.

In 1995 Barbara Walters interviewed Wise Young as part of a profile on me. She asked him point blank if I would ever walk again. Wise replied that at first there is hope, but over time hope ebbs. Two years later, when he was interviewed for *48 Hours*, he said that with adequate funding it might be possible for me to walk within five to seven years. In a front-page article about spinal cord research in the *Chicago Tribune*, he stated, 'It might be easier than we had thought.' In his laboratory at NYU he had been working with an antibody called L–1. At a fund-raising dinner in Puerto Rico in May 1997, I showed footage of rats that had been treated with this drug in Wise's laboratory after a complete transection of the spinal cord. One month later their hind legs had regained function. In fact, one rat was trying to climb out of the basin he was kept in. When the lights came up I turned to the audience and said, 'Oh, to be a rat.'

153

By the end of the year, Wise had moved to Rutgers and made even more progress with L–1. Rating movement on a scale of 0 to 14, with 0 representing no ability to move and 14 full recovery of motor function, many of the rats achieved a score of 12.5. An untrained observer would not be able to detect any abnormality. He repeated the experiment twice to make sure of his data before publishing his findings in March 1998.

With my involvement in research and fund-raising, my life became busier than it had been before the accident. I had to balance my roles as husband, father, a professional who still wanted to work in films and theater, and an activist. I established the Christopher Reeve Foundation as another way of raising money for the APA and helping with quality-of-life issues for the disabled. I made speeches all over the country, hosted fund-raisers, and lobbied in Washington. I was gratified by the last line in a *Newsweek* article that chronicled the new direction my life was taking. After listing my plans and activities, the writer concluded, 'We should all be so disabled.'

As I began to study the problem of how to raise more money for research, I realized we would have to tap the resources of the government as well as private donors. I learned that the budget for the National Institutes of Health is only a little more than $13 billion, which has to cover research into virtually every affliction affecting the American public, from Alzheimer's and Parkinson's to cancer in all its forms, as well as many others. I met a number of times with the director of the NIH, Dr. Harold Varmus, and learned of his ongoing battle with Congress for more funding. He explained that

154

the government spends $90 billion per year in Medicaid and Medicare payments to Alzheimer's patients without doing anything to cure them. $8.7 billion is spent annually merely to maintain spinal cord patients, often in VA hospitals or nursing homes.

The economics of the situation make little sense. It seems to me that the government is fulfilling a social obligation to people suffering from serious afflictions but adding significantly to the national debt while failing to improve the quality of their lives. Many families who care for a chronically ill or injured family member quickly reach the million-dollar limit on their health insurance. Then they must turn to Medicare and are usually forced to sell their homes and most of their possessions in order to qualify for it. The sad truth is that once patients are accepted into the Medicare program, they are generally relegated to nursing homes, where there is little or no therapy, and they live out their days in a kind of human parking garage. I heard of one twelve-year-old boy who suffered a spinal cord injury and was placed in a mental institution because there was no room for him at any other facility. Some patients are allowed to live at home, but with minimal care.

The fact that this occurs at a time when real progress is being made toward alleviating and curing these conditions is terrible. I once heard a scientist exclaim, 'Give us $100 million and we can cure Parkinson's.' If the budget of the NIH were doubled—raised from $13 to $26 billion—the pace of research would be greatly accelerated and therapies would come more quickly. By some estimates the government would soon save as much

155

as $300 billion annually. Unfortunately, the 105th Congress was determined to balance the budget by the year 2002, even if that required drastic cuts in a variety of worthwhile programs. The mood on the hill, the mantra for many politicians, was 'no more spending,' and it is hard for many of them to take the long view. Few could be convinced that current biomedical research is not speculative. On the contrary, it is the humanitarian and economic solution to the nation's health care issues.

Research has traditionally been considered a luxury; you throw money at scientists, who may or may not come up with something useful. Many politicians want to know exactly what their money is buying. If you order a nuclear submarine, you know what you will get. Research seems too abstract. But today this is not the case: research is quite specific, and the progress is concrete and quantifiable. In the near future there will be a vaccine for diabetes. New drugs can arrest the nerve degeneration in MS. An AIDS vaccine may soon be possible because of the money spent on research. In 1984 the NIH spent zero dollars on AIDS. In 1996 they spent approximately $1.3 billion because it had become a national issue—not a disease that affects only a small segment of the population but one that takes the lives of the sons and daughters of middle America.

I became so involved in talking to scientists and plotting strategies to increase funding for research that I began to neglect my own rehabilitation. There were no longer physical therapists supervising my progress. I had to rely on self-discipline to stay healthy and keep my body from degenerating. Breathing on my own became a

156

particularly sensitive issue. By January 1997 I was able to breathe off the vent for up to ninety minutes. I longed for independence from that machine on the back of my chair. I went to Kessler for a consultation with Dr. Kirshblum. The crucial question was whether or not my diaphragm was moving. I was injected with a special dye, and films were taken as I breathed on my own. These showed that, in fact, my diaphragm moves both voluntarily and involuntarily. In consultation with the leading expert in weaning patients off ventilators, Dr. Peter Peterson at the Craig Rehabilitation Center in Denver, we discussed what it would take for me to get off the vent completely.

The prognosis was not encouraging. Dr. Peterson said that I would have to spend ten to twelve months at their facility and have minimal contact with the outside world. He even recommended that I have no access to a telephone. I would have to get up in the morning and breathe until lunch, then breathe again all afternoon, and only be put back on the ventilator at night. He predicted my chance of success was about 30 percent; the difficulty would be in sufficiently ventilating my six-foot-four, 215-pound body. Some spinal cord patients with a C2 injury have successfully weaned off the ventilator, but all of them were much smaller than I am, and therefore had a much easier task.

On the one hand, breathing on my own would have been a huge breakthrough. Part of me longed to try it, in spite of the odds against success. On the other hand, it would have been extremely painful to be away from Will and Dana and not to see Matthew and Alexandra for that long; and I knew that if I spent a year in isolation trying to breathe, I wouldn't be able to carry on with the fund-raising efforts for research. Momentum was building and I was concerned about what might happen if I suddenly disappeared for an extended period of time.

Shortly after returning to Bedford, I was contacted by Joan Irvine Smith, a horsewoman and a great philanthropist. She was touched by the fact that I hadn't blamed my horse for the accident. She told me she was moved by my situation and wouldn't rest until I walked. She has incredible energy, and is very influential politically, both in California and across the country. Anyone running for office wants to have Joan Irvine Smith on his side.

She decided to create a chair in my name at UC Irvine, dedicated to finding a cure for chronic spinal cord injuries. She put up a million dollars of her own money, which was matched by the state. Additional funds have been coming in from the private sector; the goal is $5 million. She has also created an incentive: a $50,000 prize given annually to the scientist who has done the most to further spinal cord research in the preceding year. In the fall of '96 I presented the first award to Martin Schwab.

Even before my injury I had always thought of scientists as gifted individuals of superior intelligence but wondered why they seemed to work so slowly. I respected their need to proceed cautiously, to perform thorough investigations, and to verify their data; but I often teased my half sister Alya about the endless number of conferences and symposiums that scientists attend. When I became

158

a vent-dependent quadriplegic, my desire to resume a normal life made me more aggressive in my dealings with the scientific community. In many of my speeches around the country, I found myself referring to the *Apollo 13* mission and the now famous line, 'Failure is not an option.'

On behalf of people around the world who suffer from serious illnesses or disabilities, I often long to make the scientists understand that, figuratively speaking, *we* are in the same predicament. There is an emergency. If we fail to support cutting-edge research immediately, it will be the equivalent of saying that nothing can be done to save the lives of three astronauts about to die of CO_2 poisoning. If we insist on sticking to the standard, cautious checklist in our approach to research, if we let the bureaucracy of the FDA or the NIH prevent new therapies from reaching the public, we will have needlessly perpetuated the suffering of millions of members of the American family.

Fortunately, from the spring of 1996 on, more money has been raised and more research accomplished. In November 1996 nearly 25,000 neuroscientists met to share information and ideas at the Convention Center in Washington and in sessions in nearby hotels. It was the largest such gathering in history. In March 1997 a meeting was held of the APA's research consortium—a collaboration of neuroscientists in Europe and the United States. Dennis Choi reported on his work on cell death, Fred Gage on the growth factor NT-3, the Bunge laboratory on Schwann cell transplants, Wise Young on his progress with 4-AP and L-1, Martin Schwab on his efforts to humanize the antibody to the protein inhibitors; Lars Olson on his bridging technique. Gene therapy was discussed—the efforts to stimulate the growth of damaged axons by changing the function of an injured animal's cells to produce a growth factor at the site of the injury. It was all immensely exciting.

When I met with Martin Schwab at UC Irvine in September 1996 to give him the research award, he showed me what he'd been doing—work that hadn't even been published yet. He'd been able to take a rat who had been injured for two months and get nerve fibers to regenerate 2 centimeters. That's a long distance. With my injury at C2, you would only need to regenerate 20 millimeters to obtain functional recovery—first breathing, then arm movements, control of my hands, and so on down the line. If the regenerated nerves grew to the lumbar area, I would get up and walk. The last thing Dr. Schwab said to me as I was leaving is that by the end of 1998 we ought to be able to do things at the clinical level that had been thought impossible only a few years ago.

But when I left Kessler in December 1995, much of this work had not been accomplished. Wise Young's words to Barbara Walters—that over time hope ebbs—still haunted me. I was absolutely unwilling to give in to that way of thinking. I remember talking with Dr. Kirshblum late one night and saying that I didn't want to join the ranks of spinal cord victims who had given up. While I could certainly understand that someone who has been in a chair for thirty years would have a hard time believing in a brighter future, I had only been injured for seven months. For my own emotional well-being I had to banish negativity from my mind.

160

Lindbergh made it across the Atlantic; Houdini got out of those straitjackets; with enough money and grass-roots support, why shouldn't I be able to get out of this wheelchair? When you're trapped in a dark room, you think: Where's the exit? You find the exit by remaining calm and slowly feeling your way in the dark until you reach the door.

By the beginning of 1998 it seemed more certain than ever that victims of brain and central nervous system disorders would be able to escape from that dark room. The first fetal cell transplants into a human spinal cord were accomplished by researchers in Gainesville, Florida. Martin Schwab, having succeeded in developing the anti-body to the protein inhibitors in rats, moved into primates with similar success. After studying my latest MRI, taken at UC Irvine in September 1997, he wrote to say that I would be a prime candidate for the first human trials, which were scheduled to begin within a year. Articles about spinal cord research began to appear on the front pages of the leading newspapers around the country.

Then, on January 3, 1998, *The New York Times* carried a headline that many thought would never appear: GOVERNMENT SET TO INCREASE MEDICAL RESEARCH SPENDING. And on the continuation of the article: CONGRESS APPEARS EAGER TO INVEST IN A CAUSE POPULAR AMONG VOTERS. Beginning with a $900 million increase in the 1998 budget, the Clinton administration proposed to increase funding for the NIH by $1 billion per year over the next five years. Momentum was gathering in Congress to go further—to double the NIH budget within that period. Members were beginning to recognize the economic advantages as well as the

161

popularity of the issue in an election year.

I was particularly gratified by a comment the president made in the *Times* article. He said that this century had been devoted to discoveries and achievements in the world around us, including the conquest of outer space. In the next century we should focus on solving the mysteries and conquering the difficulties of the world within us.

If the president and Congress follow through with the vision made public at the beginning of the new year, it will be a major victory for all the advocates of research who have worked so long and hard to make this happen. I felt that a part of the speech I gave at the Democratic Convention had been validated: at first something seems impossible; then it becomes improbable; but with enough conviction and support, it finally becomes inevitable.

CHAPTER SIX

I was only fifteen, but the summer of 1968 marked the beginning of my independence. I had spent the previous summer in a theater workshop at the Lawrenceville School, just ten miles down the road from Princeton. Now I was accepted as an apprentice at the Williamstown Summer Theatre on the Williams College campus in Massachusetts. The apprentices were needed from the middle of June right through Labor Day, so there would be no time to visit either of my families, which I have to admit was a relief.

There were about sixty of us. We did everything:

ran sound, hung lights, and painted scenery; attended classes in acting, voice, and movement. And because there were eight plays to produce in a ten-week season and only fifteen Equity actors in the company, we were sometimes cast in decent parts on the main stage.

The theater was run by the wonderfully eccentric Nikos Psacharopoulos, who taught acting and directing at Yale and at the Circle in the Square Theater School in New York. He was about five feet six and usually wore a uniform of sandals, a striped sailor shirt, and a floppy straw hat. On black tie opening nights he generally went barefoot. Much like my friend Juice from Jamaica, his Greek accent had grown more pronounced the longer he lived in America.

Nikos's devotion to the theater was intense, and he knew its history and literature backwards and forwards. By the late sixties he had been at Williamstown for thirteen years and was well on the way to transforming it from a typical summer theater into the proper theater festival it is today. The choice of plays in the summer of my apprenticeship reflected his vision for the theater. We began with Euripides' *Iphigenia in Aulis*, moved on to Brecht's *Galileo*, served up a crowd pleaser with *Wait Until Dark*, then did Chekhov's *The Seagull*, Peter Shaffer's *White Lies/Black Comedy*, Tennessee Williams's *Camino Real* with a cast of fifty, repeated *Wait Until Dark*, and sent them out humming the cheery score of *How to Succeed in Business Without Really Trying*.

I was cast in a small part in *Iphigenia*. Actually I was human set dressing. John Conklin, the designer, had specified that eight soldiers should

163

stand motionless on the ramparts through the entire play, which ran for an hour and fifty minutes with no intermission. We were draped in heavy blankets, carried spears, and wore plastic helmets. During rehearsals we could turn around and watch the actors—Olympia Dukakis, Louis Zorich, Ken Howard, and Laurie Kennedy. It was exciting to see them develop such exceptional performances in Kenneth Cavander's modern translation of the play. But by opening night we had to remain frozen on the ramparts, facing upstage. The soldier to my left, Jason Robards III, often failed to hold still. Out of the corner of my eye I would notice his head bobbing and weaving, and sometimes his body would sway in an almost rhythmic motion. After a couple of performances my curiosity got the better of me, and I asked him what was going on. He showed me his helmet: taped to the inside was a small transistor radio with a wire and an earplug. During the performances he was quietly grooving to the Supremes, Santana, and Blood, Sweat & Tears.

In *Camino Real* I had a real part as one of the policemen who patrol the streets, providing a threatening presence to the people trying to escape. One day as we rehearsed a confrontation between the police and the crowd, I received a supreme compliment from Nikos. Frustrated because he wasn't getting enough noise and commotion from the extras, he stormed up onstage, pointed at me, and yelled, 'Why can't you all be like Chris Reeve? He can make the sound of a crowd all by himself.' I reveled in the moment, but later I wasn't sure what he'd meant. Maybe he was impressed by the intensity with which I

164

attacked any assignment I was given at the theater, whether onstage or off.

I think that was the purpose of that summer; it was a test of our commitment to the theater. Some of the apprentices left after a few weeks. Some didn't show up for crew calls and were asked to leave. As usual I tried to act older than I was (hardly anyone knew there was a fifteen-year-old in the midst of a group of mostly college students) and did everything expected of me, although I begged the apprentice director not to send me back to the costume shop. One week of sewing buttons and hemming sleeves had been more than enough.

We revered the Equity actors tremendously, not only for their talent but also for the discipline they showed in tackling so many parts in one short season. They in turn were interested in our development. In our acting classes we worked on scenes with Michael Posnick, a graduate student at Yale. Toward the end of the summer, ten of the best were chosen to be presented before the Equity company. I had been working on a scene from Arthur Miller's *A View from the Bridge* with a wonderful young actress from Boston named Michael Curtin. We were both thrilled when our scene was picked for the big night. I was playing the young Italian immigrant Rodolpho and suddenly worried that my Italian accent and strong characterization would be torn to pieces by the assembled Equity gurus. Michael Posnick urged me not to back down or play it safe.

The scenes were presented in one of the rehearsal rooms at midnight, after a performance of *The Seagull*. The room was packed with all the apprentices, actors, and theater staff. Much to my surprise Michael and I both stayed calm, connected with each other, and avoided the temptation to 'sell' our performances to the audience. Instead we succeeded in drawing them in.

I was especially pleased because as Michael and I had worked on the scene, I had made a number of suggestions and continually voiced my opinions about blocking, props, pace, and other details that normally are the concerns of a director. Fortunately, she didn't seem to mind. Either that, or my natural bossiness was too overwhelming.

Actually, I already had a minor credit as a director. At Princeton Day School a few months earlier I had directed *Hello Out There*, William Saroyan's one-act about a young drifter in a small-town jail who befriends the young woman who brings him his meals. Auditions were open to the whole school, but I ended up casting myself in the lead. (At least this kept arguments between the actor and the director to a minimum.) The set consisted of a single square cell in the center of a bare stage. My stepfather and I had built it ourselves. The bars were made of thin wooden dowels, which we had to be careful not to break. Sometimes after the girl dropped off my meal, the cell door would swing open and I would have to close it myself in order to remain a prisoner.

In May we were invited to join a one-act play festival at Princeton High School, where student work from many of the surrounding towns was presented over the course of a week. On the night of our performance, the jail held together, the door stayed shut, and our production won a prize. This was my first taste of directing, and I thoroughly enjoyed it.

Michael and I received a nice critique from the actors after our scene from *A View from the Bridge*. The next day I was standing at the notice board when Olympia Dukakis came up, poked a finger at me, and said, 'I'm surprised. You've got a lot of talent. Don't mess it up.'

This was very good advice because at the time only a small percentage of my attention was on acting. The rest of it was on the chorus of female apprentices in *Iphigenia*. Their costumes drove me wild: they were all running around in short, flimsy tunics. One of the group absolutely knocked me out. Her name was Alison. She was seventeen and had just graduated from Dana Hall. I was fifteen, this was my first major crush, and I was clueless. Occasionally we made eye contact—or at least I thought we did—and once, as she came out onstage, she touched my arm when she passed by. I was so excited I nearly fell off the ramparts.

Unfortunately, I was so attracted to her that I stumbled over myself at every opportunity. I had always been fairly awkward around girls, but I became particularly inept and clumsy around Alison. The problem was that, at seventeen, she was far ahead of me in every way. She dated college guys. (Rumor had it that she was involved with a student at Amherst.) A mere fifteen-year-old had an uphill climb to gain her attention.

Oh, I had it so bad. She and her roommate Trisha had a dorm room that was right in the front of the building on the second floor, and sometimes I would stand below the window trying to overhear any conversations, or just because I knew she was up there. I made mistake after mistake. One day she came down for breakfast. I didn't know that

167

she hadn't washed her hair in about three days—it was piled on top of her head with a couple of rubber bands. As she went by I said, 'Gosh, I love your hair.' She looked at me like I was some kind of crabgrass.

But I kept trying, and gradually I began to be less self-conscious around her. Finally—sheer heaven—she started to reciprocate a little as the first night of *Iphigenia in Aulis* approached. At the opening night party we started talking. I don't know where I got the courage, but I suggested that we take some food and a bottle of wine from the party and go down the hill for an impromptu picnic by the stream. It was a night of complete euphoria. We dragged ourselves back to the dorms just as the sun was coming up.

The next day she dropped me like a hot potato. Maybe Trisha and some of her other friends had seen her go off with a tenth-grader, or perhaps her college boyfriend had called. It was a summer of such highs and lows.

One night it rained really hard for a long time. By about three in the morning, the lawn in front of our dorm had become very slippery. So a group of about twenty of us stripped down to our underwear and slid across the lawn. With a good running start you could slide about thirty feet. It was wonderful. Of course the event was bittersweet for me, because it was all happening below Alison's window.

On a typical day I was in a movement class at nine, then a voice class, built a set, and had a Snickers bar for lunch. When my mother drove up from Princeton to visit, there was only enough time to take her out for a quick burger and an A & W root beer. In spite of my bewildering rejection in the romance department, it was one of the best summers of my life.

Much to my surprise, the next one topped it. I was hired by the Harvard Summer School Repertory Theater Company at the Loeb Drama Center in Cambridge, for the impressive sum of forty-four dollars a week. Nineteen dollars went to the rental of a Radcliffe dorm room, leaving twenty-one for food and entertainment. Our season included Brendan Behan's *The Hostage*, in which I had a minor part as a Russian sailor; Miller's *Death of a Salesman*, for which the set was a junkyard, symbolizing the American ethic of discarding people when they are no longer useful; and Turgenev's *A Month in the Country*, in which I played Beliaev, the young tutor at a Russian country estate. Elliot Norton, the so-called dean of American theater critics, who could make or break a pre-Broadway production with a few well-chosen words, wrote in The Boston Globe that I was 'startlingly effective.' This was good for my ego.

Even more so was the fact that the lead actress in the play—twenty-three, beautiful, and a recent graduate of Carnegie-Mellon—was interested in me. She was engaged to a fellow Carnegie alumnus, who was in California for the summer writing sketches for a television variety show. They planned to save some money and get married in the fall. He used to phone exactly at seven o'clock every Sunday evening. But before long I had moved from the fourth floor of the dorm down to her room on the second, where we'd light candles, listen to the Tchaikovsky Piano Concerto No. 1, read from *The Prophet*, and work on my education

169

as a lover. Soon she stopped answering the phone on Sunday evenings.

The summer and our relationship progressed beautifully. One morning, however, our smooth romance turned briefly into a French farce. There was a knock on the door at seven o'clock. Still half asleep she called out, 'Just leave the sheets by the door.' There was a pause, and then a male voice boomed, 'It's me!' I bolted out of bed and began a frantic hunt for my clothes, which were strewn all over the room. For a moment I considered jumping out the window; then I remembered that we were on the second floor. There was no choice but to face the music. Once we had pulled some clothes on, we took a deep breath and opened the door. There was an excruciating silence; then she said simply, 'This is my friend Christopher. But you wouldn't understand.' I quickly excused myself and retreated to the fourth floor. The two of them spent the day taking a long walk by the Charles River. That evening he caught a plane back to Los Angeles. I don't think they ever saw each other again.

In the fall I began my senior year at PDS, and she found a job with a repertory company in Providence so we could continue to see each other. Every Friday after school I would take the train up to join her for a romantic weekend, but I had to make sure to get back on Sunday in time to finish my homework. Before long something about it didn't feel right. Once again I was trying too hard. It was almost as if I had cast myself in the role of an eligible partner. The age difference hadn't seemed to matter during the summer, but now it became an issue. In late October we split up and went back to our own worlds. By the end of the year she was engaged to one of the designers at the rep company, and I was dating a girl in my class.

*   *   *

Sometimes in the winter of 1970–71 I would look out the windows of the Cornell University library and wonder what I was doing there. After graduating from Princeton Day School in June 1970, I played a season of summer stock in Boothbay, Maine. I had planned to go to New York in the fall, find a cheap apartment, and join the ranks of young hopefuls trying for a career in the theater. But my mother, who had dropped out of college to get married and start a family, always regretted that she had not gotten her B.A. She convinced me that it all didn't have to happen so quickly—that four years of study and personal growth would only help me later on. She knew that there is a big difference between taking on New York at seventeen and starting a life there at twenty-one or twenty-two.

I had also been accepted at Brown, Columbia, Northwestern, Princeton, and Carnegie-Mellon, but I chose Cornell not only for its excellent liberal arts program and theater department but because it was a five-hour drive from the city and tended to be snowed in from the end of October to the first of May. I thought this would make it easier for me to focus on my studies and avoid the temptation to drop out of school and go to New York. But on snowy nights in the library, working on a paper for Russian Literature or Philosophy of Religion, I often felt that it was all irrelevant and that I was

171

arbitrarily being forced to postpone my goal of becoming a professional actor. I wasted a number of evenings when I should have been studying by joining the group sliding on cafeteria trays down Library Slope to the dorms at the bottom of the hill. Sometimes I just sat and stared at the cinder-block walls of my room, wondering if I would ever be free.

In retrospect, my years at Cornell were invaluable—not so much for the academics but because I was given an opportunity to experiment and mature without the added burden of having to make a living in the competitive marketplace of New York. The theater department was first-rate, with acting, movement, and voice classes available to undergraduates. The MFA program was under the direction of John Clancy, a superb director and chairman of the department. Casting for the main stage productions was open to the entire university. With a student body of fourteen thousand, competition was fierce, but the productions were often exceptional. During my freshman year I saw a *Long Day's Journey into Night* that was more powerful than any I've seen in the twenty-three years since I graduated. Having nothing to lose, I tried out for the male lead in Brecht's *The Good Woman of Setzuan*, the first offering of the 1970–71 season, and got the part. Over the next couple of years I was fortunate enough to play Pozzo in *Waiting for Godot*, Segismundo in Calderón's *Life Is a Dream*, Hamlet in *Rosencrantz and Guildenstern Are Dead*, and Polixenes in *The Winter's Tale*, as well as to perform in several student projects with the MFA company.

Some of these productions were directed by

172

professors who took an academic approach; others were directed with what I call the 'acting' approach. I found the difference between the two both fascinating and frustrating. I believe that when you're acting, you shouldn't be concerned with literary themes; you need to approach the work on an instinctual and emotional level. This is what allows the audience to experience the play as the unfolding of recognizable human experience and prevents the classics from becoming museum pieces.

Peter Steltzer, a twenty-six-year-old maverick in the Theater Department, applied the latter approach. He directed *Waiting for Godot* without ever talking about themes, symbolism, or 'meaning.' The result was an original production that had aspects of vaudeville, circus clowning, classical theater, and Theater of the Absurd. It was a resounding success. I was directed to play Pozzo as a carnival barker with a Cambridge accent and my voice pitched to a high register. Often when I asked Peter for the logic behind my behavior, he explained that his main interest was in creating a novel theatrical effect. Soon I abandoned my preconceived notions about the sanctity of Beckett and gave in to Peter's innovative ideas. I found the end result surprisingly satisfying. Much as in the *Death of a Salesman* at Harvard the previous summer, the boldness of the director's vision produced something truly original.

On the other hand, the production of *Life Is a Dream* was arduous and stultifying because the director was a pure academic. Much of our rehearsal time was spent comparing the play with Hamlet and discussing its significance and place in theater history. The staging was conventional, and the translation we used was literal to the point of being boring. The story of a young prince who is banished from the kingdom because a fortune-teller predicts that he will one day murder his father could easily lend itself to a vibrant, modern interpretation. The entire cast tried as hard as we could, but we weren't able to make it come alive. Just before we opened I spent a lot of time on the phone urging my friends—especially my new girlfriend, Helen—not to come. She came anyway out of loyalty and/or curiosity. We went out afterwards and luckily had much to talk about besides my poor performance in a deadly production of an obscure seventeenth-century Spanish play.

If I had learned nothing else at Cornell, discovering this difference between drama as literature and drama as a living presence would have been worth my three years there. My mother had been right. At Cornell I triumphed and failed, learning patience and self-discipline in a safe and nurturing environment.

My newfound patience was put to the test in the fall of my freshman year, when I received a letter from Stark Hesseltine, one of the most respected agents in New York. A classy, soft-spoken gentleman with a Harvard degree, he had discovered Robert Redford when the star was still a student at the American Academy of Dramatic Arts. He also represented Michael Douglas, Richard Chamberlain, Susan Sarandon, Stephen Collins, and many other fine actors whose work was familiar to me from reading the 'Arts & Leisure' section of The New York Times every

174

Sunday while stuck in the frozen hinterlands of Ithaca.

I left the unopened letter on my desk for about a day and a half, torturing myself with speculation as to why he would be writing me. I decided there could only be two possible reasons: (a) It was a routine letter inviting me to get in touch when I graduated from college; or (b) it was a pitch for me to drop out of college now and come to New York as his client, which would violate the agreement I'd made with my mother and Tris. Finally, I opened it. Choice B was correct: he had seen my performance in *A Month in the Country* and wanted to represent me. Would it be convenient for me to meet him in New York at some time in the near future? I was tremendously flattered and excited and had to force myself to keep my mouth shut around the Theater Department. I left the open letter on my desk and frequently sidled over to see if it still said the same thing. Then I called Stark, thanked him for the note, and casually mentioned that I would be free on Monday.

That morning I left Ithaca at six and was parked in front of the offices of Creative Management Associates—at the time one of the most prestigious and powerful agencies in the business—by eleven. As I went up in the elevator in my blazer, rumpled khakis, and loafers, I felt hopelessly out of place and was sure that Stark would take one look at me and change his mind. In fact, he couldn't have been more welcoming. I was ushered into his office, and he gave instructions to hold all his calls. Then he turned to me and said, 'Well, you're too tall for films, but never mind.' I was puzzled by this but didn't say anything. I had assumed height

175

differences in movies could be manipulated by camera angles or by putting the shorter scene partner up on a box. Then he added, 'When are you available?' I explained the agreement with my parents, and was amazed when he said they'd made a wise decision. He told me how much he'd enjoyed his years at Harvard, where he was the stage manager with the Hasty Pudding Club. We decided that I would come down from Cornell about once a month to meet casting agents and producers and that we would concentrate on finding work for the summer vacations.

A recommendation from Stark Hesseltine could open almost any door. Through him I met David Merrick, Robert Whitehead, and Kermit Bloomgarden, three of the most important Broadway producers at the time; Andrea Eastman, the casting director at Paramount; Joseph Papp, who ran the prestigious Public Theater; and many others. Some executives were impressed with me. Others were not. I remember opening the door to Joe Papp's office to find him wearing a pinstriped gangster suit, his feet up on the desk, smoking a cigar. I'd taken only about two steps into the room before he looked over, dumped the ash from his cigar, and muttered, 'Christ, more white bread.' I went through my audition piece from Henry V, after which I was not invited to sit down and chat. (When they don't want to talk to you after you've done your bit, it's not a good sign.)

I left his office and ran to a phone to tell Stark that I was sorry I'd bombed, but that I'd do better next time. But Papp had already called, and soon I understood the frosty reception. He was trying to build a company of real ethnic diversity. He
176

believed strongly in nontraditional casting and wanted more actors like Raul Julia (Latino) and Cleavon Little (African-American), not an earnest WASP like me. But when Stark believed in an actor, he never gave up; I auditioned at least a dozen times during the seventies for various productions at the Public. Every time the part would be cast in a completely different way. Much later, in January 1989, when the politics of the theater had changed and directors were given more autonomy in casting, James Lapine asked me to costar with Mandy Patinkin in *The Winter's Tale*. After watching a run-through, Joe Papp took me aside and said, 'We should have used you before.'

As the summer approached I drove down from Cornell more frequently and met with some success. A day trip to New York meant ten hours on the road, often followed by pulling an all-nighter to complete a paper for a nine-thirty class the next morning; so the more I drove, the more determined I became to make the trip worthwhile. I was cast in a production of *The Lion in Winter* that was going to rehearse and perform in Bermuda for ten weeks; I was offered a small part in the film of *The Great Gatsby* with Robert Redford and Mia Farrow; and I got one of the leads in Michael Weller's *Moonchildren* for the renowned director Alan Schneider.

Unfortunately, all these productions began before the end of the school year. To have these exciting offers conflict with exam week was almost more than I could bear. But a deal was a deal, and I had to finish the semester.

By the time I was free for the summer, there were few choices left. I ended up in a touring production of *Forty Carats*, starring Eleanor Parker on the straw-hat circuit. This was a letdown compared with the earlier offers, but at least I was working, and we played in places like Cape Cod, New Hampshire, and Maine, some of the nicest spots in New England. The production was undistinguished, but I tried my best. We played each theater for a week and then moved on; one pleasant challenge was to see how many sailboats and good restaurants and delightful companions I could find in each town. The most memorable moment of the summer took place onstage at the Candlewood Playhouse in Connecticut: Eleanor Parker took a step toward me just as a fifty-pound stage light fell twenty feet right onto the spot where she had just been standing. I dutifully came out with my next line, and she tried not to react to the huge thud right behind her, but the audience freaked out. The stage manager brought the curtain down until everyone could regain composure. The rest of the lights were checked, and we picked up where we had left off.

The following March I once again began the process of finding a job for the summer. This time it didn't take long. I was offered a full-season contract with the San Diego Shakespeare Festival, with decent parts in *Richard III*, *The Merry Wives of Windsor*, and *Love's Labour's Lost* on the main stage at the Old Globe Theatre. I thought this was a wonderful opportunity and decided not to let it pass me by. I approached all my professors with a letter of support from John Clancy, and after some negotiating it was agreed that I could leave school April 15 to begin rehearsals in San Diego—on the condition that I complete all my papers and exams on the honor system and send them in on time. Having worked things out with Cornell, I was able to sell the plan to my parents without too much difficulty. I drove home to Princeton, traded my ski parka and long winter underwear for khakis and short-sleeved shirts, and soon found myself looking at palm trees and the Pacific Ocean for the first time.

Anthony Zerbe played Richard and soon became a good friend. His approach to the part was to go way overboard in rehearsals, to try anything, no matter how outlandish, then pull back later. He was never intimidated by the role; instead he took big bites out of it. His confidence and the boldness of his choices made him fascinating to watch. I was improbably cast as Edward IV, who dies of syphilis, thus making way for Richard's ascent to the throne. I had a gray wig and a complete age makeup, and I followed Zerbe's lead in attacking the part. Because the role was so far from my own age and personality, I felt free to explore and was quite secure in the characterization.

In *The Merry Wives of Windsor* I was cast as Fenton, a 'service' part that only required the actor to dress well and deliver paragraphs of exposition. Frankly I was bored by it because it seemed so dull compared with my part in Richard. Ellis Rabb, who had been the artistic director of the APA Repertory Company in New York for many years and was one of my mentors, came to see the Old Globe productions. (As a teenager I had seen all of his productions and become friends with him and many of the actors in the company.) His comment to me in the dressing room was brief and to the

179

point: 'Your Edward is acceptable; your Fenton is a mess.' Later a group of us went out for something to eat, and I cornered him for an explanation. His point was that as I progressed in my career it would be more valuable to learn how to play parts closer to myself; that it would rarely if ever be necessary to put on tons of makeup and play so far against type. There were opportunities with Fenton that I hadn't explored because I'd decided that it didn't require 'acting.' He argued that a greater challenge than playing Edward IV would have been to find something original and interesting in Fenton instead of allowing my condescending attitude toward the part to come across the footlights.

I rank that conversation as one of the most important of my whole career. I understood that without being typecast an actor can and must bring his own personality, emotional life, and physical attributes to the work. These are assets, not liabilities. I learned that acting is about being truthful and figuratively naked onstage, as opposed to trying to disappear into some clever but remote characterization.

The season at the Old Globe was so exciting and enlightening that I dreaded the approach of Labor Day weekend, which would bring it to a close. I also realized how reluctant I was to go back to Cornell. I was still willing to get my undergraduate degree, but I needed to take some time before returning to university life. I wanted to see more top professional actors at work in both modern and classical plays and had a strong urge to travel. With money I saved from my job at the Old Globe, I took a three-month leave of absence from Cornell, packed a knapsack and a small bag, and headed for

England.

I bought a copy of *Europe on Five Dollars a Day* and made a rough plan for the trip. The cheapest fare I could find was on Icelandair, which landed in Glasgow rather than London; so I decided to begin my theater tour in Scotland and work my way south.

The very first production I saw was the Brecht-Weill *Threepenny Opera* at the Citizens' Theatre in Glasgow. The production was first-rate, but what impressed me most was that the name of the theater reflected its role in the community. Tickets were cheap, and the theater was filled with working-class people. Too many American rep companies are patronized primarily by affluent subscribers. Even at the Old Globe and Williamstown, during curtain calls we were almost always looking out at a sea of gray hair—well-to-do retirees with plenty of free time. Where were the students and the small shop owners, the taxi drivers and the gas station attendants? In Glasgow they were all there, mingling comfortably with the doctors, lawyers, and university professors. I imagined what it must have been like for Shakespeare: his plays had to appeal to everyone, from the commoners in the pit to the gentry in the upper circle.

From Glasgow I made my way north to Inverness and Aberdeen, then south to Pitlochry and Edinburgh, where I managed to catch some of the 'fringe' productions at the end of the Edinburgh Festival. Working my way south, I saw an amazing *King Lear* at the Every-man Theatre in Liverpool (another theater that lived up to its name), Ibsen's *Brand* at the Octagon Theatre in

181

Bolton, and productions of Pinter, Chekhov, Albee, Williams, and many others in places like Nottingham, Sheffield, and Derby. In Manchester I came across a production of Wycherley's *The Country Wife* with Albert Finney, who was a little heavier but just as dashing and charismatic as he was in the 1963 film *Tom Jones*. At each town I would usually find the actors in the bar after the performance. I had no hesitation about introducing myself as an admiring and curious American actor. At first some of them were taken aback by my direct approach, but it's pretty much true of actors anywhere in the world that if you compliment their performance and ask them how they did it, they will soon launch into a monologue and often tell you even more than you wanted to know.

I was particularly impressed by the commitment so many of them had to theater in and of itself. Many of their American counterparts feel stuck in a rep company while they wait for a good film role or even a TV series to come along. The actors I met in the UK seemed not to care if or when film work turned up. They lived simply, enjoying the rehearsal process and the satisfaction of deepening and enriching their performances over a long period of time. Most of them had attended drama school and were extremely versatile. They could move and speak well and had obviously developed acting technique. They could play Shakespeare or Miller or Alan Ayckbourn, just as a musician in an orchestra can play Haydn or Berlioz or Stravinsky.

I also found the clichéd notion that British actors are 'technical' while American actors are 'natural' to be completely unfounded. That may have been true several generations ago, but not now. I saw many performances (one of the best was Finney's) that were both technically adroit and absolutely truthful. It was also a pleasure to find that the younger actors felt honored to have been chosen for these companies; they weren't just 'passing through.'

I reached London the third week of October and stayed at the flat of an actress I'd met who was performing at Nottingham Rep. Occasionally she came to town on her days off, making my stay even more enjoyable. I saw dozens of productions, from the West End to pub theater in Camden Town and Hammersmith. I saw Olivier in *Long Day's Journey into Night* at the Old Vic. I was very starstruck watching him perform, but I still thought the Cornell production was better. Afterwards, as usual, I talked my way backstage and met the other actors.

I struck up a conversation with Dennis Quilley, who had played Jamie Tyrone and was in rehearsal for *The Front Page*. He confided that he and some others in the cast were having trouble mastering their American accents. They found it particularly difficult because the 1920s Hecht and MacArthur comedy had to be played at breakneck speed. The next day I found myself in the large rehearsal room at the OldVic, sitting next to the director in front of a cast of thirty, charged with taking notes and making suggestions. I had assumed that the company would have any number of dialect coaches available at all times, but for some reason there were none in sight. I wasn't being paid but didn't care. I took copious notes in case an actor asked for advice. Sometimes the director asked me to stand in front of the company and read the newspaper aloud. The actors always paid close attention, and some of them tape-recorded the sessions. It was a tremendous honor to be useful to them.

At the end of November I went to Paris on the final leg of my journey, before returning to Princeton for the holidays and then back to academia. I had studied French from third grade all the way through my sophomore year at Cornell and was fairly fluent. As I crossed the English Channel I made a quiet agreement with myself not to speak English from the moment we docked at Calais until I boarded a plane for New York. I had an introduction to the great French actor Michel Lonsdale and the phone number of a young college student, Jacqueline, who had been the au pair for my half brothers Jeff and Kevin a few summers before. I stayed at a youth hostel near the Pont Marie and often went with Jacqueline to her classes at the Faculté des Sciences at Jussieu, where she was a biology major. Since I'd always been bored by the subject in English, my eyes glazed over as I sat in the back of a large lecture hall listening to an ancient professor drone on in French. Every Sunday night I joined Jacqueline's family for dinner in their comfortable apartment in the sixteenth arrondissement.

I managed to get in touch with Michel Lonsdale and thoroughly enjoyed watching him rehearse Pinter's *Old Times* at the Théâtre de l'Odéon. Through him I was introduced to the company of the Comédie-Française. Because their stagehands were on strike, they had moved into a tent in a nearby park, where they were preparing a production of Molière's *Le Bourgeois*

Gentilhomme. As I watched rehearsals I was surprised to find that the director was mounting an extremely traditional production. Actors would come forward and declaim their lines, playing directly to the audience as they did in the seventeenth century. I talked to some of the company and discovered that they felt Molière must be done 'properly,' not reinvented for a modern audience. From studying the play in high school, I remembered it being extremely funny, and I'd seen productions in the States that were fresh and inventive. The Comédie-Française production was unbelievably boring, a real disappointment. On opening night I left after the first act.

I spent a lot of time roaming the city. Because I spoke French, I was treated better than many Americans. I could chat with people in restaurants, ask anyone on the street for directions, and catch up on the news by reading Le Monde instead of the International Herald Tribune. At Jacqueline's apartment on Sunday evenings, I confidently joined the discussions over dinner led by her father (a lawyer), who was usually challenged by her mother (a schoolteacher). Sometimes the whole family stayed at the table for two or three hours, enjoying lively arguments. Before I knew what was happening, I was becoming more French. I took to wearing a fisherman's sweater and baggy pants, and spent many afternoons in a bar smoking a pipe and writing in my journal. I have no idea who I thought I was, but I was still experimenting with different identities, both onstage and off. I tended to immerse myself in any new environment. In San Diego I looked like a surfer; at Cornell, a dyed-in-the-wool preppie; and now in France I was becoming some kind of generic bohemian.

The trip abroad had been stimulating and rewarding, but I had also been lonely. It was hard not having someone to share my experiences with me, and I sometimes wondered why I had taken the trip alone. Helen and I were writing each other several times a week. Every day I would go to the nearest American Express office to see if a letter had arrived. When there was one it was the highlight of my day. When there was nothing for me I would wander aimlessly out into the streets. Why weren't we together? By mid-December I fully realized how much I missed her, and my friends, and even the student life at Cornell. I wanted to change my flight and come home sooner, but I couldn't afford the difference in price. At last the return date arrived. After three months of meeting strangers and having no particular structure in my life, I felt the need to do something productive instead of just being an observer. I was ready to go home.

CHAPTER SEVEN

It would be nice to report that when I returned to Cornell in January 1973 I settled in, studied hard, and readjusted completely to campus life. Unfortunately it didn't happen that way. I found it hard to concentrate and I wanted to study acting exclusively, certain that it would be my life. Intellectual History, Physics, and several other courses I had to take seemed more irrelevant than ever. The trip to Europe had strengthened my desire to become a serious classical actor, and I felt I couldn't wait any longer.

Jack O'Brien, who had hired me for the Shakespeare season in San Diego, was now on the faculty of the Juilliard School in New York. The three-year-old Drama Division was already attracting some terrific young talent, and its reputation was on a par with the best drama schools in the country, such as Yale, Carnegie-Mellon, and Northwestern. I had a long talk with John Clancy, arguing that as a theater major I would achieve more at Juilliard (if I could get in) than I could by staying at Cornell. I managed to convince him and the dean of the College of Arts and Sciences. We agreed that my first year at Juilliard would count as my senior year at Cornell. I was ecstatic. I would be able to keep my agreement with my parents while making greater progress in my chosen career.

Now the problem was how to get into Juilliard. Jack O'Brien recommended me to the faculty and to the legendary John Houseman, the director of the Drama Division. Still, I was fully aware that every year two thousand students auditioned for twenty places in the freshman class. Only an additional two or three were accepted into the Advanced Program. These were students with professional experience who entered the school at the third-year level. I was trying for one of these places.

My Juilliard audition was more nerve-wracking than any arranged by Stark Hesseltine. Ten faculty members sat in a row in the school theater. The seats sloped upwards from the stage level, which gave the audience a superb view, but as I looked up

187

at the row of distinguished teachers sitting on high ready to pass judgment, I felt small and insignificant. Houseman, of course, was the most intimidating. Here was the man who had cofounded the Mercury Theater with Orson Welles and, after a long and distinguished career as a producer, was now enjoying success as an actor. He had just won an Academy Award for his role in *The Paper Chase*. There was supposedly an avuncular side to his personality; those who knew him well spoke of his warmth, kindness, and generosity. As a stranger I had a completely different impression.

I had heard he was notoriously impatient. Each prospective student had to present two pieces, one classical and one modern, not to exceed a total of five minutes. If Houseman was unimpressed, he would boom out a resounding 'Thank you' from the darkness above, and the aspiring young actor would have to apply elsewhere. Some probably returned to Indiana or Texas, reconsidered their parents' advice, and chose a more stable profession.

I felt particularly pressured because of Jack O'Brien's recommendation. What if I didn't live up to my advance billing? As I walked onto the stage I knew that somehow I had to get control of the situation. Experience had taught me that it's impossible to perform well if you feel like a temporary—and perhaps unwelcome—visitor. You need to believe that you have something special to offer and that your time and talent deserve respect. When you rehearse in your living room you own the space, and that comfort informs the work. The challenge is to create the same feeling during an audition in an unfamiliar setting before an audience of jaded producers, casting directors, or teachers who may have already had a long and frustrating day. It's hard to watch a new young hopeful come in the door every five minutes.

Fortunately the last applicant had left a few chairs and a table onstage. They were in my way, and I took my time clearing them aside, breathing deeply all the while, until the stage was bare and my heart rate had returned to double digits. Then I began a quiet monologue from *Life Is a Dream*, the very production that had gone so badly at Cornell. But I had worked on a passage in which Segismundo wonders out loud why he has been so harshly punished simply for existing. I hoped that this material might be unfamiliar to the faculty and would be a welcome relief from the standard Shakespeare soliloquies that many students presented. I took my time and didn't panic. Houseman didn't interrupt. My next piece was from *A Month in the Country*, an old friend that had lightness and humor and provided a nice contrast to the painful introspection of the other scene.

When I finished Jack O'Brien was beaming. Houseman said nothing, but Marian Seldes, one of the warmest and most supportive acting teachers a student could hope for, called out, 'Thank you, that was lovely.' During the five-hour drive back to Cornell, I replayed the whole experience again and again. I thought I had done well, but I had no real idea where I stood. Maybe Marian was just being polite. Why hadn't Houseman said anything?

Three weeks later the official letter came from Houseman himself. One other actor and I had been accepted into the Advanced Program. Classes

189

would begin September 15.

*   *   *

The first person I met at Juilliard was the other advanced student, a short, stocky, long-haired fellow from Marin County, California, who wore tie-dyed shirts with track suit bottoms and talked a mile a minute. I'd never seen so much energy contained in one person. He was like an untied balloon that had been inflated and immediately released. I watched in awe as he virtually caromed off the walls of the classrooms and hallways. To say that he was 'on' would be a major understatement. There was never a moment when he wasn't doing voices, imitating teachers, and making our faces ache from laughing at his antics. His name, of course, was Robin Williams.

As 'advanced' students we had several classes together, just the two of us. One of my favorites was a 9:00 a.m. session with the much-revered Edith Skinner, who for nearly six decades had been one of the world's leading voice and speech teachers. She had taught at every drama school in the country and was in great demand as a dialect consultant at theater companies everywhere.

Edith must have been in her mid-eighties when Robin and I crossed her path, and she had no idea what to make of him. She taught dialects the proper, academic way, using the phonetic alphabet and identifying key vowel changes and substitutions so an actor could meticulously master a new voice. But Robin didn't need any of this. He could instantly perform in any dialect—Scottish, Irish, English, Russian, Italian, and many of his own invention. Meanwhile, I was dutifully marking my text with the phonetic corrections, barely managing to learn one new accent at a time.

Michael Kahn, our primary acting teacher, was equally baffled by this human dynamo. Every two weeks we were expected to perform a scene for the rest of the class. Our group was talented, and there was a lot of good work, but nobody was prepared for a scene Robin performed from *Beyond the Fringe*. He played a somewhat dim-witted preacher delivering a Sunday sermon. Most of us were familiar with this monologue by Peter Cook, but Robin's version was even funnier than the original. His characterization, timing, and delivery were impeccable. Usually there was silence at the end of a presentation, then the floor would be open to a discussion of the work. But when Robin finished we all applauded. Michael Kahn, however, was not impressed. He said that Robin had taken the easy way out; this was not proper scene work but facile stand-up comedy. He urged Robin to try something more challenging instead of mimicking someone else's performance to make us laugh.

The first production of the third-year class was Tennessee Williams's *The Night of the Iguana*. Robin's performance immediately silenced his critics. His portrayal of an old man confined to a wheelchair was thoroughly convincing. He simply was the old man. I was astonished by his work and very grateful that fate had thrown us together. We were becoming good friends. Many of our classmates related to Robin by doing bits with him, attempting to keep pace with his antics. I didn't even try. Occasionally Robin would need to switch off and have a serious conversation with someone,

191

and I was always ready to listen. For a time he had a crush on a girl in our class who thought he was an immature goofball. Robin was able to share his real feelings with me, and I always did the same with him. This has remained true for twenty-five years.

My first role at Juilliard was Dr. Johnny in *Summer and Smoke*, also by Tennessee Williams. Dr. Johnny's relationship with his father is a key issue, and I identified strongly with him. I was able to draw on certain truths in my own life, and my performance went well. Afterwards I was called into Houseman's office for a private critique, which was standard operating procedure in the department. Houseman was still a daunting figure to most of us. He was in his early seventies, and the sternness evident in his Smith Barney commercials (with the now-famous line, 'We make money the old-fashioned way; we earn it') was exactly how he came across to his students. He could stop you abruptly during a poor audition or boot you out of school for a bad performance. Houseman would say, 'It's not worth our time to train you. Good luck!' and a student would be gone, just like that.

I was shown a seat in his office. He closed the door and settled into his rocking chair. After a long pause, he intoned, 'Mr. Reeve. It is terribly important that you become a serious classical actor. (Pause.) Unless, of course, they offer you a shitload of money to do something else.' I loved John Houseman from that moment on.

Then he offered me the opportunity to leave school and join the Acting Company, the graduate arm of the Drama Division. If you were invited to join the company, which was considered quite an honor, you went on a bus and truck tour of the hinterlands for twenty-six weeks a year. The stars at that time were Kevin Kline, Patti LuPone, David Ogden Stiers, and David Schramm. I was very flattered by the invitation to join their ranks, but I worried that I would be resented by my classmates, especially since I had only appeared in one production. I also felt an obligation to complete the year in order to receive my B.A. from Cornell. And I was enjoying the school atmosphere and working with my classmates—among them Mandy Patinkin, Bill Hurt, Diane Venora, and, of course, the amazing Mr. Williams. I politely declined the offer and stayed in school.

The highlight of my Juilliard experience came in the spring of 1974, when ten of us toured the New York City school system in Molière's one-act *The Love Cure*. We performed in every borough, often for sixth- and seventh-graders at inner-city schools who had never seen a live theatrical performance, much less Molière. But the play was easy for the kids to understand and genuinely funny. I was the dashing but none-too-bright romantic hero, and Stanley Wilson (now a film producer and a lifelong friend) was my servant. As in many Molière comedies, the servant is much brighter than the master and continually has to get him out of some scrape.

We were at first apprehensive but then delighted by the response from our audiences. They were mesmerized by the story, laughed in all the right places, and hung on every word. At one school in the Bronx, I received the greatest ovation of my entire career, although it came at an unexpected moment. The action called for me to leap up on a bench, raise my sword, and make some romantic declaration. I leapt on the bench, drew my sword with a flourish, and demolished most of a row of lights just above me. Glass flew everywhere, the lights went out, and the students roared their approval at this reckless destruction of school property. There was no way to get them back under control, so we were forced to retreat into our station wagon and head back to Juilliard.

I finished the year and then returned to the Loeb in Cambridge to play Macheath in *The Threepenny Opera*. This time Elliot Norton was less impressed. He wrote that an otherwise 'masterful' performance was ruined by the fact that I had no singing voice.

I had planned to return to Juilliard, but Tris was having a hard time financially. He was responsible for eight children, and I learned from my mother that it would have been a hardship for him to continue to put me through school.

Before the summer I had auditioned for a soap opera called *Love of Life*. In those days I'd try out for everything just for the practice. I was offered the part of Ben Harper, a charismatic 'bad boy.' I spoke to Houseman over the summer, trying to work out an arrangement that would allow me to do the soap opera and finish my second year at Juilliard at the same time.

The producers of the soap opera had originally promised that I would perform only a couple of days a week, and that I would always be finished by one o'clock. Houseman reluctantly agreed to this arrangement because he understood it was a financial necessity. I started working at CBS in late July 1974. By mid-August my character had become very popular. Soon the ratings began to go up, and the brass attributed it to Ben Harper.

Ben was the tennis pro at the local country club, but this was only a cover. He arranged kickbacks for the mayor's office, had a scheme to extort a half million dollars from his mother, and was married to two women at the same time. One wife was Betsy, the wholesome girl next door; the other was a low-rent pickup named Arlene, whom Ben had married on an impulse in Las Vegas. Most of my scenes involved hopping from one bed to the other and trying to keep Arlene hidden away. She, of course, wanted to cause as much trouble as possible and to drag me away from my cozy, affluent hometown.

The role of Ben Harper marked the end of my anonymity, because soap opera stars have huge followings. Guys on the bus would always say, 'Man, that Arlene, she's hot. You go for her. Don't you be going with that Betsy; she's square. But that Arlene, whew, she's hot. You make it with her, man, you got it.' But the women I met would usually say, 'It's really a shame what you're doing.' And I wanted to say, 'Hey, I don't write this stuff.'

But people get very involved in these soaps. In late August I was driving down Route 93 in New Hampshire and pulled into a service station to have an ice cream cone. I was sitting on the hood of my car when suddenly a woman came over, took a vicious swipe at me with her handbag, and screamed, 'How dare you treat your mother that way!' There was no opening line, no 'I've seen your show,' just whap! I decided to take it as a compliment.

As the ratings went up the producers began to write more scenes for Ben and his wives. I reminded them of our initial understanding, but

195

they pointed out that there was nothing in writing about limiting my appearances. I felt they had reneged on a promise but had to admit I was having fun. I was making a living and becoming well known.

Another benefit of the soap opera was that I was learning to act in front of a camera. I was fairly comfortable when the director pulled the camera back for a wide shot, but whenever he moved it in for a close-up, I became very self-conscious. Sometimes the lens was only a few feet away, and I found it almost impossible to concentrate. Close-ups are essential because they let the audience know what the character is thinking and feeling; unfortunately, they also reveal any tension or uncertainty in the actor. Although I still had a lot to learn, and much of my work was barely acceptable, after a few weeks I began to relax and enjoy it. Many of my fellow actors see a soap opera as the modern equivalent of the old-fashioned touring companies: the material isn't great, so you've got to make something of it, and you've got to work very quickly.

A lot of talented people were alumni of *Love of Life*: Warren Beatty, Jocelyn Brando (Marlon's sister), and Bonnie Bedelia, among others. If it was good enough for them, it was certainly good enough for me. And the $250 a day was unbelievable.

Finally the soap opera schedule forced me to drop out of Juilliard. This gave me enough time to try out for plays around town—Off and Off-Off Broadway. I took acting classes at the HB Studios, performed at the Theater for the New City, and starred in a limited run of Berkeley Square, a

196

romantic piece from the twenties that became a surprise hit.

It took a lot of energy, but then I had a lot of energy. I was only twenty-one; I lived alone in a fourth-floor walk-up on West Eighty-third Street near the park, and was now making almost a thousand dollars a week. Some of this went into the bank, but I spent the rest on enjoying the city and getting my pilot's license.

Love of Life was 'live on tape,' which meant we didn't stop unless somebody really screwed up. Gradually I became less self-conscious and developed my technique in front of the camera. If I simply concentrated on the other actor and the action of the scene and didn't care whether it was being filmed, the result was the ease and naturalness I always hoped to achieve.

On a typical day we had to learn nearly twenty-five pages of dialogue. Before long I discovered that if I wasn't absolutely certain of the lines, my performance was more spontaneous and less 'presentational.' The actors I admire most make you feel that anything could happen. I found that unpredictability draws the audience in. I didn't mean to be subversive; I was always careful to give the other actors the right cues. But as I experimented with an improvisational approach, my work improved. Soon I started to learn my lines on the bus on the way to the studio in the morning. I found I was able to absorb twenty-five pages of the script in about half an hour. By eleven o'clock I was ready for the taping, but I tried not to 'freeze' my performance, so that there would be room for new and unexpected moments as we filmed.

I never lost touch with the theater. At the

Theater for the New City, we did a very interesting play by Jacques Levy called *Berchtesgaden*, about the goings-on at Hitler's summer retreat. I played a young officer in the Elite Guard at the compound.

If this young man had grown up in Iowa, he might have been a 4-H Club-er or a varsity swimmer; but he grew up in Nuremberg in the 1930s. In several monologues he talks about Hitler's vision for the country—that he will turn the economy around, pull Germany out of the Depression, and restore national pride and unity.

The play was superbly directed by Elia Kazan's wife, Barbara Loden. She asked me to play the character calmly and rationally. She said, 'You look like a Nazi. So when you come out and talk about opportunity and pride and speak warmly and simply to the audience, it will be all the more chilling.'

Her advice has helped me in many parts over the years. Remembering what she told me, I underplayed *Superman*. I was six feet four, strong, and physically imposing; so I played against that, making him as casual as possible, letting the audience sense an implied power. Contradictions are always more interesting than playing the part 'on the nose.'

Barbara was a mentor to me. She was really my first coach, and she helped me steer around clichés. When she died of cancer at a young age, I was devastated.

In the fall of 1975 I had the opportunity to audition for *A Matter of Gravity*, a new play by Enid Bagnold starring Katharine Hepburn. The second lead was the part of her grandson. Every white male actor between twenty-five and thirty-five wanted to try out for it. Much to her credit, Miss Hepburn read nearly two hundred of them. The auditions were held at the Edison Theater on Forty-seventh Street. I walked out onstage to find the producer Robert Whitehead, his casting director, and Miss Hepburn herself sitting somewhere out in the dark. I had to read with the stage manager, who couldn't have been more pleasant but was not one of the greatest actors I've ever come across. I was extremely nervous. This would be a highly visible Broadway production, because Hepburn onstage after a twenty-year absence was big news.

Once again I knew I needed to gain control of the situation. I was going to face Katharine Hepburn in the dark, which is an intimidating experience. (Katharine Hepburn in the light is also intimidating.) So before I began, I called out into the darkness, 'Miss Hepburn, I would like to bring you greetings from my grandmother Beatrice Lamb; I believe you were classmates at Bryn Mawr.' There was a long pause. Then out of the darkness came the reply, 'Oh, Bea. I never could stand her.'

Now I had two choices: disappear or go to work. I fought to regain control after the Bryn Mawr setback. I started to direct the stage manager and to move furniture around. He was stunned. He'd been sitting in a chair all day feeding lines to potential grandsons, and now I was asking him to be a proper scene partner. My aggressiveness forced him out of his complacency, and my nervousness dissipated. I knew the words, felt comfortable in the space, and managed to snatch victory from the jaws of defeat. As I was walking out, that famous voice called to me from the dark: 'Rehearsals begin September seventeenth.'

Stark was blown away. This was unheard of. I felt relieved that doing the soap opera and leaving Juilliard had not 'ruined' me, as some of my teachers had predicted.

But now I faced a huge logistical problem. I was cast in *A Matter of Gravity* in September 1975, but my contract with *Love of Life* ran until July 1976. I had already had to give up my final year at Juilliard because of the soap opera contract. How would I be able to rehearse and play in the Hepburn production in tryout cities from Toronto to Washington and still hop from bedroom to bedroom as Ben Harper?

By begging. I went first to our producers and then all the way up the line to Darryl Hickman (brother of Dwayne Hickman, aka Dobie Gillis), the head of daytime drama at CBS. The *Love of Life* cast—especially my two wives—was very supportive. Any one of them would have fought tooth and nail if given a similar opportunity. The CBS brass, however, were unmoved. What was a Broadway play compared with a hit show on their network? I explained my problem to Miss Hepburn, who immediately called Darryl Hickman and shredded him into small pieces. By the end of the day I had two jobs and soon was racing back and forth between the *Love of Life* studio and rehearsals for the play at a Broadway theater.

From September 1975 through June 1976 I had to manage both. After a month of rehearsals we opened in Philadelphia, then went on to Washington, New Haven, Boston, and Toronto before coming to New York. Most days I would

200

catch a train to New York at 6:00 A.M., learn my lines on the way, tape scenes from several episodes, then travel back in time for the evening performance out of town. Occasionally we would tape *Love of Life* on Sundays as well, which was my only day off from the play. I rarely had time for meals and lived mostly on candy bars and coffee. But I had just turned twenty-two and thought I could handle it all because I had unlimited reserves of energy.

One highly melodramatic moment in New Haven proved me wrong. I'd finished a day of taping in New York. I'd been up since five, filmed all my scenes by three-thirty, caught the train back to New Haven, and arrived at the theater by seven-fifteen, ready to go on at eight o'clock.

My first entrance in the play had been generously set up by Hepburn: she was downstage left as I entered through the French doors center stage. In the first act my character, Nicky, a student at Oxford, occasionally comes home to visit his grandmother for the weekend, and they're always delighted to see each other. The direction called for me to burst through the French doors calling out, 'Grandma!' then cross down left to embrace her. On this particular evening I burst through the French doors, managed to call out 'Grandma!' and passed out cold. I bounced off a nearby table as I went down on the floor.

Hepburn turned to the audience and said, 'This boy's a goddamn fool. He doesn't eat enough red meat.' She had the curtain brought down, and after a moment I came to. I was then helped to my dressing room and the understudy went on. I had to lie there listening to him go through the entire
201

performance. I was checked out by a doctor, who told me I was suffering from exhaustion and malnutrition. I promised him that I would take better care of myself and assured everybody that I could still do the show. On the way to her dressing room, Hepburn stuck her head in the door and said, 'You're just goddamn lucky you're a little bit better than he is.'

I think that she cared about me, and for that I'll always be grateful. She invested so much time in me, always pushing me to do more. Hepburn never expressed affection in a direct, loving manner, but she always brought us things from her summer home on the Connecticut shore. She'd pass around strawberries, tomatoes, and corn and say to me, 'You're going to be a big star, Christopher, and support me in my old age.' And I'd say, 'I can't wait that long.' She even forgave me for collapsing onstage.

I adored her, but she scared the pants off me most of the time. On a good day, though, I could stand up to her, which I think she respected. I believe I was fairly close to what a child or grandchild might have been to her. A gossip column in the Boston papers even suggested that we were having an affair. She was sixty-seven and I was twenty-two, but I thought that was quite an honor.

She was always a fantasy figure to me. When we were rehearsing in New York, I would go to see her old films, like *Alice Adam, Bringing Up Baby*, or *Holiday*, at art houses around the city. As I watched her on the screen, I knew that if I'd been an eligible bachelor back in the thirties, I would have done anything to meet her. Then at work the next

202

morning she was sixty-seven again, coping with Parkinson's, sometimes crotchety, and always unpredictable.

For many years after the play closed, she would invite me for tea, and I would send her my latest news along with pictures of my kids. Once I ran into her at Lincoln Center, where Robin Williams and Steve Martin were doing *Waiting for Godot*. At this point I hadn't seen her for quite a while. I came down and stood in the row below her during intermission. I was about to say, 'Hi, Kate, nice to see you,' but she preempted me with 'Oh, Christopher, you've gotten fat.' She had a knack of throwing people off balance; she was a master of the unexpected.

In the fall of 1984, when I was in Hungary on *Anna Karenina*, my friend Steve Lawson was staying in my apartment. He, too, experienced the unexpected when the phone rang and it was Kate calling. At first he wondered what friend was doing such a good impersonation. Finally she convinced him she was Katharine Hepburn and asked, 'Where's Christopher?' Steve replied, 'Oh, he's overseas.' Then she said, 'Tell him I'm calling to say he was absolutely marvelous in *The Bostonians*. He was absolutely captivating.' Steve quickly wrote down this extravagant praise. Then she asked, 'What's he doing now?' Steve told her that I was in Budapest shooting *Anna Karenina* with Jackie Bisset. To which Hepburn responded, 'Oh, that's a terrible mistake. He shouldn't be doing that. Goodbye.' You're up one minute and down the next.

When we were doing *A Matter of Gravity*, my father took a huge shine to Kate. And she thought

203

he was just the most charming, the most intelligent, the most attractive man she'd met in a long time. He was teaching at Yale and lived nearby in Higganum, so it was easy for him to come to the performances. When I think about it, they're quite similar, Kate and my father. Two perfectionists: loving, charismatic, charming, and able to undercut you in a second.

But I have such wonderful memories of what she could do on-stage. In Act 2 of *A Matter of Gravity*, Nicky has decided to marry a young girl who's half black and half white. They plan to move to Jamaica; the grandmother thinks he's throwing his life away. The two of them are alone, just before he leaves. Then she says, 'You are my last piece of magic. I have so loved my portrait in your heart.' Nine actresses out of ten would say that directly to the grandson, with tenderness and poignancy. Hepburn played it straight out front, never looking at me, to underscore her disappointment and to indicate that she no longer respects him. There was nothing left for me to do; I had to walk off in silence. At that point, at most performances, she broke down, suddenly realizing that wasn't how she had wanted it to end. Sometimes she would move upstage toward the door wanting to call Nicky back, to embrace him one last time. But it was too late. It was a completely original and surprising way to play the scene.

Hepburn often used to say to me, 'Be fascinating, Christopher, be fascinating.' I used to think: That's easy for you to do; the rest of us have to work at it. But over the course of rehearsals, the out-of-town tryout, and the Broadway run, I learned that she was talking about unpredictability, about revealing the contradictions. She told me that if you're playing a character who's usually drunk, you have to find moments of complete sobriety in order to add dimension to the role. Not even a chronic alcoholic is drunk all the time. And she talked about how important it is to bring your own life experience to the work. She once said, 'You are already real; the character is fiction. The audience must see your reality through the fiction.'

As I studied her acting it seemed that she was always Katharine Hepburn and the character at the same time. Over the years I had the good fortune to perform with other brilliant actors who work the same way, like Paul Scofield, Vanessa Redgrave, Gene Hackman, and Morgan Freeman. Gene Hackman, for example, never goes to great lengths to change his outward appearance for a role; instead he transforms himself inside. In spite of your initial awareness of seeing the familiar Gene Hackman appear on the screen, you quickly accept him as whatever character he is playing because his work is so truthful. In *Gravity* I had the privilege of spending nine months working with one of the masters of the craft.

When we opened in New York, Kate got the bulk of the reviews, and I was favorably mentioned. The *Times* said that our scenes were the best, although the play itself didn't make much sense. The reviewer wrote that when Enid Bagnold tired of a character she sent him offstage for no good reason, but that it was great to see Hepburn in person and that I showed promise.

I wish I'd made more of an effort to stay close to her over the years, instead of just sending notes back and forth and often declining her invitations to tea. But from the moment we started working together, the uncertainty of our relationship was difficult for me. I guess it was too much like the roller coaster rides within my own family. The play had been a tremendous learning experience, but now I felt a need to break away. In the summer of 1976, when the production moved to Los Angeles, I dropped out.

Kate was very disappointed in me for doing that. When I went to see the new production, I got a chilly reception backstage. I felt as if I'd betrayed her. We'd created something, a special relationship, and then I hadn't stayed the course.

I had another reason for leaving: I was enticed by movies at this point. If the play had been truly wonderful, I would have stayed with it. But it was really her vehicle, a chance for the audience to see Katharine Hepburn live. While the rest of us were not exactly set dressing, we were not absolutely essential to the proceedings. I felt I needed to move on.

Stark convinced me to go to Los Angeles after the New York run, in June 1976. He arranged for me to be represented by Bresler, Wolf, Cota & Livingston, a small but prestigious agency that represented a select number of film and television actors. Jack Nicholson was their star client. All of the partners in the agency were very enthusiastic about working with me, but as they sent me out on auditions I realized we were not in sync about the kind of work I wanted to do.

Mike Livingston, who became my 'responsible' agent, was ecstatic when I was offered the starring role in a television series called *The Man from Atlantis*. The character was part man and part fish.

The $14,000 a week certainly appealed to me, but when Mike told me I had to go to an optometrist to be fitted for green contact lenses and then go over to the studio to be measured for webbed feet, my heart sank. I had wanted to get my feet wet in Hollywood, but this was definitely not what I had in mind. I told Mike that I needed to think it over. Then I drove out to my favorite little airport in Rosamond, near Edwards Air Force Base, hopped in their Pilatus B4 sailplane, and spent the afternoon playing in the clouds over the Tehachapi Mountains. I passed on the fish-man (Patrick Duffy, later a star of Dallas, took the part). When my agents called with other unappealing ideas, I would always head back out to the desert to find relief in soaring.

Finally I did take a small part in the film *Gray Lady Down*, with Charlton Heston and Stacy Keach, about the efforts to rescue the crew of a sunken nuclear submarine. I played a young lieutenant aboard the rescue ship and always stood as close as possible to Stacy Keach in order to have more time on-screen. It was a pleasant experience spending several weeks on Navy vessels off the coast of San Diego, but the script was mediocre, and most of us (and later the critics) referred to the film as 'a disaster about a disaster.'

By October I'd had enough of avoiding auditions for parts I didn't want. I threw my few belongings into the backseat of my Cherokee 140 and headed back to New York and the theater.

When I arrived home I called my friend Bill Hurt and asked if he knew of anything interesting that was casting. He said that he had just been offered the lead in *My Life* by Corinne Jaecker at the Circle Repertory Company, and the small but important role of the grandfather was still open. He arranged for me to audition for the director, Marshall Mason. Two weeks later we started rehearsals.

I was thrilled to be part of the first production of a brand-new play and to be working with Bill. I was also his understudy. One Sunday late in the run he came in with laryngitis. Suddenly I was on. I had to wear Bill's costumes, which was fine, until the character had to change into a bathing suit and go for a swim in a little onstage pool. The bathing suit was the one item that didn't fit—it was much too small. As I climbed dripping out of the pool, there was no place to hide. I had to carry on for the next few pages oblivious to the buzzing in the audience, until I could go offstage to change. Fortunately, this was my only experience as an understudy.

In late January, Stark called to say that I had been asked to audition for the lead in a big movie for a major studio. The casting director, Lynn Stalmaster, had pleaded with the director for a meeting. Three times he put my picture and resumé on the in pile; each time the producers put it back on the out pile. Finally he persuaded them to bring me in for a meeting. Stark told me the chances of my getting the lead in this big-budget movie were remote, and he had doubts about the project because no one had seen a script. But the interview was set for the following Saturday afternoon at the Sherry-Netherland Hotel on Fifth Avenue. I agreed to go because Stark had always said, 'Audition for everything, then make your choices afterwards.' And because I had plans to catch a five-thirty train at Grand Central (a straight shot down Fifth Avenue) to visit my father.

I truly believe that if the meeting had been in another part of town, I wouldn't have gone. Everything about the project seemed so unlikely. But at three o'clock that Saturday afternoon in January 1977, I rang the doorbell of a plush suite at the Sherry-Netherland and was ushered in to meet Ilya Salkind and Richard Donner, the producer and director of *Superman*.

CHAPTER EIGHT

When I finally arrived home from Kessler on December 13, 1995, we started our preparations for Christmas, keenly aware how different this one would be. We also realized that the house would have to be extensively modified if I was to have any kind of freedom and mobility. We set up a hospital bed in the dining room and brought down a mattress for Dana. The rooms were cozy and inviting, but there were steps everywhere, and it was very frustrating to have to put down a metal ramp every time I wanted to move into the living room or cross through the dining room into the kitchen.

Matthew and Al came over for the holidays, and we all went to Williamstown, where the renovations had already been completed. I was free to roam from one end of the house to the other, which gave me a real sense of independence. I missed skiing together at Jiminy Peak and sledding down the hill above our front yard, which was how we usually spent most of our time between Christmas and

New Year's. Staying by the fire and watching the others enjoy the outdoors was very difficult for me. I tried to keep my spirits up by reminding myself that, even with all the limitations, I was home with my family and had begun a new life.

Today I spend much of my time traveling around the country giving speeches, visiting rehab centers, lobbying in Washington for more money for biomedical research. Whenever we arrive in a new city, people are amazed at how efficiently our team of nurses and aides transports me in and out of airplanes, vans, and hotel rooms. But as I began life at home in early '96, I was reluctant to make these trips; not only because they would be mentally and physically challenging but because I was not eager to be seen in public.

In addition, the new year had begun with a serious medical set-back that made the idea of travel even more daunting. In January I developed a urinary tract infection, which the doctors at our local hospital decided not to treat with antibiotics because over time the bacteria can become resistant to them. The doctor in charge of my case recommended drinking large amounts of cranberry juice, but the infection, left untreated, caused serious repeated episodes of dysreflexia. At the worst point I was having bouts of high blood pressure and excruciating headaches twice an hour. I was admitted to the hospital and was extremely relieved when Dr. Kirshblum drove up from Kessler once again to take a firsthand look at the situation. He immediately prescribed antibiotics, and as they began to take effect, the dysreflexia stopped. But I had had to spend five days in the hospital, which could have been prevented. Lying in a bed in intensive care once again sent me into an emotional tailspin despite Dana's and Will's best efforts to comfort me. All I could think of was how soon the next attack of dysreflexia would come, hoping it wouldn't be strong enough to cause a heart attack or a stroke. At that point I was in no condition to consider traveling anywhere.

Even after my release from the hospital, I was still reluctant to leave the house because that winter we were experiencing some of the worst weather in years. As I recall we had seventeen major snowstorms. (One afternoon one of our intrepid nurses arrived for her shift in a snowplow.) And my two appearances in public—the dinner for Robin and the APA fund-raiser at the Waldorf— had both been stressful, despite their success. I had no desire to put additional pressure on myself.

A real turning point came in February 1996, when the producer Quincy Jones asked me to make a special appearance on the Academy Awards at the end of March. I was extremely grateful for this invitation because it was a gesture of inclusion by the film industry—a gesture I took to mean that I had not been forgotten by my peers after nearly twenty years in the business. We talked for a while about my moment on the Oscars. I would speak briefly about socially relevant films and urge the Hollywood community to remember how influential and necessary such work can be. I told Quincy I was flattered and would certainly think about it. Then, on a wild impulse, I accepted on the spot.

As soon as I hung up the phone, it dawned on me that I had just agreed to appear live in front of two billion people, in a wheelchair, breathing on a

211

ventilator, and with no way of knowing whether my body would remain still during my five to seven minutes onstage. If I hit a bump as I wheeled on, I might spasm and end up slumped in an awkward position, and there might not be time to put me back together again before the curtain went up.

I rolled into the kitchen and told Dana what I had just agreed to do. One of the things I love most about her is that she gives instinctive, honest answers to even the most difficult questions. Without missing a beat, she said, 'Do it.'

Every possible consideration—hotel rooms, security, vans, and a private jet—was extended to me and Dana and our large staff of nurses and aides in order to facilitate the trip. Several times I considered backing out, but the part of my personality that likes challenges finally won the debate. I knew it would be risky, but 'the successful outcome of the maneuver would not be seriously in doubt.' If I spasmed onstage I planned to ad-lib some line about wanting to dance—feeble perhaps, but a way to let the audience know I was all right. I worked on my speech, told Dr. Kirshblum about the trip, and was relieved when he said there was no medical reason not to go. We were given the names of doctors, pharmacies, and ventilator service companies in Los Angeles in case of an emergency.

My appearance on the telecast was kept secret. This would not only create a greater dramatic impact but would also leave me a way out if I developed some physical problem that would make it impossible for me to be there. But as the day approached my confidence grew, and there was no reason to turn back.

212

While I was rolling into position onstage at the Dorothy Chandler Pavilion, I went a little too fast and bumped over the threshold of a doorway. Just what I'd been afraid of. Miraculously, my body didn't move an inch. I felt I was 'in the zone.' My name was announced, a curtain went up, and I was revealed center stage in my chair. I looked out at a sea of friendly faces; everyone was standing, reaching out to me. I felt truly embraced by the audience, strangers and old friends alike. The applause died down into the same intense silence that had greeted my first appearance, at the tribute to Robin. I knew I had to put the audience at ease. Luckily an idea came to mind and I said, 'What you probably don't know is that I left New York last September and I just got here this morning. I'm glad I made it, because I wouldn't have missed this reception for the world.' After that my speech and the introduction of several film clips Quincy and I had chosen was a piece of cake. I felt as euphoric as the day our PDS hockey team beat the mighty Kent School and I had a 2–0 shutout.

The Academy Awards appearance gave me the courage to accept the many public engagements, both live and on film, that have now become such an important part of my life. But another completely unexpected benefit came out of the Oscar adventure. During my stay in Hollywood I entered hotels and buildings through garages, kitchens, and service elevators, and met cooks, waiters, chambermaids, and maintenance crews. Many of them said they were praying for me. Others looked me right in the eye and said, 'We love you, *Superman*. You're our hero.' At first I couldn't believe they meant it. Then I realized that they were looking past the chair and honoring me for a role that obviously had real meaning for them. I didn't feel patronized in any way. Clearly a part I had played twenty years before was still valued. The fact that I was in a wheelchair, unable to move below my shoulders, and dependent on the support of others for almost every aspect of my daily life had not diminished the fact that I was—and always would be—their *Superman*.

*   *   *

The morning after my meeting at the Sherry-Netherland, a three-hundred-page script for two *Superman* movies was messengered to my apartment. This had never happened before; I was used to picking up the material myself at the casting director's office. I raced to my desk and devoured the pages. As I read I was genuinely surprised and delighted. This was not a comic book or corny science fiction but a piece of American mythology with a captivating blend of humor and heroics. At about eleven Stark phoned to say that the meeting had gone extremely well and that the producers wanted me to fly to London immediately for a screen test. He also casually mentioned that *Superman*'s father would be played by Marlon Brando and that Gene Hackman would play his arch-enemy, Lex Luthor.

Down at Circle Rep there was great excitement about my news. The trip to England was scheduled for the coming weekend, so there would be time to rehearse another actor to cover for me as the grandfather. As a skinny WASP with light brown hair, I didn't think I had much of a chance of actually being cast. So I decided to think of the trip as a free minivacation and promised to bring back presents for everyone from Harrods and Fortnum and Mason. Once I was on the plane, however, I began to seriously consider how I would approach the part. My first insight was that the role was really *two* parts. I remembered seeing George Reeves on TV in the fifties and wondering why Lois Lane didn't instantly recognize Clark Kent as *Superman*. How could a thick pair of glasses substitute for a believable characterization? Right away I saw a great opportunity: I would attempt to create more of a contrast between the two characters. After all, Lois Lane shouldn't have to be blind or dim-witted.

I also felt that the screenwriters, Mario Puzo, Robert Benton, and David and Leslie Newman, had provided a basis for playing *Superman* in an understated, offhand way. If the special effects could be truly convincing, if the flying scenes were realistic, then it would not be necessary to strike unnatural, 'macho' poses or attitudes. It seemed to me that in the fifties the image of what a man ought to be had come from icons like John Wayne, Richard Widmark, Kirk Douglas, and Burt Lancaster. These movie heroes projected stoicism; they faced adversity without needing anyone's help. Women tended to get in the way (witness Newman's and Redford's attitude toward Katharine Ross in *Butch Cassidy and the Sundance Kid*).

By the late 1970s the masculine image had changed. People expected marriage to be a genuine partnership. Now it was acceptable for a man to show gentleness and vulnerability. It was even

215

admirable for him to cook dinner, change diapers, and stay home with the kids. I felt that the new *Superman* ought to reflect that contemporary male image. A perfect example is a scene in which Lois Lane interviews *Superman* on the balcony of her apartment. At one point she asks him, 'How fast do you fly, by the way?' In the fifties he might have quoted a Mach number; in our script his response was, 'Oh, I don't know ... I never carry a watch. Why don't we find out?' Then he gently takes her by the hand and they step off the balcony together for a romantic aerial tour of Metropolis by night. For me this scene illustrates the difference between the two eras. When Lois Lane asks, 'Who are you?' *Superman* simply responds, 'A friend.' I felt that was the key to the part: I tried to downplay being a hero and emphasize being a friend.

I based the character of Clark Kent on the young Cary Grant. There's a wonderful scene in *Bringing Up Baby* in which he plays a paleontologist working on a dinosaur, and he's up on a ladder that is rocking back and forth. He looks terribly awkward and afraid, while Katharine Hepburn looks brash and fearless as she comes to his rescue. He has a shyness, vulnerability, and a certain charming goofiness that I thought would be perfect for Clark Kent. He even wears the same kind of glasses. Of course I knew I couldn't *be* Cary Grant, but there was nothing to prevent me from stealing from him.

By the time my plane landed in London, despite a sleepless night over the Atlantic, I had something to offer the creative team of the movie. Once again the instinct to gain control of the situation served me well. Sheer adrenaline carried me through the screen test. On the way back to my hotel my driver

216

said, 'I'm not supposed to tell you this, but you've got the part.'

Filming *Superman* was sometimes tedious and exasperating. I spent months hanging on wires for brief moments in the movie that would then have to be reshot. But ultimately it was a wonderful experience. One of my favorite memories is of running into John Gielgud in a hallway at Pinewood Studios. We had met before at a social occasion; now I was dressed in full *Superman* regalia. As he shook my hand he said, 'So delightful to see you. What are you doing now?'

The more I worked with Dick Donner, the more he seemed like a fifty-year-old kid in a candy store. With his deep, booming voice and infectious laugh, you wanted to follow him anywhere. On the wall of his office was a plastic *Superman* in flight carrying a banner that read, 'Verisimilitude.' He respected my desire to make the character as human and natural as possible.

Most of the time we had fun. Once I had to appear on Fifty-seventh Street in New York in my costume. We were filming a scene in which *Superman* catches a burglar climbing up a building with suction cups and brings him down to the street. The burglar and I both hung from wires below a construction crane about ten stories above the sidewalk. The live action would later be cut together with footage of the burglar attempting to break in a window, shot on a soundstage at Pinewood Studios. As the crew prepared for the scene, I waited in a trailer on Fifty-eighth Street with a couple of enormous bodyguards. (I wondered who they worked for when they weren't needed on a movie set. And I thought it was sort of funny that *Superman* would need bodyguards, but Donner was worried about my safety.) Finally they were ready to shoot, and I came out of my trailer with my two guardians. There was nobody there— absolutely no one in sight. I thought: We're a flop. Nobody cares. We walked through a passageway to the front of the building on Fifty-seventh Street. As I came around the corner, I suddenly saw several thousand people jamming the sidewalks on both sides of the street. When the crowd spotted me in the *Superman* costume, a huge cheer went up. I was stunned, relieved, and suddenly quite nervous.

The wires were lowered from the construction crane. I shook hands with the burglar and was hooked up to the harness underneath my costume. Donner called for a rehearsal. I double-checked that the hooks were closed and locked, then gave the thumbs-up to indicate that I was ready. As I was hoisted up, the crowd roared their approval. They didn't care about the crane or the wires; they were willing to look past all of it. There was *Superman*, flying up the side of the building. That's when I knew the movie would work.

The following week we shot a scene in which *Superman* rescues a little girl's cat from a tree. The setting was a cul-de-sac in Brooklyn Heights with a spectacular view of the East River and the Manhattan skyline in the background. The action called for *Superman* to swoop down from the sky, gently pick the cat off a branch, and return it to the anxious little girl on the sidewalk below. We started rehearsing in midafternoon in order to be ready to shoot just after dark. The shot was fairly complicated: the crane had to swing in a carefully calculated arc so that I wouldn't crash into the tree.

218

At the same time I had to descend at the right speed in order to scoop up the cat. My flight path took me past the seventh-story windows of an apartment building. I was wearing street clothes and the flying harness with my hair done *Superman* style as I flew over and over again past the same windows. At around five o'clock a kid of about seven pulled up the window in his room and called out, 'Hey, *Superman*, how ya doing?'

About an hour later we were still rehearsing, and now I was in full costume. As I flew past him again, he called out, 'Hey, *Superman*, my mom says come on in, we're having spaghetti!' I thanked him but said I still had work to do. At about eight I was still rehearsing the shot (one of our problems was that the cat was getting restless), when my young friend opened the window again and said, 'Hey, *Superman*, take care, I gotta do my homework.' Finally, we started to film the scene. Take after take this kid would look up from his desk and wave as I floated by, trying to catch the elusive white cat. At eleven o'clock we were still shooting. (By this time the cat had been replaced by a dummy.) The window opened one last time. 'So, *Superman*, I gotta go to bed. I'll see ya!' I guess from his point of view it was just a normal day in Metropolis.

When the movie finally came out in December 1978, it was accepted by ordinary people, die-hard *Superman* fans, and critics alike. I think I was the right actor for the part at the time I played it, but I think the role is larger than any particular actor and should be reinterpreted from generation to generation. As Kirk Alyn was right for the '40s and George Reeves was right for the '50s, I was the temporary custodian of this icon of American pop

219

culture in the '70s and early '80s. Now rumor has it that Nicolas Cage will be the *Superman* of the late '90s.

I approached the role seriously. I've always felt that an actor should never judge a character but should commit fully to the process of bringing him to life. In this respect *Superman* and Henry James and Chekhov and a French farce are no different from the actor's point of view. I always flatly refused any invitation to mock the *Superman* character or send him up.

With the success of *Superman* came innumerable invitations for public service as the character. I wasn't about to let *Superman* interfere with the progress of my career, but I was willing to make productive use of the *Superman* image in certain circumstances. Through the Make-a-Wish Foundation, I visited terminally ill children whose last request was to meet *Superman*. I joined the board of directors of Save the Children, a charity dedicated to helping needy children all over the world. In 1979 I served as a track and field coach at the Special Olympics in Brockport, New York. One of the other volunteers was a charismatic former football star named O.J. Simpson.

In 1985 I was asked to host *Saturday Night Live*. Although I had never poked fun at the character, I thought of a *Superman* sketch that seemed irresistible. I played *Superman* at an old-age home; Billy Crystal was an old-timer named Izzy. The two of us sat on the porch on a summer evening reminiscing about our youth. I wore a bathrobe with the *Superman* costume underneath. The leotard was wrinkled and baggy, but the famous red-and-yellow *S* was still featured prominently on my chest. Silver hair and bifocals completed the picture.

As I talked about the old days I said, 'I used to be faster ... faster than ... uh ...' Then Billy would finish the line. Then I'd go on, 'And I could leap ... um ... tall ...,' and the sentence would trail off. *Superman* with Alzheimer's may have been in poor taste, but the audience roared. At the end of the sketch the nurses and some other residents of the old-age home came out with a cake covered with candles and a big *S* in the middle. They sang 'Happy Birthday, dear *Superman*,' kindly indulging an old man's delusion. Then Julia Louis-Dreyfus as the head nurse gently suggested (with a wink to the others), 'Now blow out your candles, *Superman*.' With a look of tremendous concentration, I drew in a breath and blasted the cake off the porch and across the studio. Blackout.

The sequels to the first two *Superman* movies were not up to the earlier ones. I think *Superman II* may be the best of the series, because it has some effective comedy (in one of my favorite scenes, Lois and Clark pose as newlyweds) but it also has Donner's 'verisimilitude' and respect for the mythology. Dick Donner didn't receive the directing credit for *Superman II*, but he had set it in motion and shot much of the footage while we were filming Part I. In the scenes where the sets doubled, we went back and forth in our three-hundred-page script. But by the end of production in October 1978, Donner had had a serious falling out with Ilya Salkind and his partner, Pierre Spengler, and could not be persuaded to resume filming Part II in September 1979. Richard Lester, who had directed *A Hard Day's Night* and *Help!*

221

with the Beatles, as well as *Petulia* and *The Three Musketeers*, was brought in to complete the job. I liked him tremendously, but I thought it was unfair to ask such an accomplished director to imitate the tone and style of someone else's work. Nevertheless, he succeeded in bringing his own brand of humor to it.

Superman III was to be Dick Lester's own movie, but in my opinion he was hamstrung by a decision made by the producers. One night on the Johnny Carson show Richard Pryor raved about the *Superman* films and said how much he'd love to be in one. When they heard about it, Salkind and Spengler were excited by the idea that they might get Pryor to play some kind of comic villain in *Superman III*. They approached him and received an immediate yes. David and Leslie Newman, the only writers left from the original group, were hired to write a movie that became more a Richard Pryor comedy vehicle than a proper *Superman* film.

In the first draft of *Superman* was a scene in which *Superman* sees a bald man walking down the street. Thinking it's Lex Luthor he swoops down to collar him and take him away. But it's Telly Savalas, who says, 'Who loves ya, baby?' to the startled *Superman* and offers him a lollipop. This was the kind of inane material that Dick Donner got rid of immediately. Unfortunately, gags like this resurfaced in the script for *Superman III*. The Newmans wrote a scene in which Pryor, wearing skis and sporting a pink tablecloth as a *Superman* cape, zooms off a little ski slope on the top of a high-rise. He falls down the side of the building and lands—miraculously unhurt—in the middle of traffic on a busy street, then waddles toward the

222

sidewalk, oblivious to all the honking horns and staring pedestrians.

I personally found all that in poor taste. I missed Donner tremendously, and what we'd created just two years earlier. I did enjoy the sequence in which *Superman* has become an evil version of himself and tries to kill Clark Kent in an automobile junkyard. That scene stands alone; I think the rest of *Superman III* was mostly a misconception.

The less said about *Superman IV* the better.

*   *   *

After the success of *Superman*, one of my greatest problems as an actor was that my agents and many Hollywood producers wanted me to be an action hero, which didn't interest me. I found most of the scripts of that genre poorly constructed, and I felt the starring roles could easily be played by anyone with a strong physique. My eyes glazed over with boredom when two producers and a studio executive once pitched the idea of my playing Eric the Red in an epic adventure about the Vikings. I could just imagine myself with an iron helmet and horns on my head. There were stories set in outer space, westerns, and futuristic fantasies, all of which struck me as formulaic. Sometimes I got the sinking feeling that I had inadvertently closed the door to my future as a legitimate actor. I made it clear to everyone who worked with me that I was still interested in the theater and that I wanted to play parts that were complex and challenging. I told them I would rather be in a good film that might not make a lot of money than a lousy film that grossed a hundred million. By the spring of '79

223

there were more choices.

Over the next few years I discovered that *Superman* had actually opened many doors; the question was how to make the best use of these opportunities. While some producers would not cast me because I had played *Superman*, others cast me because I had. I was offered the lead in *American Gigolo* for Paramount; I passed on that because John Travolta had bailed out of the project and they wanted me to start in less than a week. An entire film unit was ready and waiting, but I wanted time to prepare. Then I was offered Roberta, the ex-football player who'd had a sex-change operation in *The World According to Garp*, for the esteemed director George Roy Hill. I passed on that too (an enormous stretch—for both me and the audience—after *Superman*), and the role made my friend John Lithgow a star. When I was offered the lead in *Body Heat*, I turned it down because I didn't think I could be convincing as a seedy, small-town lawyer. My friend Bill Hurt, of course, was brilliant in the role.

In 1982 David Lean—the David Lean, director of *Lawrence of Arabia, Dr. Zhivago, The Bridge on the River Kwai*, and many other classics—invited me to join him and the great producer Sam Spiegel for a 'chat' at their hotel one September afternoon. Without much preamble Lean announced that he was going to do a remake of *Mutiny on the Bounty*, with Anthony Hopkins as Captain Bligh. Would I like to play Fletcher Christian? Kate Hepburn had recommended me and persuaded him to see *Superman*. How this led to my being cast as the first mate aboard a British merchant ship in 1787 was beyond me. I decided that the always unpredictable

224

Hepburn must have badgered Lean into submission on my behalf.

I agonized for more than a week about joining an all-British cast in a role that had already been played by Clark Gable and Marlon Brando, opposite the distinguished Anthony Hopkins, who I thought would probably blow me off the screen. Gae and I went to the Bahamas for a few days to try to relax, but even as I fished and scuba-dived and walked on the beach, I couldn't reach a decision.

No sooner had I arrived back in New York than I received a call from Anthony Hopkins (whom I'd never met) urging me to stop procrastinating and accept the role. I was extremely flattered, but I finally decided I would be miscast. I thought Charles Dance or Jeremy Irons would be much better. Ultimately David Lean had a falling out with the studio and did not direct the picture. Fletcher Christian was played by a young Australian named Mel Gibson.

My first role after *Superman* turned out to be a delicate romantic fantasy for Universal called *Somewhere in Time*, based on the novel *Bid Time Return* by Richard Matheson. It is the story of a young playwright who falls in love with a portrait of an actress (loosely based on Maude Adams) and manages to travel back in time to meet her at the height of her fame and beauty in 1912. Jane Seymour was cast as the actress Elise McKenna, and I was Richard Collier, the lovestruck young writer. Our producer, Stephen Deutsch, and our director, Jeannot Szwarc, found a perfect location: Mackinac Island on Lake Michigan. Just to visit the island is to journey into the past. The most

225

prominent landmark is the Grand Hotel, built by railroad money in the mid-nineteenth century. It still looks brand new. No cars are allowed on the island, although we received special permission to bring our equipment trucks over on a barge. When you finish dinner at one of the restaurants, you call for a cab, and soon a horse and buggy arrive to take you to your lodgings. Over the years I've met hundreds of people who have the same feelings about Mackinac that I had: it is an enchanted island where time has stood still.

We began filming in late May 1979, and the location quickly cast a spell on our entire company. The real world fell away as the story and the setting took hold of us. I've rarely worked on a production that was so relaxed and harmonious. Even the hard-boiled Teamsters and grips from Chicago succumbed to the charms of the island and the mellow atmosphere on the set.

When the film was completed and test screenings were held a year later, audiences loved it. The finished product looked beautiful and was greatly enhanced by John Barry's score. In addition to using a recurring piece by Rachmaninoff, he had composed a main theme that captured the essence of the story perfectly. Early reviews were extremely favorable, especially one in *Daily Variety* that praised everyone involved. But when the film opened in October, it bombed. Later I often joked that it left a crater on the street. Vincent Canby in *The New York Times* wrote, 'This film does for screen romance what the Hindenburg did for dirigibles' and 'Christopher Reeve looks like a helium-filled canary. One more role like this and it's back to the cape forever.' Audiences stayed away in droves, and the film disappeared within a few weeks.

Needless to say, this was a huge blow. I had never failed so visibly before. Of course, I blamed myself entirely. In retrospect, I think that because I had worked on *Superman* for so long, my characterization of Clark Kent may have crept into Richard Collier. We had such a wonderful time filming *Somewhere in Time*, but maybe we lost our objectivity. In any case, we were devastated by the public's rejection of our work. Cast and crew alike moved quickly into other projects.

Over the years, however, a miraculous transformation took place. Cable television spread across the country, and people began to discover our little movie. Charles Champlin, a critic for the *Los Angeles Times*, hosted a film series on a local station, and soon people began talking about *Somewhere in Time*. We became the most popular and requested offering on Z Channel and soon developed a cult following. More than ten years after the film's release, a die-hard fan, Bill Shepherd of Covina, California, founded INSITE—the International Network of *Somewhere In Time* Enthusiasts. Today it has thousands of members. Bill publishes a newsletter four times a year, and every October the Grand Hotel hosts nearly 700 members who come for a special *Somewhere in Time* weekend. Dana and I attended the gathering in the fall of 1994 and enjoyed an overwhelming reception. Thanks to persistent pressure from INSITE members, the Hollywood Chamber of Commerce gave me a star on the Walk of Fame, seventeen years after the film's debut.

When the filming of *Somewhere in Time* was

completed in August 1979, I bid a fond farewell to the magic island and immediately returned to London to begin filming *Superman II*. Gae and I bought a house that dated back to 1850 on Redcliffe Road in Chelsea. I resumed my routine of hanging on wires in front of a blue screen at Pinewood Studios during the day, followed by two hours of weight training every evening, while Gae continued to work with Laraine Ashton's modeling agency. We enjoyed a very active social life. Because *Superman* had been such a success, we were never short of invitations to parties, benefits, opening nights, and charity events all over town. Richard Lester was always cheerful and full of good suggestions, which made going to work enjoyable. He worked at a faster pace than most directors, often using two and three cameras at once to film a scene, so time passed quickly. But the real highlight of 1979—in fact, the highlight of my entire life up to that point—was the birth of my son Matthew on December 20.

He was born at the Welbeck Street Clinic in Mayfair. Gae had checked in the previous night, and I had stayed with her, expecting Matthew's imminent arrival. But by ten o'clock the next morning, the doctors thought it might be false labor and even considered sending us home. Laraine Ashton and her father invited me to lunch. We agreed that I would check back at the clinic in the early afternoon.

We had just started the main course when the headwaiter raced to our table with the message that the baby would be born any moment. I ran out of the restaurant, and miraculously there was a cab waiting right outside the door. (Usually it's so difficult to find a cab in London when you need one that you call to book in advance. Finding one right in front of a restaurant seemed like a sign from the gods.) I told the driver that I would pay him double the meter if he would take me to Welbeck Street as quickly as possible without getting us killed. He was more than happy to oblige, but I'll always remember his calming remark, 'Relax, Guv. When my first was born I was at the track. Much nicer place to be.' He continued to chat pleasantly about fathers and sons while driving at breakneck speed toward Mayfair, sometimes literally driving on the sidewalk.

I took surviving the ride as another sign from the gods. I rushed up the stairs and into Gae's room just as Matthew appeared. As soon as he was breathing, I had the privilege of handing him to Gae, who was crying from both exhaustion and joy. Instead of bawling at the top of his lungs, as I had expected, Matthew snuggled in quietly and drifted off to sleep. But just before he dozed off, he opened one eye and looked right at me. It seemed to me that he was asking, 'Who are you?' And then, satisfied that I was meant to be there, he fell asleep. I think that look of complete acceptance from my first child within moments of his birth somehow taught me the most important lesson about being a parent: unconditional love is everything.

After I finished *Superman* II the following spring, Gae and I took Matthew and his nanny to Los Angeles and set up camp in another rented house in the Hollywood Hills. I got my instrument rating in my new airplane, an A36 Bonanza, read a lot of scripts, and floated Matthew in the crook of my arm around the shallow end of our swimming pool. I wasn't able to find a project I liked, and by June, tired of our Hollywood lifestyle, I picked up the phone and called Nikos Psacharopoulos in Williamstown. Would it be possible for me to join the festival at some point during the summer? I had been rejected there for years because I had become a professional when most people my age were still students and didn't have to be paid. But now Nikos welcomed me with open arms.

We agreed to do *The Front Page* by Hecht and MacArthur, to be directed by Robert Allan Ackerman, one of the hottest Broadway directors at the time. Edward Herrmann and Richard Burton's daughter, Kate, still a drama school student, would be the other leads, and Celeste Holm was cast in a cameo as my prospective mother-in-law. Gae and Matthew and I packed our bags again, closed the door on our rented life, and I was soon reunited with the WTF family.

Robin Williams came up to visit during the run and seemed to enjoy it tremendously. One evening we went out to a local seafood restaurant, and as we passed by the lobster tank I casually wondered what they were all thinking in there. Whereupon Robin launched into a fifteen-minute routine: one lobster had escaped and was seen on the highway with his claw out holding a sign that said, 'Maine.' Another lobster from Brooklyn was saying, 'C'mon, just take da rubber bands off,' gearing up for a fight. A gay lobster wanted to re-decorate the tank. People at nearby tables soon gave up any pretense of trying not to listen, and I had to massage my cheeks because my face hurt so much from laughing. Later Robin would use this material for

230

his appearance at a huge gala for the Actors Fund at Radio City Music Hall.

The Front Page turned out to be one of the biggest successes of the summer, and I was delighted to be back onstage after a four-year absence.

In the fall I was asked to do Lanford Wilson's *Fifth of July* on Broadway. We bought a duplex apartment on Seventy-eighth Street and Columbus Avenue, and Gae furnished it while I began preparing for the part. The play had originated at Circle Rep, where Bill Hurt had distinguished himself once again as Ken Talley, a former schoolteacher and Vietnam vet who is now a bilateral amputee. I felt honored to have been asked to take over the role when the play moved to Broadway. My first task was learning to simulate walking on artificial legs. To me one of the most exciting things about acting is doing the homework: learning whatever is necessary to be convincing in the role.

The research for *Fifth of July* took me to a VA hospital in Brooklyn and into the world of the disabled. A Vietnam vet named Mike Sulsona became my coach. In 1969 Mike was an eighteen-year-old soldier finishing his second tour of duty and scheduled to go home just one week later. Then he stepped on a mine that blew off both his legs. At first I was awkward and self-conscious around him, but he soon put me at ease. He explained that before he went to 'Nam, he was a high school dropout hanging out on the street. Now he was married, the father of two children, and a budding playwright. The accident had given meaning to his life. He taught me how to stand up, sit down, and move like an amputee. Braces were made to keep my legs rigidly in place. I had to be especially careful not to move my toes and spoil the illusion. That physicality—the technical requirements—got me into the part.

Ken Talley was a breakthrough role for me. I was able to put together bits and pieces from school, from Hepburn, from film work, and from my own experience and bring all of it to the work. Having mastered the technical demands of the role, I tried to be spontaneous, truthful, and 'in the moment.' This is an acting term, which means the opposite of planning in advance. You know the lines and have rehearsed the scene, but at each performance you go with what you are actually feeling at the moment rather than trying to re-create something that happened during rehearsals or at yesterday's performance.

One of a bilateral amputee's greatest fears is of falling backwards, because the amputee has no way to protect the back or spinal cord. In Act II of *Fifth of July* another character bumps into Ken, and he falls straight back. That scene produced unexpected results at every performance. Even though the words were always the same, my experience was different every time. Sometimes I felt anger and denial. Then my attitude was: Don't help me, I don't need anybody. Sometimes I cried, and would reach out for help. Sometimes I tried to pretend it hadn't happened. The dialogue never changed; but you can say 'pass the salt' and load the words with any number of meanings, depending on what's happening within you.

During the previews at the New Apollo Theater, Ellis Rabb materialized again. His advice to me was as concise and to the point as it had been in San Diego: 'Your performance is brilliant; your curtain call is a disgrace.' He told me that I was cheating the audience by coming out at the end as if I was in a hurry to go home. He reminded me that I was billed above the title and taught me how to take a proper curtain call. He coached me not to rush the entrance: once you arrive center stage, you stand at your full height and take time before you bow. Most important of all was what you should be *thinking* during a curtain call: you look to the balcony on one side, to the balcony on the other side, to the right side of the orchestra, to the rest of the orchestra, and each time, you think: Thank you for being here, it was a pleasure to perform for you, and then you bow. I tried this the next night, and the result was a standing ovation. I understood what made the difference: I was embracing the audience. Instead of implying, Yes, I was in it, now I'm out of here, my new thought was: We shared this, didn't we? I busted a gut here for you tonight, and I'm glad you noticed. What he suggested sounded egotistical to me until I learned that when people have witnessed a good performance, they want a chance to applaud. A proper curtain call completes the experience of the play for actors and audience alike.

Fifth of July received outstanding reviews. I was happy because I felt it confirmed that I could play complex characters, play against type, and be successful. My next role was even further away from the conventional leading man than Ken Talley. I played a psychopathic student opposite Michael Caine in Sidney Lumet's film of *Deathtrap*. The twisted relationship between the two

233

characters in this Ira Levin thriller shocked many of our fans, but Michael and I played the parts without apology, and the film was well received. When I look back on it now, the performance still holds up.

Deathtrap prepared the way for James Ivory's film of *The Bostonians*. (He was one of the directors who cast me *because* he had liked my work in *Superman*.) I was offered the lead role of Basil Ransom, an impoverished writer from Mississippi who comes to New York in the 1870s. Although he fails to find a publisher, he succeeds in wooing and winning Verena Tarrant, a rising star in the feminist movement. The budget was only about $2 million, but the cast included Vanessa Redgrave, Jessica Tandy, Wallace Shawn, and Linda Hunt. Jim Ivory and his producing partner, Ismail Merchant, had worked with the novelist and screenwriter Ruth Prawer Jhabvala since the mid-1960s, and had established a reputation for elegant and intelligent films like *The Europeans, Bombay Talkie*, and *Heat and Dust*. I was thrilled by the offer; this was exactly the kind of film I wanted to do.

Ismail could only afford to pay me $100,000, less than a tenth of my established price at the time. I insisted that money was not an issue, that this was the kind of work I ought to be doing, but my agent told me, 'If you do that picture with those wandering minstrels, it will be one foot in the grave of your career.' (Years later, after the tremendous success of *A Room with a View* and *Howards End*, the very same agency took Jim and Ismail on as clients.)

I cheerfully ignored their advice and went to

work on my Mississippi accent. My coach was a gentleman named Haley Barbour III, a prominent lawyer from Yazoo City, who later served as chairman of the Republican National Committee. I sent him a phrase book that I had from my Edith Skinner days at Juilliard. He recorded the sentences, sometimes adding items from newspapers and magazines, then sent the tapes to me up in Williamstown, where I was working again at the festival. I reported for filming in Boston in August 1983.

James Ivory's films are so well crafted that most people think the scripts are set in stone and the actors have to do exactly as they are told. In fact the opposite is true. He gathers talented artists on both sides of the camera who are committed to the project and full of their own ideas. Then he culls the best of what everyone has to offer and turns out a polished gem. Ruth Jhabvala used to say that her screenplays were merely blueprints; she left it to the filmmakers to build the building. I don't think she ever even visited the set. Jim was so relaxed, confident, and easygoing that he brought out the best in the entire company. He was always ready to take advantage of what was actually taking place in front of him. As a director, he, too, was 'in the moment.'

One day we were filming a scene on a beach on Martha's Vineyard. Basil Ransom is telling Verena (Madeleine Potter) about his difficulty getting published, complaining that no one listens to his ideas. As Madeleine and I ran the lines and Jim lined up the shot, a young cocker spaniel came over to us. I casually picked up a stick and threw it for him while we continued to rehearse the dialogue.

He brought the stick back, so I threw it again. We played back and forth until Jim was ready to shoot. I started to coax the dog out of the shot, but Jim suggested we keep playing the game. On the first take, as I was talking about what a failure I was and how hopeless life seemed in New York, I threw the stick, and my new friend chased it as usual. But this time he took it and ran off. I called out for him to come back, but he continued running down the beach, so I turned to Madeleine and said, 'See? *Nobody* listens to me.' Jim liked it and used it in the film. Then he polished the scene with a cutaway shot of the dog running away. This sort of thing happened nearly every day. Working with Jim, I learned that a good film needs these 'lucky accidents.'

The Bostonians succeeded beyond everyone's expectations. *Daily Variety* ran a long article about it under a banner headline that read, ART HOUSE PIC SHOWS SURPRISING B.O. STRENGTH. It opened in a few selected cities, but soon the distributor, Almi Pictures, needed to make additional prints. This time Vincent Canby raved in *The New York Times* about all the performances (especially Vanessa Redgrave's, which earned her an Oscar nomination). At the end of his review, he concluded that our film was 'the best adaptation of a literary work yet made for the screen.'

*　　　*　　　*

One of the most enjoyable aspects of filmmaking for me was the opportunity to go on location all over the world without feeling like a tourist. In Rome, Budapest, Zagreb, Paris, or Vancouver, we got to know the locals and were often invited into their homes and their private lives.

I also enjoyed keeping up with my various sports interests during production. While we made *The Bostonians* I lived aboard *Chandelle* on a mooring in Vineyard Haven. Every day I would row ashore and wait on the dock for the crew van to pick me up. Sometimes on weekends my brother, Ben (who lives on the Vineyard), and I would take cast and crew members sailing. Once Jim Ivory came with us for a nighttime sail. I don't think he'd ever done anything like that before; he seemed impressed that we could navigate confidently in the dark. I took him flying as well and was grateful that he trusted me to bring him back in one piece.

During the shooting of *Superman III*, I raced my sailplane on days when the weather was right— puffy cotton-ball clouds from a cold front are ideal. Otherwise I would make my way down to Redhill, in Surrey, home of the Tiger Club. Like going to Mackinac Island, this was a journey into the past. The club was a group of genuine aviators, many of whom had served in the Royal Air Force and flown in the Battle of Britain. The 'Tiger' referred to the Tiger Moth, a vintage World War I combat plane; several of them, as well as other open cockpit biplanes like the Stampe and the Stearman, were still maintained by the club. I showed the club president my American license and was thrilled when I was invited to join as an Overseas Member. Before long I too was wearing a flight suit with a leather jacket, a helmet, and goggles, and joining in mock dogfights over the sleepy English countryside. Occasionally five or six planes would fly in tight formation. Sometimes we would have

237

balloon-bursting contests: balloons were released from the center of the air-field, and we would maneuver to hit them with our propellers before they climbed out of sight.

I especially loved flying inverted. Even though I was strapped in by a seat belt and shoulder harness and was wearing a parachute, as I flipped the plane upside down I always had that little moment when I felt I was going to drop straight out of the cockpit and land in a cornfield below. One crucial thing to remember before turning upside down was to switch to the inverted fuel tank; otherwise there would be a brief coughing and sputtering of the engine followed by a chilling silence. If you were lucky, you could flip the plane upright again and the engine would restart; if not, you would have to make a dead-stick landing in a field. I never had any difficulty flying these vintage aircraft, but I was prepared for 'outlandings' from my experience in sailplanes.

It was a complete coincidence when I received a script called *The Aviator*, about a taciturn airmail pilot in the 1920s on the route between Elko, Nevada, and Boise, Idaho. The mail was carried in the front compartment of a Stearman. The producers had no idea that I could actually fly a Stearman but agreed with me that if I did my own piloting, we would have opportunities to make the film more realistic than if we had to use a double. I could throw a couple of mailbags into the plane and then hop in, start the engine, and take off, all in one shot. We would also be able to film air-to-air from a helicopter instead of having to cut to close-ups shot in the studio.

We filmed near the town of Kranjska Gora on

the border of Yugoslavia and Austria. My favorite days involved flying, acting, and a little directing as well. A camera would be mounted on the wing, and I would take off with instructions from the director of photography to find a suitable location to film myself on the mail run. The director and crew would hang around the airfield until I returned a couple of hours later.

One afternoon I landed and was given the message that my daughter had just been born in London. Gae and I had been hoping for a weekend, but the baby had decided to arrive a few days early. Before dawn the next morning I drove across the border into Austria and down to the city of Klagenfurt, caught a flight to Vienna, then one from Vienna to London, followed by another high-speed cab ride to the hospital in Wimbledon. I felt extremely guilty about having to race back to work the next day, and also that Gae and I had not decided on a name. Finally, after a month of phone calls and visits between London and Yugoslavia, we decided to call this tiny blond creature with the huge blue eyes, Alexandra.

Anyone looking at a picture of me and Gae and these two beautiful little children would have thought it a Christmas card portrait of a perfect young family. But I still had not overcome my reservations about marriage. Even though Gae and I made a genuine, valiant effort to build the bond between us, I still felt unsettled and restless. I was frequently away from home, busying myself with film projects, sports, and work for various social and political causes. Now I had responsibilities that had come to me sooner than I had expected. Even though I was uncertain about my future with Gae, I adored these two little people—and still do. I was determined that no matter what happened, I would always try my hardest not to subject them to the kinds of family difficulties I had faced as a child.

As I journeyed back to Yugoslavia, I was in turmoil—elated over the birth of Alexandra but confused and anxious about the direction my life was taking. I continued to brood through the night without finding any solutions. I was greatly relieved when the alarm went off at 6:30 and it was time to go back to work.

CHAPTER NINE

Throughout the 1980s I kept the commitment I had made to avoid action pictures in favor of smaller films with more complex roles. Whenever I couldn't find a good film project, I went back on the stage. In 1984 I appeared with Vanessa Redgrave and Dame Wendy Hiller in *The Aspern Papers* in London's West End. The play, based on the Henry James novella, was written by Vanessa's father, Sir Michael Redgrave, who had played the lead himself in the 1950s. It was Vanessa's idea to revive the play as a tribute to him for his seventy-fifth birthday. He never came to rehearsals, but on opening night he took the place of honor in the royal box. This put him so near the stage that as I played his part in his play, it was hard to concentrate because he was watching me so intently. When I met him at the party afterwards, all I remember him saying was, 'Keep your head up.'

Vanessa and I enjoyed continuing the working relationship we had begun on *The Bostonians*. I was awed by her range. In the film we were archrivals for a young girl's affections. In the play she was a sequestered spinster who is flattered by the attentions of a young American literary sleuth who arrives in search of the private letters of the romantic poet Jeffrey Aspern. She was completely convincing as both characters. I felt privileged to share the stage with her.

In the summer of 1985 I had a great time chewing up the scenery as Tony in *The Royal Family* at Williamstown, then played the Count in an off-the-wall production of Beaumarchais's *Marriage of Figaro* at the Circle in the Square in New York. The clothes were from the '30s and all white, until the last act, when the director, Andrei Serban, dressed us in proper eighteenth-century costumes, but all in black. Some characters zoomed around the polished floor of the set on roller skates. I made my first entrance on a bicycle, then spent most of my scenes striding around in riding clothes, carrying a crop. When an actor would ask Andrei for the logic behind an action, he would simply reply in his thick Romanian accent, 'I like. Is *interesting*.'

In early '86, still trying to find a decent film project, I was looking through my bookshelves and came across a script called *Street Smart*. It had been sitting there for years; I couldn't even remember where it had come from. As I reread it I liked it immediately and wondered why I hadn't responded to it before. The lead character, Jonathan Fisher, is an amoral yuppie who fabricates a profile of a pimp in order to keep his job on the staff of a slick New York magazine. As he does research for the article, he crosses paths with a real pimp named Fast Black and soon finds himself drawn into a dangerous underworld. The script makes it clear that the smarmy young writer and the treacherous pimp are much alike but that the pimp is actually more honest.

I took the project to Cannon Films and was given a green light. Jerry Schatzberg, who had directed the gritty urban drama *Panic in Needle Park* with Al Pacino, was brought in to direct. The role of Fast Black was offered to Danny Glover; he liked the script but after *The Color Purple* didn't want to play another unsympathetic character. Jerry knew of a talented actor who had not yet gained the recognition he deserved and whose steady job at the time was playing Easy Reader on *The Electric Company*. At the first read-through I knew I would have to work very hard to keep up with him. This was my introduction to Morgan Freeman.

Because of the low budget of *Street Smart*, we had to shoot in Montreal, and the art department had to make it look like New York. When we worked on the street, all the signs in French were covered up and the prop people littered the sidewalks with newspapers and garbage. We did film in Harlem for three days, and I was amazed that this footage blended so well with the scenes shot in Canada.

I was not aware that Morgan was a grandfather. One evening as I was waiting to shoot a scene, he and his wife pulled up at the location in a big station wagon with a cute little girl sitting behind them in a baby seat. They had driven all the way from New York during his week off, typical

242

American tourists on a summer vacation. I watched as he kissed them fondly and sent them off to their hotel. Then he disappeared into his trailer. A half hour later the grandfather was gone and out came the dangerous pimp, with the flashy clothes and gold-capped tooth. Even though I had worked with him for weeks, I was startled by the transformation. Later that night we shot a scene in which the pimp drags Jonathan Fisher into the bathroom of a Harlem restaurant, smashes his face into the sink, and puts a gun to his head. That kind of threat has been used in countless films without producing a real impact: the viewer knows that the star of the movie probably isn't about to be blown away. But Morgan could take a clichéd moment and make it real. As we shot the scene I actually felt he might kill me any second. No one was surprised when he was nominated for an Oscar and his career took off.

Menahem Golan and Yoram Globus, the owners of Cannon Films, produced and financed *Street Smart* on the condition that I play *Superman* in at least one more sequel. They had bought the rights from Ilya Salkind and his father, Alexander, the financier, over dinner in Cannes the previous May. While we were filming in Montreal, the writers Larry Konner and Mark Rosenthal were busy churning out the script for *Superman IV*. The premise this time (based largely on input from me, I'm sorry to say) was that *Superman* would intervene in the nuclear arms race. *Superman* had been used as a morale booster for the troops in World War II. Now, when President Reagan was referring to the Soviet Union as 'the evil empire' and summit talks with Mikhail Gorbachev were at an impasse, I thought the character could be used effectively in the real world once again. Big mistake.

We were also hampered by budget constraints and cutbacks in all departments. Cannon Films had nearly thirty projects in the works at the time, and *Superman IV* received no special consideration. For example, Konner and Rosenthal wrote a scene in which *Superman* lands on Forty-second Street and walks down the double yellow lines to the United Nations, where he gives a speech. If that had been a scene in *Superman I*, we would actually have shot it on Forty-second Street. Dick Donner would have choreographed hundreds of pedestrians and vehicles and cut to people gawking out of office windows at the sight of *Superman* walking down the street like the Pied Piper. Instead we had to shoot at an industrial park in England in the rain with about a hundred extras, not a car in sight, and a dozen pigeons thrown in for atmosphere. Even if the story had been brilliant, I don't think that we could ever have lived up to the audience's expectations with this approach.

Often my work provided a welcome distraction from the complexities of my private life. Not this time. Not only was the film a mess but my relationship with Gae was deteriorating. In spite of the tremendous sorrow I felt about leaving the children behind, Gae and I could no longer keep up appearances. When the production ended in February 1987, I moved back to New York. Gae and the children remained in our house on Redcliffe Road.

The next few months were truly miserable. I came back to an empty apartment and an empty life. My friend Michael Stutz and I went to Barbados for a week, but even as I went scuba diving and met a number of available women, I couldn't lift myself out of my depression. I realized that what I needed wasn't a vacation but time to grieve.

Still trying to pull myself out of the depths, I went to Williamstown in the dead of winter and literally did something constructive: I met with a local architect and drew up plans to expand and improve the house. The builders started to work in the early spring. I was always amused that they had coffee and donuts at seven, but at about nine-thirty they switched to Budweiser. By the end of the day they had finished a couple of six-packs. I didn't mind, however, because even though they built my house with a slight buzz on, the framing was excellent and all the corners were square.

My half brother Jeff moved in early in the spring and got a job as a Little League coach in Pittsfield. In the evenings we shared takeout food at a card table in the partly finished dining room. I flew to New York occasionally for meetings and picked up a few jobs to keep an income flowing. When I hosted a documentary about the future of aviation at the Smithsonian in Washington, I recorded my trip on video for Matthew and Alexandra. But they were unimpressed. Gae told me over the phone that the shots of the Washington Monument and Lincoln Memorial had bored them. They watched for a while, then turned it off.

One of the clear indications that I was still deeply depressed was that I lost the willpower to make my own decisions. I had switched agents in the fall of '85 because I wasn't getting the roles I wanted. The first project my new agents at ICM had put together for me was the *Street Smart/Superman IV* deal, which turned out to be a disaster. Golan and Globus had spent no money on advertising and promoting *Street Smart*, so it quickly vanished from sight despite excellent reviews. *Superman IV* was simply a catastrophe from start to finish. That failure was a huge blow to my career. Now I let my team of agents talk me into the third lead in *Switching Channels*, yet another remake of *The Front Page*. The movie would star Kathleen Turner and Michael Caine.

I thought doing a comedy might cheer me up, and it had been great fun working with Michael on *Deathtrap*. In the 1940 version of the story, *His Girl Friday*, Ralph Bellamy is sincere but too square for Rosalind Russell. The idea this time was to make him a vain buffoon: a rich tycoon obsessed with clothes and the color of his hair. Thrown in for good measure was a fear of heights, which the creative team felt would be an amusing takeoff on my *Superman* image.

My big moment as Blaine Bingham III takes place in a glass elevator. When it gets stuck between floors in a shopping mall he has a major panic attack. Everyone assured me this would be hysterically funny. Before I knew what was happening, I had signed a contract and found myself on location in Toronto making a fool of myself. I had taken the job as a distraction from pain, which made it all the more difficult to be a light comedian at work every day. To make matters worse, after two weeks of filming with Kathleen, we learned that Michael Caine would not be able to join us. He was filming *Jaws IV* in the Bahamas, and the mechanical shark had broken down; the film was delayed indefinitely while they waited for new hydraulic parts to be sent from Ohio. Burt Reynolds was brought in to replace him. Unfortunately, he and Kathleen couldn't stand each other, so I had to take on the added burden of being a referee. Trying to be funny while dealing with personal problems and a tense atmosphere on the set was absolutely exhausting.

Gae's brother Jonathan lived in Toronto at the time, so when she brought Matthew and Al over during their spring vacation, they had a place to stay. The kids spent a few nights with me at the Sutton Place Hotel. They loved room service, playing in my trailer at work, and tossing a ball around in the park. But underneath I think they couldn't understand why their parents were in two different places in the same city. Part of me was tempted to put all the pieces back together again; it certainly would have been easier and more convenient. But every time I thought about doing that, I was stopped by the realization that ease and convenience can't be the basis of a permanent relationship. I knew that somehow I had to get through this difficult period, and I believed that in the long run we would all be the better for it. Later that year Gae and I worked out an amicable agreement that provided for joint custody of the children and financial security for the three of them. I'm extremely grateful that in the years since our separation we have never had a serious disagreement about any aspect of the children's upbringing.

Switching Channels was doomed from the start by a number of factors: material that was too broadly written, the lack of chemistry between Burt and Kathleen, and my own overexertions in the role of Blaine Bingham III. For the first time in my career I had accepted a job for all the wrong reasons, without any genuine creative purpose. And I learned the hard way that doing comedy doesn't necessarily pull you out of depression. At the preview that fall I could tell by the audience's halfhearted response that *Switching Channels* would go down the drain. Coming so soon after the debacle of *Superman IV*, it marked the end of my nine-year tenure as an above-the-line movie star.

I retreated to Williamstown once again and immersed myself in rehearsals for *The Rover* and the completion of the house with its octagonal bedroom. Jeff left his job in Pittsfield to coach a team in town. My other half brother, Kevin, joined us and found work as a carpenter. We spent many afternoons knocking fly balls out toward the pasture. One day we took turns hitting the ball as far as we could from the front porch. I marked the winning spot and decided to put a fence there, turning the expanse in between into our front lawn. I called the children frequently in London and waited anxiously for them to visit as soon as school ended in the third week of July. With rehearsals going well and enjoying the company of my two younger half siblings, I began to feel a bit better about life in general, and to socialize occasionally with some of the other actors. And then, on the evening of June 30, I went to the cabaret and saw Dana.

*   *   *

Since the accident I've had time to look back—much more time than I would have liked. I could never have imagined that in my forties I would have the time or the inclination to dwell on the past when my future seemed so bright and full of potential. But during those long afternoons at Kessler, and even now when Will and Dana are out and about, I can't help thinking about the past and discovering certain patterns. One image that keeps coming to mind is a bar graph with three columns. Column A is talent and skill. Column B is career. Column C is personal life. I often imagine that ideally the three columns should remain equal, progressing steadily upwards. In my case—and I guess the same is true for most people—the graph presents a very different picture. Beginning with my first real commitment to acting when I was a teenager, Column B took the lead. It seems that I succeeded very quickly, perhaps too quickly, in my career. The bar rose steadily as I journeyed from the McCarter Theater and Williamstown to Cornell, Juilliard, Broadway, and film stardom. By the age of twenty-five, I was recognized everywhere and seemed firmly established on the Hollywood A list. But Column A, talent and skill, progressed more slowly, somewhat hampered by the way the system works: when you become a star many directors and producers assume you will automatically work magic for them without any guidance. I walked onto many film sets at the height of my career and was treated like royalty—certainly good for the ego, but damaging to growth and to the creative process. It's easy to let yourself be spoiled and skim over the part instead of digging in and doing the kind of work that you had to do to prove yourself as an unknown. Column C, my personal life, was often relegated to the background. My desire to succeed and to maintain my independence seemed more important than my relationships.

By the late '80s and early '90s, one door had slammed shut in my face. I was no longer an A-list actor; now my agents had to fight for meetings. Sometimes I had to audition, which had not been necessary for over a decade. When I tried out for the part Richard Gere played in *Pretty Woman*, I prepared three scenes from the film for the director, Garry Marshall. But when I arrived at the production office for my appointment, I was told that Julia Roberts had other business to attend to and would not be there to read with me.

I had to play the scenes with the casting director, who kept her nose buried in the pages and read about as well as a reject from some community theater. Halfway through the second scene, anger, frustration, and humiliation got the better of me. I ripped the pages in half, dropped them on the floor, told Garry Marshall and the producers that they had no right to treat any actor this way, and stalked out of the room. Many times my agents, Scott Henderson and Arnold Rifkin (I had switched to William Morris in 1988 and have been happy there ever since), would submit me for a part only to be told that even though I was right for the role, the producers wanted 'a fresher face.'

But I was always able to find some kind of work, though I have to admit I thought it was ironic that my film career had bottomed out just as I was making real progress in my development as an actor. Sometimes I did a TV movie of the week to

250

pay the bills, but even then I worked diligently with Harold Guskin, my extraordinary coach, to make the most of it. Some projects, like the film *Morning Glory*, and *The Rose and the Jackal* and *The Sea Wolf* (both for TNT), were pieces I really believed in and still think of as some of my best work.

And where one door had closed, another had opened. Dana's and my marriage was blossoming, and my personal life became more important and satisfying than ever. Now when I went on location, my contract always included a house big enough for all of us: Dana and me, Will, the nanny, and Matthew and Al when they came to visit. I made sure there was always something for everyone and activities for the whole family. This was a radical change from the old days, when location work was so often a means of escape. When I filmed *The Sea Wolf* in Vancouver in the summer of '92, Matthew and Al spent every day with me aboard the schooner that stood in for the *Ghost*. In the evenings we would all take turns trying to soothe six-week-old Will, who was suffering from colic. The next summer I spent ten weeks in Calgary doing *The Black Fox* for CBS, a western set in Texas in the 1860s. Al played the daughter of one of the families in the fort, while Matthew made a little money directing traffic and playing a young sheriff's deputy. On weekends we drove up to Banff and went hiking in the Rockies. One afternoon I carried Will on my back as we all climbed up to a secluded lake for a swim, then hiked back down to the Banff Springs Hotel for a family supper. Al and I went riding together; Matthew and I played tennis; Will enjoyed being a part of any activity but especially loved it when I gave him his bath.

In October 1992 there was a brief period when my professional and personal life seemed perfectly balanced. That spring Dana and I had attended the premiere of *Howards End* at Lincoln Center and sat behind Jim Ivory and Ruth Jhabvala. I thought the film was brilliant. When the lights came up I tapped Jim on the shoulder and said, 'Any part in your next film, it doesn't matter what it is.' The next morning he called and offered me the part of Lewis, a young American congressman, in *The Remains of the Day*, which was to begin filming in England in September.

Now everything came together. I was reunited with the Merchant Ivory group for the first time since *The Bostonians*; I was co-starring with Anthony Hopkins and Emma Thompson; the script was one of the best I'd ever read; Dana, Will, and I were together in beautiful old hotels and inns in the West Country, near Bath and Gloucester, and Matthew and Al made frequent trips by train from London to be with us.

After only a few days of shooting, it was obvious to everyone involved that Tony and Emma were giving the performances of a lifetime. My spirits soared with the realization that I was contributing, even in a small way, to a film that was certain to become a classic. Jim was as generous and open to suggestions from everyone as he had been when we worked together nine years earlier.

In one scene Lewis is frustrated by his inability to get a French diplomat (played by the very same Michel Lonsdale I'd met in Paris twenty years before) to stop worrying about his swollen feet and join him in taking a stand against the Nazis. Lewis

252

urges him to recognize the rising threat to all of western Europe, but the diplomat is more concerned about ordering a basin of hot water for his feet. On the first take I impulsively pulled his shoe off and dropped it on the floor in disgust. That action was not in the script, but it seemed appropriate, and Jim used it in the film.

Later, at dinner, Lewis accuses the assembled English gentry of being political amateurs who have no idea of what is happening in the real world. He offers a toast to 'the professionals,' meaning American pragmatists like himself who are not stuck in a nineteenth-century perspective. After we shot this speech it seemed to me that it might be a good idea for Lewis to apologize to the host (James Fox) to make it clear that the cutting remarks at dinner were not meant to be taken personally. Jim and I added some dialogue about how I had loved England since I was a child and always enjoyed visits here with my family. As the cameras rolled I approached our host with my apology. James Fox had not expected me to come over, so his look of polite bewilderment was absolutely genuine. Once again, as he had done with the dog on the beach in *The Bostonians*, Jim appreciated the spontaneity of the moment and used it in the final cut.

When *The Remains of the Day* premiered in the fall of '93, it was hailed as a masterpiece and received eight Oscar nominations. I had been included in the press junket in Los Angeles—two days of seclusion in a hotel suite doing round-table interviews with journalists from all over the world. I went along willingly because I felt that my performance as Lewis was one of my personal best and hoped the role might begin the resurrection of my film career. The press was polite and listened attentively as I answered their questions. But when the articles and reviews came out, I was scarcely mentioned. All the attention was focused on Tony, Emma, Jim, and their astonishing collaboration, which had followed on the heels of *Howards End*. I had the satisfaction of being part of an undeniably great film, but it did nothing for my career.

Once again the three columns were out of sync. Column B, career, failed to advance. I was proud of Column A, talent and skill; in a couple of interviews I expressed relief that the *Superman* years were behind me and said that I felt my best opportunities as an actor still lay ahead. In my forties and fifties I expected to find challenging, satisfying work both in films and in the theater. Column C, personal life, was soaring far beyond my dreams. Dana, Will, and I moved to Bedford, and for the first time it was a real pleasure to spend time at home, just enjoying our life together.

I was also fortunate in having other passionate interests that helped sustain me during the reversals in my career. In the late '80s I began to take riding more seriously, eventually training five and six days a week to prepare for competing in combined training events. Dana and I had the *Sea Angel* built and roamed from the Chesapeake to Nova Scotia, sometimes by ourselves but often with friends or with the children. I also continued finding great satisfaction in working on political issues. I campaigned for Sen. Patrick Leahy of Vermont, a strong advocate for the environment and the arts, and made speeches around the state on his behalf. I became a board member of the Charles Lindbergh Fund, which provides grants for environmentally sound new technologies. I lent my support to Amnesty International, the Natural Resources Defense Council, and People for the American Way.

I joined the Environmental Air Force, using my plane (now a Cheyenne II, a seven-seat turboprop) to give government officials and journalists a firsthand look at hidden areas of environmental damage. I took them on a number of trips over the Maine woods. The aerial view revealed a common practice of the lumber companies: they would clear-cut hundreds of acres of timber but leave the perimeter intact to conceal the devastation.

In the fall of 1987 I was asked to participate in a political action that was far more dangerous. Seventy-seven actors in Santiago, Chile, had been threatened with execution by the dictator Pinochet if they did not leave the country by November 30. Ariel Dorfman, the exiled Chilean novelist and playwright, contacted me in Williamstown and explained that only the presence of internationally recognized artists in the days preceding the deadline could save their lives. I joined a small group of actors representing Germany, France, Spain, Argentina, and Brazil. As a council member of Actors' Equity Association, I represented 38,000 of their counterparts in the United States.

For years the Chilean people had suffered under a reign of terror. Dissident students and prominent citizens who opposed Pinochet were simply 'disappeared' at night by his death squads. Because they performed thinly disguised political satire and had the support of the people, the actors in Santiago were considered subversive and threatening to the dictator. Their ability to

255

influence public opinion became more and more of a problem for Pinochet as he prepared for a referendum the following April that would determine whether he remained in power. His open declaration of his intention to execute so many members of the opposition signaled a new level of oppression, even by the standards of Pinochet. Telegrams and letters of protest poured in from governments and private citizens all over the world. When I met with many of the threatened actors at various locations in Santiago, I was always accompanied by six bodyguards. There was genuine concern that any one of the visiting artists might be the target of a reprisal by the military.

On the Saturday evening of my week-long visit, several thousand people gathered at a sports arena for a rally *'Por Vida y Arte'* (For Life and Art). Permission had been granted for the performance, but just before it began the military attacked with fire hoses and beat the crowd back from the entrance gates. We retreated to a garage, and the performance took place as planned, even as sharpshooters surrounded the building. In halting Spanish I expressed the support of actors and ordinary citizens in the United States. There were songs of protest, readings from the works of Pablo Neruda, and a message of solidarity from the widow of Salvador Allende, who had been murdered in the military coup in 1973.

During my trip abroad in 1972, in places like Glasgow, Liverpool, and Leeds I had seen strong relationships between the theater and the local community. But in Santiago I witnessed something much more profound: the power of art to speak for the oppressed and disenfranchised.

The next morning one of the newspapers ran a cartoon on the front page that showed me carrying Pinochet by the scruff of his neck, with the caption 'Where will you take him, *Superman?*' I returned home somewhat shaken by the intensity of the experience but gratified that we had made such an impact. When the November 30 deadline passed and all the actors survived, it was the first time a threat by the dictatorship had not been carried out. The people of Chile began to believe that Pinochet could be overthrown. The plebiscite that was supposed to give a rubber-stamp approval to his leadership went against him. In April 1988 he was forced to resign, although he remained as commander in chief of the army. Several months later elections were held. Patricio Alwyn, the leader of the Christian Democratic Party, became president.

The experience in Chile was a dramatic example of how celebrities can make a significant difference. I knew that a number of my colleagues felt the same way. During his campaign for the presidency in 1988, Michael Dukakis had enlisted the aid of several well-known actors to help draw crowds and gain more attention from the media. My friend Ron Silver, a longtime political activist as well as a recognized name, was appalled at how inarticulate and uninformed many of these celebrities were. It was his idea to form an organization that would help prepare celebrities to speak knowledgeably on the issues. Susan Sarandon, Alec Baldwin, Blythe Danner, and I were early members of the group. We decided to call ourselves The Creative Coalition and to open our membership to anyone in the arts. Within a few months we were joined by agents, publicists, writers, stagehands, and opera singers, all with different aspirations for the group. We agreed that we would be most effective if we focused on three or four important issues to be chosen by the board of directors and ratified by 75 percent of the membership.

Our first major undertaking was to defend the National Endowment for the Arts against attacks by conservative Republicans like Jesse Helms, who were outraged that taxpayer dollars were being used to fund art they considered obscene. We argued successfully that in its twenty-five-year history the NEA had given over 90,000 grants to artists and only about a dozen had ever provoked any controversy. Considering the cultural and economic benefit to the country and the provisions of the First Amendment, we felt this was a small price to pay. It was also our contention that politicians do not have the right to impose content restrictions on federally funded art. The peer-panel review system—artists judging the merits of other artists—had always worked effectively. The NEA survived that attack by Helms in 1990, but the issue has remained a source of controversy.

In 1994 Blair Brown and I were elected copresidents. We tried to de-emphasize the importance of our celebrities and to create more opportunities for our general membership. Working with Robert Kennedy, Jr. (who became such a good friend after my accident), we launched an initiative to protect New York City's water supply. Unless the upstate reservoirs were protected from pollution, the city would have to install filtration systems costing billions of dollars that it could not afford. After appearing at town meetings, working the media, and lobbying in Albany for nearly two years, we managed to convince Governor Pataki and the state legislature to spend $1 billion to protect the greater New York City watershed area. We were also instrumental in starting residential recycling in the city, over the objections of sanitation workers and the city administration. On several occasions when the administration tried to scrap the program because of budget constraints, we fought back with hard-hitting subway posters and radio spots, and funding was restored.

It wasn't long after the formation of TCC that our work was noticed both in Albany and in Washington. Soon we were besieged with requests from a wide variety of advocacy groups and politicians to help their causes or campaigns. One afternoon on my way back to the airport after testifying on behalf of the NEA, I was cornered by three officials of the Democratic Party who urged me to run for Congress. They hoped I might fill the seat representing the district in Massachusetts (including Williamstown) that had been vacated by the death of Rep. Silvio Conte. I immediately replied, 'Run for Congress? And lose my influence in Washington?' I had learned that a member of the House has to worry constantly about money and the handling of special interest groups, whereas I and my colleagues at TCC were free to speak from the heart without obligations to anyone and would receive more coverage in the media. Unfair perhaps, but that's the way the system works.

During this period my friends at William Morris

phoned frequently with various offers, but none was terribly interesting. John Kimble, one of the top television agents, was the most persistent caller, because the three major networks were all interested in my doing a series. Most of the scripts were pretty poor; some of them reminded me of material I had rejected in the summer of '76 (though none were as bad as *The Man from Atlantis*). One or two, however, were very well written. I particularly liked the pilot scripts for *Picket Fences* and *Chicago Hope*. CBS also offered me carte blanche to develop my own series. But any of these projects would have meant moving to Los Angeles, which neither Dana nor I wanted to do. It was always comforting to know that if Matthew or Al needed me for any reason, I could hop on the Concorde and be in London in a few hours. Sometimes I flew over to watch a soccer match or just to spend a weekend. I never missed either of their birthdays. Los Angeles would have added another three thousand miles to the distance between us.

But I didn't mind making brief trips out west for a film or television project. I went to New Mexico for a few weeks to shoot *Speechless* with Michael Keaton and Geena Davis. And the whole family particularly enjoyed the time we spent together in Point Reyes, just north of San Francisco, while I did a remake of *Village of the Damned* for John Carpenter.

One film, a project for HBO called *Above Suspicion*, took me once again into the world of the disabled. In *Fifth of July* I had learned to simulate a bilateral amputee; now I was cast as a police officer who sustains a bullet wound and becomes a

260

paraplegic. I did research for the part at a rehab hospital in Van Nuys, a suburb of Los Angeles. I learned how to get in and out of cars and how to use a sliding board to transfer from a wheelchair onto a mattress in the physical therapy room. I spent most of my time with a young woman who had been crushed under a bookcase during a recent earthquake. She had a halo screwed into her head and was just beginning to walk again. In contrast to Mike Sulsona, my coach on *Fifth of July*, she was still deeply depressed and having real difficulty dealing with her condition. I tried to control my emotions as I watched her struggle to hold herself up on parallel bars while she took tiny, painful steps forward. At the end of these sessions I would retreat to the comforts of the Sunset Marquis Hotel, thinking all the while: Thank God that's not me.

So it went until the spring of '95. Dana auditioned for a number of projects in New York. I got up at six most mornings to train Buck before a full day in my office, often putting business aside to take Will to Water Babies or Gymboree in Mount Kisco. We launched the *Sea Angel* as usual in early April, and even went sailing one weekend in a snowstorm. My good friends the Halmis of Hallmark Entertainment offered me the lead in *Kidnapped*, to be shot in Ireland. Dana and I held each other close one night and decided that Ireland would be a perfect place to conceive our second child. Matthew and Al could come over from London and perhaps bring friends along, too. When we returned to Bedford in the fall, I would direct my first project for the big screen, a romantic comedy called *Tell Me True*. Our plans for the year

261

were falling into place beautifully. Then one evening in May I went downstairs to fill out an entry form. The following Friday we were off to Culpeper.

CHAPTER TEN

At home in Bedford I began a routine of exercising in the morning and doing office work in the afternoon. I was approached by Senator Jeffords of Vermont about an amendment to a bill in the Senate that would raise lifetime insurance caps from $1 million to $10 million. The Jeffords amendment was attached to the Kennedy-Kassebaum bill, which provided insurance coverage for individuals with preexisting conditions and portability, meaning that you would still be insured if you changed jobs. I wrote a letter to every senator explaining that the increased insurance caps would not be a hardship on employers; the cost (approximately nine dollars a year per worker in a medium-size company) could be split between management and the employees. Businesses employing fewer than twenty people would be exempt, and the legislation would not go into effect until 2004.

I spent over a month on this issue, giving interviews and making follow-up calls, trying to keep the amendment alive. Finally we were able to bring it to a vote. Jeffords had expected support from about eighteen of his colleagues. When the roll call was taken, the tally was forty-two votes in favor. Even though we lost, the margin was much smaller than expected, which meant that the issue could be reintroduced later, either attached to other health care legislation or as a separate bill.

I also worked on several approaches to increase funding for research at the NIH. I appealed to President Clinton, reiterating the thrust of my speech at the Democratic Convention: that spending a reasonable amount now on good science would save billions in the long run. I joined forces with Senators Tom Harkin and Arlen Specter to propose legislation that would require companies that offer health care insurance to donate one penny of every premium paid by the consumer to research. The conservative estimate was that this 'tax' would generate $24 billion a year. When Harkin and Specter called for a sense of the Senate on the bill, the result was 98 to 0 in favor. Gratified by this response, they called for an official vote. It was defeated 65 to 33. To my mind this was a perfect example of the duplicity of most politicians. They know what's right, but when pressured by a powerful special interest group such as the insurance lobby, they fail to vote their consciences. The latest proposal for raising research money is to impose a tax of $1.50 on cigarettes, a measure that is more likely to pass because it's safer for the politicians now that public opinion is running against the tobacco companies.

During the first few months of 1996, the combination of being home with my family, working on these political issues, preparing for my appearance at the Oscars, and maintaining my health kept me extremely busy. Even though I'd decided not to go back into rehab for an all-out attempt to wean off the ventilator, I still breathed on my own nearly every morning. By February I could manage ninety minutes off the hose before becoming too exhausted to continue.

Gradually Dana and I assembled a staff of nurses and aides to provide me with the twenty-four-hour care I needed and to allow us a more normal family life. A psychologist at Kessler once said to me, 'Don't turn your wife into your nurse or your mother.' We considered ourselves very lucky to be able to follow that advice; in many cases the patient's spouse has to become the primary caregiver, and the stress on the marriage is intense.

I was adjusting reasonably well, but in spite of all this activity I longed for some kind of creative outlet. In early April, Michael Fuchs, the former CEO of Home Box Office, came to the rescue. We had been friends since the early days of The Creative Coalition, when he lent his support to our fledgling organization and gave us office space in the HBO building. He had built HBO into the pre-eminent cable company by developing exceptional material, taking risks with his programming, and drawing talent away from films and the other networks.

Michael joined my friend and former agent Andrea Eastman and her husband, Richard, for a social dinner with Dana and me one evening. He had recently been fired in a shake-up at Time Warner, HBO's parent company. He had to leave a number of scripts behind, including one that was nearly ready for production called *In the Gloaming*. Michael knew of my interest in directing; in fact, I had been slated to direct *Family Album* for HBO several years earlier, but the executives and I could not agree on casting, so I bowed out and the film was never made. Now, even as he was being shown the door, he pitched *Gloaming* as an ideal project for my directorial debut.

Colin Callender, the executive in charge of HBO films produced on the East Coast; Keri Putnam, his second in command; the producer Fred Zollo; and Will Scheffer, who had adapted the screenplay from a story in *The New Yorker*, all descended on our house in Bedford one afternoon in early May. I think they needed reassurance; I doubt any of them had ever considered hiring a vent-dependent, quadriplegic first-time director. Meanwhile, I had my own agenda: I had read the script, and while I liked the premise very much, I felt there were a number of problems that needed to be addressed.

As soon as they were comfortably arranged in my living room, I launched the meeting by stating that I was grateful for their interest and felt that this would be the perfect project for me, both in terms of the emotional content of the story and the logistics of undertaking the production. (My experience at auditioning had taught me that it helps to take charge.) Then I risked losing the job immediately by stating bluntly that I thought the script needed a substantial rewrite—the father lacked dimension, the mother-and-son relationship was inappropriately romantic, and there were too many clichés about the gay lifestyle. I half-expected the team would make a quick exit; instead, I learned later that my direct approach had given them confidence in me. Will Scheffer volunteered to start work immediately. After the executives left, we had a quick lunch, then turned to page 1 and began to revise. I was very grateful that he was so willing to consider my ideas. Many writers are defensive about their work, especially when they've already been told it's brilliant.

In the Gloaming is the story of Danny, a young man suffering from AIDS who comes home to die. His return has a profound effect on his family, particularly his mother. After a long period of estrangement, a new bond forms between them. His father and younger sister, who have never accepted Danny's homosexuality, have a much more difficult time. During the last four months of his life, Danny helps to bring about healing and reconciliation in his dysfunctional family.

The first important task was to reexamine Danny's character. I felt that in the original script he was too sarcastic, bitter, and judgmental about his family. It seemed to me that a quiet dignity would make him much more sympathetic. Perhaps I felt a strong connection with Danny because of my own experience. After having nearly died twice, I felt no anger toward any of my relatives, even those with whom I'd had difficult relationships. I felt no need for 'justice' or retribution. Issues in my two families that had troubled me for years now seemed much less significant.

I suggested to Will that when Danny gets his mother to talk about her life in a series of conversations in the twilight, his motivation is to understand rather than to criticize. Our working relationship was deeply satisfying. Will seemed genuinely affected by all I had learned and experienced in the past year. We spent the last two weeks in May working together in Williamstown. By June 1 we had a script that we were both proud of, and we had no reservations about showing it to anyone.

The rest of the summer was spent fighting the Casting Wars. My primary concerns were (a) to find first-rate actors, and (b) to create a believable family. HBO was sympathetic, but they also wanted to cast big-name actors who are seldom, if ever, seen on TV. For the first few days as we bandied names around, I hoped this wouldn't be a repeat of my experience with *Family Album*. Many first-time directors are so eager to get their films made that they cave in on casting. I felt strongly that if directing was going to be my second career, I didn't want it to begin with serious compromises.

Whenever HBO and I reached an impasse, I offered to step down. We did agree that no one could play the mother better than Glenn Close. I reached her on location in Australia, and she accepted the part within twenty-four hours of reading the script. I was thrilled, but then I was asked to approach Gene Hackman to play the father. Notwithstanding his tremendous talent (and our friendship that dated back to *Superman I*), I simply could not imagine Gene and Glenn as a married couple. I tried to convince HBO that Janet and Martin had to be about the same age or there would be no logic to the story, and their reconciliation at the end would not be effective.

The Name Game went on for nearly three months, more time than it takes to cast many big-budget feature films. After Glenn was cast there were endless discussions about every role with the exception of the one played by Whoopi Goldberg. I called her on the set of *Ghosts of Mississippi* to discuss the part and make sure she understood it was just a cameo. She asked only one question: 'Am I a maid?' I replied, 'No, you're a nurse.' I offered to overnight a script, but she said it wasn't necessary and signed on immediately.

By late August I was fairly exhausted by the struggle, but we had signed up the perfect cast. I had gotten my first choice for every role. I was grateful that actors of the caliber of Glenn, Robert Sean Leonard, Bridget Fonda, David Strathairn, and Whoopi had decided to trust me, and was very glad I had sent them a polished script rather than a work in progress.

The crew fell into place much more easily than the cast under the capable supervision of our line producer, Nellie Nugiel, who ran the day-to-day logistics of the shoot. I hired my cousin Nick Childs to be my assistant, which raised some eyebrows until the executives discovered he was more than qualified for the job; then they made him postproduction supervisor as well. Fred Elmes, a superbly versatile director of photography who had worked several times with David Lynch, loved the script and quickly agreed to join us. Glenn's daughter Annie and my son Will were cast as young Bridget and Robert in the opening credit sequence—a little harmless nepotism. We found the ideal location, a house in Pound Ridge, just ten minutes from my home. Andy Jackness and his crew decorated it perfectly. By the third week of September everything was set to go.

We began with a table reading of the script at our production offices in Bedford Hills. The night before I lay awake thinking of moments in my life when I'd been in a position of leadership. I remembered screaming at my crews during my racing days as a young teenager and the humiliation of the Seamanship/Sportsmanship

Award. I recalled a couple of directors who had frustrated me with their inability to communicate. I thought about Jim Ivory's skill at being 'in the moment.' I had learned how important it is to lead but also to get out of the way.

Now it was my turn. As I wheeled into position at the head of the table, all eyes turned toward me. This was it. We had assembled an exceptional group of artists on both sides of the camera, and I eagerly looked forward to the gifts they would bring to our film. We turned to page 1 and began.

The night before shooting Glenn threw a party for the whole company and made a very moving speech, saying that she was delighted to be part of this new adventure in my life. I felt tremendous warmth and support from everyone in the room. That night I was able to go home and sleep soundly instead of staring at the ceiling, wondering what I had gotten myself into.

The next morning Nick drove me to the set in my van, making sure to arrive fifteen minutes early. (I made a point of being early every day so no one would worry about me.) Neil Stutzer, our accessibility adviser, designed a forty-foot ramp that extended from the sidewalk to the front porch. This was my entrance to the set, but it had to be taken apart when we shot exteriors, then reassembled so I could leave the house at the end of the day. Once I was inside I parked myself in front of a monitor; the script supervisor, my nurse, Nick Childs, the producers, and visitors from HBO would soon join me in what came to be known as Video Village.

We began each day by reading the first scene to be shot as soon as the actors were made up and dressed. The crew was ready with the lighting because we set the actors' positions each evening before going home. Working with the art department during preproduction in early September, I had gone into every room, both upstairs and down, to make decisions about the placement of furniture and possible camera positions. This involved lifts, ramps, and my occasional transfer into a seventeen-inch-wide aisle chair so that I could negotiate the narrow hallways. I had to be strapped in with my arms crossed, my knees tied together, and my head bound to the back of the headrest with tight Velcro straps so that I wouldn't slump sideways out of the chair if I had a bad spasm. I often joked that I looked like Gary Gilmore and suggested that they pin a big red heart on my chest and shoot me. Once I was strapped in I usually quoted his famous final words: 'Let's do it,' whereupon the grips would carry me upstairs or wherever I needed to go.

When it came time to shoot, I could stay in my chair in front of the monitor, the mayor of Video Village. Fred Elmes had a viewfinder that transmitted directly to my TV screen from anywhere in the house or on the property. We used microphones and speakers so we could discuss camera angles and choices of lenses as easily as if I were next to him on the set. This technology is often used by able-bodied directors as well. Francis Ford Coppola is famous for directing actors from the inside of a bus, and I heard a rumor that Steven Spielberg directed some of the sequel to *Jurassic Park* via satellite linkup from his home on Long Island to the sound-stage in Los Angeles. I only used this technology because I had to; on shooting

270

days we would have wasted a lot of time hauling me upstairs and finding an out-of-the-way place to put me. Also the whooshing of my ventilator would have distracted the actors and ruined the sound track.

The set was very calm, and there were few distractions. I think that my being in a wheelchair helped everyone to focus on the work. Glenn came in one day with walking pneumonia. She should probably have been at home in bed, but she performed brilliantly as usual, using the time between setups to hook herself up to an IV drip of antibiotics. I remember Bobby Leonard saying one day, 'You're not going to hear many people complaining. It's like, "I'm *tired*." Yeah? Well, see the man in the wheelchair? ... It puts things in perspective.'

I particularly enjoyed shooting the exteriors, because then I could wheel down to the set and be closer to the actors. One of my favorites was the scene in which Glenn as a young mom plays tag with her two children on the front lawn. We used this during the opening credits to establish immediately that she prefers the son over the daughter, creating a lasting jealousy. I asked Glenn to organize the game with Annie and Will and told Fred to quietly turn on the camera on a signal from me. But Will found a starting spot, put his hands on his knees, and waited. I called to him to start playing, but he shot back, 'Aren't you going to say, "Action"?' Glenn and the crew tried not to crack up, but it was hopeless. Will, now four, had learned that 'Action' means start and 'Cut' means stop, and he wanted to be directed properly. The concern I had about him being self-conscious in front of the camera was obviously unfounded. He even slowed down at the right moment so that Glenn could catch him and pick him up for a hug. He later confided to me that he could easily have outrun her, but he knew that wasn't in the script.

One of my most difficult challenges was to make sure that the father, played by David Strathairn, did not come across as a stock figure—stern, strict, and pompous. I also needed to convince Bobby Leonard that stillness is not boring; in fact, it makes the character more interesting: the viewer is intrigued and wants to know more about what's going on inside him. I asked David to search for ways to be with his son instead of avoiding him. When he comes into the sickroom with Danny's tennis trophies from high school, he should hope to be invited to stay. The result was an awkwardness that I thought was very effective, and even painful to watch. And as Danny resisted the temptation to challenge his parents or criticize their behavior too harshly, I witnessed the emergence of a courageous and dignified young man.

Many times the actors would come over to Video Village to discuss a particular moment or to make suggestions. One afternoon we were shooting one of the most important scenes in the film, in which Glenn comes into the sickroom for the first time. Following Whoopi's lead, she learns to overcome her fear of touching her son and helping with his care. When we filmed the wide shot of the scene, I experienced a mild anxiety attack; Whoopi was clearly uncomfortable and having trouble with the business of connecting a catheter and starting an IV. She was only available for two days. We had already shot the easy scenes, but this one was absolutely critical and had to be in the can within the next four hours. After a couple of takes she pulled up a chair next to me to talk things over. I asked her if my nurse, Tracy DeLuca, who had cared for many AIDS patients, could help. Some actors would have been insulted by this suggestion, but Whoopi immediately took Tracy by the hand, and the two of them went off together.

Fifteen minutes later Tracy came back and gave me a thumbs-up. Whoopi took her seat at Danny's bedside and asked if we could shoot right away. I decided not to reshoot the wide angle but to push in for the close coverage. As usual Fred was ready. We rolled the camera, and I said 'Action' with no idea what to expect. That take was technically perfect, which was a great relief because Whoopi was now completely convincing. She had not only mastered the mechanical problems but had found the right way to respond to a grieving parent. I did one more take for protection and finished the day knowing we had just captured one of the best moments of the film.

We finished principal photography in late October and celebrated with a lavish party at Luna, a New York City–style restaurant in Mt. Kisco owned by my friend and fellow TCC board member Susan Liederman. The next day I began to edit the film in our little office next to the Bedford Hills train station. David Ray, whose distinguished credits included editing *A Bronx Tale* for Robert De Niro and *Billy Bathgate* for Robert Benton, had already assembled a rough cut. I had been told by a number of directors, from Mike Nichols to Jonathan Demme and Dick Donner, that the first time you see the film put together, you come away

273

depressed and wonder if there is any hope of fixing it. I have to admit that I had the opposite experience. Some of the scenes seemed choppy, and the pace and rhythm needed a lot of work. But as I watched it unfold, I was moved by the performances and once again felt very grateful for the talent and generosity of the cast and crew.

David and I spent the next six weeks looking at every take, moving scenes around, featuring different characters at certain key moments. The Avid computer system we used allowed us to make immediate changes, a far cry from Stuart Baird's cutting room on *Superman*, with its strips of film hanging everywhere waiting to be spliced together with tape. By the middle of November we were ready to show the film to HBO. We had cleaned up the soundtrack and added temporary music cues borrowed from a little-known Irish film that we had discovered after listening to nearly a hundred scores.

The reaction was mixed. When the lights came up Fred Zollo said the film was ready for an immediate release; Bonnie Timmerman, our casting director and coproducer, was crying so hard she had to leave the room. I was pleased that the film 'held'—no one squirmed in their seats or left to use the phone (which actually happens sometimes at these early screenings). Colin Callender was polite but left quickly for New York. The next day I received a memo from him describing the work as 'a promising first draft' along with about ten pages of notes and comments. I found that I disagreed with many of them, so I decided the best course of action was to have David make the requested changes to see if they

274

improved the film, rather than defend my choices point by point. Meanwhile Colin brought in another editor, Kathy Wenning, as a consultant. They had worked together successfully on a number of projects, and he trusted her implicitly. She had also edited several films for Merchant Ivory, including *The Bostonians* and *Howards End*, so I was glad Colin had chosen her. Perhaps I *had* ruined the film, or at the very least failed to make the most of it. A fresh look at the material by someone so sensitive and skilled could be helpful.

Kathy began by looking at Colin's version, then my original cut. I fully expected her to side with Colin, assuming that she had been hired to endorse his point of view. But after seeing both versions she recommended that we use my cut as the basis for the finished product. I was deeply gratified and reassured; after all, the work David and I had done closely followed the script, which had been admired by everyone involved in the project.

Originally Kathy was hired to work on the film for a couple of weeks. She had made it clear that she was attending architecture school and no longer editing. But once she and David and I huddled together around the computer screen and started fine tuning, she couldn't tear herself away. I was especially impressed by David's willingness to take suggestions from her. I considered myself lucky to have input from both of them, which helped me tremendously.

I agonized particularly about Danny's death scene: the question was whether to stay on a spectacular close-up of Glenn as she realizes that her husband may still be in love with her, or to cut back to Danny for a moment as he takes his final breath. We talked about it at length, tried it both ways, left it for a week and came back to it, played different music cues underneath the scene—the process of getting that moment right seemed to go on forever. But the collaboration was exhilarating. I thought again of how Jim Ivory absorbed suggestions, giving everyone free rein to speak his or her mind, then making the final decision. I remembered a famous maxim of Nikos's, which I first heard all those years ago as an apprentice at Williamstown: 'Theater is a democracy where the director is king.'

After nearly three weeks of agonizing about the death scene, I decided to incorporate the brief cut of Danny, because in the best take you couldn't be sure if he was dying or merely drifting off to sleep. I thought the ambiguity captured this crucial moment perfectly. I also thought that if I stayed on Glenn throughout it might seem as if I was servicing the star rather than telling the story.

In January I developed a blood clot behind my left knee and had to be hospitalized for a week on IV blood thinners. Kathy and David brought the computer to the hospital so we could continue working. As soon as I was out of danger, I returned to the editing suite; but in February I developed another blood clot in the same leg and had to go back to Northern Westchester Hospital (my home away from home) for five more days.

The film was scheduled to air on April 20. All the disagreements that had made the editing process so challenging were now behind us. Dave Grusin had provided the final touch with his simple but eloquent score. I was tremendously relieved that the final result was satisfying to everyone.

HBO (and especially Colin Callender) now gave their full support to the film and threw a lavish screening and reception at the Museum of Modern Art on a Monday evening a few weeks before the television premiere. Dana and I looked forward to an exciting night out.

But on Saturday afternoon, as I was being transferred from my exercise bike back into my wheelchair, the nurse and the aide working with me had trouble with the lift. Instead of landing smoothly in the center of the seat, I came down on the front corner, balanced precariously for a moment, then fell straight over the side onto the floor. Dana helped the two of them pick me up and put me back in the chair, but I could sense that something was wrong with my left arm: it seemed looser and far too flexible.

The next morning we went back to Northern Westchester for an X ray, which revealed that the bone between my shoulder and my elbow, the humerus, had broken cleanly in two. The doctors decided that the best thing to do would be to drill a hole through my shoulder and insert a titanium rod inside the bone to hold the pieces together.

The problem we faced was that I was still on blood thinners and might lose a critical amount of blood during the operation. All day Sunday I sat around hooked up to an IV designed to reverse the thinning process, waiting for the clotting factor to reach a level that would make it reasonably safe to operate. Finally at 8:00 P.M. I hit the magic number. The surgeon was paged at home, left his dinner table, and scrubbed in. I stayed in my wheelchair, and a plastic sheet was draped over me so that I wouldn't end up looking like a victim in a splatter film.

At first they tried 10 milligrams of Versed, a mild anesthetic. This dose would be enough to make most people quiet and comfortable. However I was still chatting away and looking rather apprehensively through the sheet, watching Dr. Levin assemble a hammer, a chisel, and a drill. They kept increasing the dosage of Versed until they reached 22 milligrams (probably enough to sedate a 300-pound gorilla), but I still showed no signs of drowsiness. Tracy suggested they bring out 'the good stuff,' meaning Diprovan. Five minutes later I was out cold, which was a good thing, because I had been all too aware of what was coming. I'm glad I didn't have to watch the actual procedure.

First Dr. Levin entered the shoulder and the top of the humerus with the drill, spraying blood on the floor and all over himself and the team of nurses. Once he had access to the inside of the bone, he literally tapped the titanium rod into place with the hammer and chisel I had watched him prepare. But in less than forty-five minutes it was all over, and I was relaxing in the recovery room. The operation had gone flawlessly, and the postop X ray showed that the bone had been perfectly reconnected. I was free to go home.

The next morning I told Tracy that I was more tired than usual. She wasn't surprised, because I had lost four pints of blood—one-third of normal capacity. She suggested I relax in bed until it was time to get ready for the evening gala. I was only too happy to comply, which was unusual for me, because normally I hate having to spend a beautiful day indoors. At about four-thirty Tracy and one of my aides began the process of getting me up and out the door. I was still not quite myself but was eager to go because the whole cast would be there, as well as many friends, relatives, and acquaintances, some of whom I hadn't seen in years.

So many people had accepted the invitations to the screening that the film was shown simultaneously in two theaters. Colin Callender and Fred Zollo made generous introductory remarks. I particularly appreciated Fred's observations that I had been 'as difficult and opinionated as any other director' and that he would work with me again in a second. Dana, Alexandra, Ben, and my mother, all seated in the row next to me, gave me looks of encouragement as the film came up on the screen. I worried that since it was made for television, it wouldn't play in a theater, but it held up well. Fred Elmes's cinematography looked much more beautiful than it had on the computer-generated Avid display, and I saw nuances in the performances that I hadn't noticed before.

At the end of the film the camera pulls away from the house as Dana sings the title song. The final credits begin halfway through the second verse, over a shot of the now empty bench where mother and son had some of their most intimate conversations. I was surprised and deeply gratified when no one moved or started talking, even as the credits continued to roll silently over black for nearly two minutes. When the lights came up the audience turned toward me and the cast and gave us a standing ovation. To be given such a reception less than two years after I lay in a hospital bed

279

wondering if I would ever work again was overwhelming.

At the party a steady stream of well-wishers stopped at our table, including a few directors with kind things to say. Calvin Klein came over and was just about to talk to me when he caught sight of Alexandra, sitting on my left, looking absolutely stunning in a dress bought especially for the occasion. I could almost see the dollar signs rolling around in his eyes as I introduced them. Peggy Siegel, the publicist who had organized the party, practically had to drag him away. On the way home Al and I joked about Klein's reaction to her. I asked her how she felt now about modeling, a subject that had come up before, and I was relieved that she still had no interest in it. How lucky I am to be the father of such a beautiful but unspoiled teenager.

In the Gloaming premiered on April 20. It got respectable ratings, but the reviews were extraordinary. As an actor I sometimes felt that my choices were wrong or that I had failed to do justice to a role; I often wished I could do a part over again and fix my mistakes. But in my first outing as a director, there were no such regrets. I had thoroughly enjoyed making dozens of decisions every day, relying mostly on instinct. I loved making suggestions to the cast and crew, and never minded making changes or deferring to someone with a better idea. My experience working with Jim Ivory had served me well. I even found a way to pay tribute to one of my favorite scenes in *The Bostonians*: every day Glenn came to work with her little dog, Gaby, who followed her everywhere. As soon as I noticed this, I cast the dog in the film.

When I told Dick Donner that I was going to

direct a film, his response was, 'So what's new?' Obviously he remembered that during the seemingly endless shooting of *Superman*, I had bombarded him with questions about lenses, camera angles, and lighting. In my spare time I had driven around in my golf cart to the various departments—the flying unit, the model unit, the mechanical effects unit, and especially the editing suite—making a nuisance of myself as I tried to learn all I could from the experts who were working with us. That year and a half was like going to film school. Although I didn't realize it at the time, it helped prepare me to be a director.

With *In the Gloaming* I made a transition from one aspect of my career to another. So many people who sustain injuries like mine are forced to give up what they love doing most. Musicians or painters or carpenters may never work in their chosen fields again. But I was lucky enough to find another creative outlet and to do something that had interested me since I was a teenager. The fact that this new venture succeeded so well was just the icing on the cake: we were nominated for five Emmys and won four Cable Ace awards, including Best Dramatic Special. Even though I was still in a wheelchair, I had taken a big step forward.

CHAPTER ELEVEN

The door to our bedroom slides open, and Will comes in just as it's light enough to make out the trees above our skylight. He knows I can't speak to him because my trach has been inflated for the night, cutting off the air to my vocal cords. He waves to me, and I make a clicking sound in return as he passes by and jumps on Dana's bed, telling her it's time to get up and play floor hockey. They go out together, and soon I hear Will's play-by-play of the action as he and Dana go one-on-one with plastic golf clubs for sticks and a bottle top for a puck in the family room down the hall. It's just past six o'clock, too late to go back to sleep. Sometimes I try to doze, but mostly I watch the trees taking shape above me and prepare myself for the day.

Will continues playing hockey by himself while Dana makes him breakfast and the lunch he takes to school. At eight the nurse and aide on the morning shift come in. The nurse counts out my twenty pills, which I take in one swallow of cranberry juice: some are vitamins, some are to help control my spasms, the rest are to keep my bladder from shrinking and to maintain the proper functioning of my bowels. I treat myself to a single cup of coffee, which I drink all at once through a straw, and then we begin the painful process of moving my body from the position I've been in all night.

My joints and muscles are frozen, and I can barely turn my head because my neck is so stiff. Usually I have a tingling, burning sensation in both legs and pain behind my left knee where the blood clots were. I sleep with splints on both feet to prevent foot drop; if the tendons and ligaments are not flexed and are allowed to atrophy, it will never be possible to stand or walk. There are splints on my arms, too, which keep my fingers in a natural position. Otherwise they would clench into fists and ultimately never straighten out.

282

Once everything is removed I am rolled onto my back. But my body rebels no matter how gently they try to move me; my arms and legs flail wildly, and my chest tightens, making it difficult to breathe. The nurse turns on the oxygen that is always ready at the bedside. Because my muscles are still strong, it often takes the full weight of both the nurse and the aide to control these spasms and force my body to lie still.

Will comes in, carrying his lunch box and wearing my purple knapsack, which is now his. He climbs over the side rail of the bed and gives me a kiss. I tell him what my plan is for the day; maybe when I've finished my work, late in the afternoon, I'll watch him play basketball in the driveway. Or maybe after supper we'll watch a hockey game together, or maybe I won't be back 'til after his bedtime because I have to fly somewhere to make a speech or attend a fund-raiser. If it's a city with a professional sports team, I always bring him back a jersey or a puck or a helmet. Whenever I'm away I always miss our morning hug and our little conversations about sports, or whales, or the solar system. To stop myself from brooding about these missed moments, I ask whoever is on duty that morning to turn up the radio just to have some noise to distract me.

Then we begin ranging, very slowly moving all four limbs. The nurse holds down one leg, while the aide stretches out the other one, first working it almost ninety degrees out to the side, then pushing my knee up to my chest, then straight up, and finally doing the 'frog': pushing the knee from side to side in a bent position. All the while the nurse is looking intently for any red spots that might

283

indicate the first stage of a skin breakdown. The redness is almost always caused by some kind of pressure: the heel of a shoe, or the outside of a knee pressing too tightly against the wheelchair. If these pressure sores aren't immediately given proper treatment, serious problems, like the decubitus ulcer I had in my sacral area, can develop very quickly.

In June 1997 a red spot appeared on the outside ankle of my left foot, probably caused by irritation from a shoe. A dermatologist and Dr. O'Hanlon, my podiatrist and a specialist in wound care, both examined it but did not recommend a course of treatment. By the middle of July it had opened to a little more than the size of a quarter and was nearly half an inch deep. Then the wound became infected. When the infection penetrated the bone, I had to face the possibility of having my foot amputated to prevent it from spreading through my body. We were in Williamstown at the time, just a short distance from the Albany Medical Center, where Scott Henson is now the chief of neurosurgery. I called and asked for his help.

Two days later my ankle was examined by an orthopedic surgeon, a physiatrist, a wound care specialist, and a vascular surgeon, all assembled by Dr. Henson as a personal favor. I watched him cut away the dead tissue, a process known as debriding. As he worked I noticed how delicately he held the scalpel and how carefully he cut into my skin. I kept thinking: This man, one of the top neurosurgeons in the country, who had assisted Dr. Jane in the unprecedented operation on my shattered vertebrae, is treating my ankle himself.

I was put on a ten-day course of industrial-strength IV antibiotics that my nurses could administer at home. Although I hated sitting out on the deck in Williamstown attached to a pole while Dana, Will, Matthew, Al, and various friends played soccer or volleyball on the front lawn, the treatment worked. There were ups and downs, including allergic reactions to the medication, but by mid-August there was no more infection in the bone, and the wound had begun to shrink. By December, through proper nutrition, elevating the leg, and wearing T.E.D. hose to prevent swelling, the ankle was just about healed.

The morning ranging typically takes about an hour. If we're on a tight schedule, as we were most days during the filming of *In the Gloaming*, we can do it in half the time, but then I'm likely to have more spasms during the day. After the ranging I'm given a sponge bath from head to toe. The bandages around the trach are changed, and new dressings are applied to my ankle and at the site of my superpubic catheter. This kind of catheter is surgically inserted directly into the bladder and allows for continual drainage, eliminating the need for a catheter change every four hours. It also allows me to drink as much as I want, which is essential for the health of my kidneys.

By this time I've been worked on for nearly an hour and a half, and I'm finally ready to be dressed. Because my clothes have to be put on while I'm still in bed, I particularly hate days that end with a black tie gala. These events are definitely worthwhile, but I have to admit I wish there weren't quite so many of them. The aides are only available for the morning and nighttime care, so on formal occasions I have to dress for the evening at nine in the morning. Sometimes I rebel and wear more comfortable clothes. When I arrive at the venue I apologize profusely for having misunderstood the dress code.

Even on days when I can stay at home, getting dressed takes time and, more important, the ability to accept not being able to do any of it by myself. When two people have to roll you back and forth in order to put on your underpants at age forty-five, it's a difficult lesson in patience and acceptance. I pick out my wardrobe, but I have no choice about one part of it: to promote better circulation in my legs, I always have to wear the hated T.E.D. hose. Finally I'm ready to be lifted into the chair. The entire ordeal of getting up can take as much as three hours.

And there are times I have to stay in bed longer than required by the regular routine. Every three weeks the trach has to be changed, which involves pulling the old one out, cleaning the site thoroughly, and putting a new one in. Tracy does this better than any of the doctors who used to perform the procedure. I will never forget the first trach change, attempted by two pulmonologists a week after I came home. I was given a mild anesthetic; the doctors pulled the trach out, cleared away some granulation (healing) tissue in my throat, then couldn't get the new trach to go in. By this time I had been off the hose for nearly two minutes; my lips were turning blue, and my eyes were bulging. I couldn't breathe because the air I took in through my mouth escaped through the open hole in my throat instead of getting to my lungs. One of the doctors ran to the phone to call an ear, nose, and throat specialist; the other one kept asking, 'Are you all right?' Tracy stepped in and with one hand shoved the new trach down my throat and into place. As she reconnected the hose from the ventilator and I started breathing again, one of the doctors berated her for interfering with their work and for touching the trach without a glove. Matthew and Al, who had just arrived for the Christmas holidays, watched in horror from the kitchen; they had never seen an emergency before. The two pulmonologists packed and left in silence, taking their egos with them.

That was not the first time Tracy had taken matters into her own hands and proven her skill. Within days of my arrival back in Bedford, Dr. Kirshblum asked her to remove the picc line from my chest. This requires a special certification, which of course Tracy had. It had been a traumatic experience when it was put in at UVA, but I understood that it was needed for the quick delivery of drugs or blood into my body. They insert the line into a vein in the arm, then snake it up over the shoulder and down into a major artery right next to the heart. The fact that the procedure was performed by a specialist was not enough to reassure me.

Now as Tracy prepared to remove the picc line, I started to lecture her about the danger involved. I told her that the end of the line was in a critical artery, and that if she wasn't extremely careful she could cause serious internal bleeding. I suggested that on second thought it might be better to go to the hospital to have it taken out. Just as I was finishing these rather condescending remarks, Tracy held up the picc line. It had taken her about a minute to remove it, and I hadn't even noticed.

When I'm not on a tight schedule, I always do some kind of exercise as part of the morning ritual. We keep a chart of each day's activities so that every muscle group is worked equally. Apart from the physical benefits, I have found that exercising the body helps me focus on the future. No matter what kind of mood I'm in, I always make myself do something that will help prevent my physical condition from deteriorating. It's just like the first few months of 1977, when I was training for *Superman* and told my driver to take me to the gym even if I said I wanted to go home. Once I was there, there was nothing to do but change into my workout clothes and start lifting weights.

Now, facing muscle atrophy, loss of bone density, osteoporosis, and all the other side effects of a spinal cord injury, I use the same technique—only I'm the driver. There's no one standing over me cracking a whip, nothing to prevent me from lying in bed until late in the morning. I have to rely on self-discipline and faith, although my faith is based on science rather than religion. The very real possibility that an injured spinal cord can be repaired is a testimony to the dedication, perseverance, compassion, and skill of a few great minds. The least I can do is try to match their dedication as they achieve the seemingly impossible in the laboratory. I have faith that they will succeed, in spite of the fact that there is no certainty.

The morning routine of dressing and exercise is usually finished by eleven o'clock. I eat a light breakfast of cereal or a piece of toast with tea, and occasionally an omelet to keep my protein levels up. Sometimes I wish that I still couldn't stand food, because it's extremely difficult to stay thin. I often joke with Dana and the nurses about the weight I put on in the spring of '97. I remind them that in the pictures of me receiving my star on the Hollywood Walk of Fame I look like Marlon Brando—and not the Marlon Brando from *Streetcar* or *On the Waterfront*.

I consider myself extremely fortunate because my schedule is so varied. Many patients have no choice but to become stuck in a routine, which of course makes it hard for them to be optimistic about the future. But I'm able to travel, to visit scientists in their laboratories and hear about progress in research months before the results are published in scientific journals. Thanks to the generosity of groups that hire me for speaking engagements, I've appeared all over the country, sharing my experiences and creating more awareness about the disabled. Often I speak at rehab centers and talk about what I've learned with other spinal cord patients. I had the opportunity to direct a film, which gave me great creative satisfaction and kept me from thinking so much about myself.

I spend much of my time planning events to raise money for the Christopher Reeve Foundation. In our first year of operation we raised more than $750,000; 70 percent of it went to the APA and the rest to groups dedicated to quality of life issues of the disabled. I was also involved in the creation of a paid commercial called *Circle of Friends* to benefit the APA. I approved the script and called friends like Paul Newman, Mel Gibson, and Meryl Streep as well as a number of scientists to ask for their participation.

Much of my time is spent on the phone and corresponding with members of Congress about funding for research. As of this writing the effort is continuing to double the budget of the NIH, in spite of the first vote against it. The Harkin-Specter bill that would require insurance companies to donate one penny per premium for research is still alive, and I've been meeting with executives of several companies to enlist their support. Often I refer to my great-grandfather Franklin d'Olier, who was the CEO of the Prudential Insurance Company in the 1920s. I truly believe that he not only would have backed the legislation but would have pressured his colleagues at other companies to do the same. I'm still working with Senator Jeffords on the bill that would increase insurance caps to $10 million, as well as on the legislation that would fund biomedical research by means of a tax on cigarettes. I correspond regularly with President Clinton, urging him to follow the example of FDR's initiative with polio and call for sufficient funding for an all-out war against Alzheimer's, MS, stroke, Parkinson's, and spinal cord injuries. Because cures for these conditions are so imminent, his leadership on this issue could be an important part of his legacy.

The minute there is a lull in the action, my assistants Michael, Sarah, and Rachel come up from the offices downstairs armed with faxes, letters, messages, and the appointment book. There is always enough work to keep me busy all day, but I generally attend first to the items we consider 'crashing and burning.' Business that involves the American Paralysis Association, the Christopher Reeve Foundation, or political activity in Washington gets top priority. We also try to answer as many requests as possible from the spinal cord community. Often when I can't attend an event, I record a video message to be played at the dinner or symposium. On those days our house is overrun with equipment and crew. (We're running out of ways to rearrange our living room so it doesn't look exactly the same in every video.) Sometimes when my obligations on a particular day seem overwhelming, I take time to go outside, lean back in my chair, and enjoy the view of the Gonzaleses' farm below our house. The goats and sheep graze contentedly in the pasture near the pond, while the chickens and guinea hens scurry around in the safety of the front yard.

Actually, they are not always so safe. In the fall of '97, Jay Wiseman, a family friend, came to stay with us as a part-time baby-sitter for Will and aide to me. Along with him came the world's friendliest dog, Oliver, part Belgian shepherd and part St. Bernard, who became a great pal to Will. Even though he was only nine months old, he was the perfect houseguest. When he needed to go to the bathroom, he went up into the woods rather than make a mess on our carefully manicured lawn. He was so well behaved that we let him have free run of the house and our property.

Usually he stayed nearby. But one day as I was working in my office, I looked out the window and saw him trotting up the hill with one of the Gonzaleses' chickens in his mouth. Jay made Oliver drop the mangled fowl and tied him to a tree while Dana and I agonized about how to break the news to our neighbors. She called them that evening, apologizing profusely and promising it would never happen again. Lynn, their teenage daughter, who answered the phone, wasn't nearly as upset as we thought she'd be. (This was a surprise to me, because I thought the chickens were beloved family pets.) She simply said that if Oliver were to attack again, all would be forgiven as long as she was invited up to meet Robin Williams the next time he came to the house.

I try to finish the workday by 5:30 so I can spend time with Will, and with Dana if she's back from her appointments in the city. We eat dinner at about six-thirty or seven o'clock at the latest; usually fish or red meat with spinach, broccoli, or salad, which I need to keep my hemoglobin and albumin levels up. This is necessary to promote healing of any skin breakdowns and to maintain my over-all health. After dinner Will and I race around the driveway if it's not too cold. My wheelchair is no match for his bike, even if he gives me a head start. But I love the fact that he enjoys beating his dad, just like any other kid. Aside from opening doors for me and sometimes moving furniture out of my way, he doesn't cater to my disability, which I deeply appreciate. In the winter we watch the New York Rangers on TV, and we always go to several games a season at Madison Square Garden. I started teaching Will to play hockey when he was two years old, before he had ever put on a pair of skates. Now he is obsessed with the game and can tell you the names of the star players on every team in the NHL. When Dana comes into the kitchen first thing in the morning, she usually finds Will already at the table reading the sports section of *The New York Times*. Then he comes into the bedroom and reports to me on the latest stats of his favorite teams, as well as the scores and highlights of last night's games. When he plays floor hockey in the family room, I often come through in my wheelchair and we pretend that it's the Zamboni; I drive back and forth resurfacing the ice.

When we're at home I generally go to bed at 9:30, which is very much against my nature. When I was on my feet, I never went upstairs until 11:30 or midnight. But now I have to go in early because the process of putting me to bed takes nearly two hours. A nurse and an aide share the workload. First they take the legs and the left arm off the wheelchair. Then the aide gets a firm grip on the canvas lifting pad that remains underneath me at all times and positions himself to carry my upper body. The nurse gets a grip under my knees. On a count of three they lift together and set me down gently (most of the time) on my bed. Coordination between them is crucial, and if the lifting pad slips I could easily be dropped on the floor in the space between the chair and the bed. Having been dropped once during the transfer from the bike to my chair, I am always slightly anxious. But I think that accident served as a warning to everybody who works with me. Now the lifts are almost always perfect.

Next comes the process of undressing me, which I have finally come to accept; I used to have to control my anger with myself for having ended up in this situation. Often I listen to music or watch TV so I don't have to think about being taken care of like a baby. Once my clothes are off I'm given another sponge bath, and every other day the nurses wash my hair. This involves leaning my head back into a small plastic tub filled with water at the head of the bed. After I'm shampooed and conditioned the water is drained into a bucket and dumped into the sink. About once a week I'm transferred onto a special plastic chair and treated to a proper shower. Unfortunately that takes a lot of time, and the transfer from the bed to the shower chair is fairly dangerous; since the chair's arm can't be removed, I have to be lifted over it. While all the aides are good, I naturally feel more secure with some than with others.

After I'm clean I choose a T-shirt to sleep in, and I decide on the number of blankets, depending on my temperature. Because the connection between my brain and the nerves in my spinal cord has been disrupted, my body frequently responds inappropriately. People around me might be dropping from the heat while I'm asking for a space heater and more blankets. Almost every night I wake up at four in the morning feeling that I've been placed in a broiler. Dana, sleeping next to me, seems perfectly comfortable under a pile of covers.

Once I'm settled in bed the aide ranges me again, taking extra time to stretch and flex all the muscles. After twelve to fourteen hours of immobility in the chair, this is a great relief and one of the highlights of my day. Unfortunately this is immediately followed by one of the low points: the bowel program. I often joke that it's one of my favorite shows, right after *NYPD Blue* and *Law and Order*.

I'm turned on my side, and the aide pushes on my stomach with his fist in order to force stool down through the intestines and out onto plastic sheets placed underneath me. Part of the rehab process is training the bowels to release stool on a schedule. It takes nearly a month for this conditioning, and there are many accidents along the way, until the body learns to produce results at a specific time. Again, this is a time when I let my mind drift far away. The nurses and aides are always extremely professional, but all of us recognize what a personal invasion this is, and what an indignity. Sometimes it can take nearly an hour to complete the bowel program, and it seems like an eternity. When I'm unable to detach myself mentally, I still can't help agonizing over the accident and the twist of fate that caused me to end up this way.

When the whole regimen is over, Dana joins me in the narrow bed, and we spend intimate time together until we say good night and she has to move to her own bed beside me, because there isn't room for both of us in mine. By now it's nearly midnight. I take my 'sleepers'—a Benadryl tablet and a 10-milligram tablet of Ambien, a mild sedative. I hate having to take any kind of drug at bedtime, but without them my body would spasm during the night. Within a half hour I'm dreaming, whole again and off on some adventure.

*   *   *

People often ask me what it's like to have sustained a spinal cord injury and be confined to a wheelchair. Apart from all the medical complications, I would say the worst part of it is leaving the physical world—having had to make the transition from participant to observer long before I would have expected. I think most of us are prepared to give up cherished physical activities

295

gradually as we age. I certainly wouldn't be competing in combined training events in my sixties or skiing nearly as fast as I used to. If I went sailing in my later years I wouldn't go single-handed. Stronger arms and more agile bodies would be needed to raise and trim the sails or steer in a heavy sea.

The difference is that I would have had time to prepare for other ways of enjoying the things I love to do most. But to have it all change and have most of it taken away at age forty-two is devastating. As much as I remind myself that being is more important than doing, that the quality of relationships is the key to happiness, I'm actually putting on a brave face. I do believe those things are true, but I miss freedom, spontaneity, action, and adventure more than I can say. Sometimes when we're up in Williamstown I sit out on the deck looking across our pastures to Mount Greylock, and I remember how I used to be a part of it. We hiked up the mountain, swam in the streams, rode our horses across the open fields, chopped our own Christmas tree from the woods above the house. Now it's just scenery—still beautiful, but almost as if cordoned off behind velvet ropes. I feel like a visitor at a spectacular outdoor museum.

When I first moved to the Williamstown house in the summer of '87, the trailer for my sailplane was parked beside the barn. As soaring gave way to riding, a horse trailer took its place. Over the next few years the three stalls were home in turn to Valentine, Abby, Hope, Dandy, Denver, and Buck. I taught Al to ride, and we spent many happy hours cleaning tack together, bringing the horses in from their turnout, getting up at six for the morning feed. Bill Stinson kept all his gardening equipment in the other half of the barn, so he was always coming and going. Many times Matthew and Al would play with their friends in the hayloft above, making forts out of bales of hay and attacking each other with tennis balls. The barn was always cool and inviting on humid August days.

Now the stalls are empty. The barn is all closed up, and my van, full of ramps, oxygen tanks, and emergency supplies, is parked where the horse trailer used to be. We all remember how it was, but we don't talk about it much. The barn, too, has become scenery. Al continued to ride for about a year after my accident, and I coached her once at a local show, but now she's given it up. As I write this she's just turned fourteen. Her schoolwork takes much more of her time, she enjoys spending weekends with her friends, and the phone is ringing more and more as boys her age are beginning to work up the courage to ask her out. There may be other reasons why she's stopped, but I don't ask. Dana doesn't ride anymore either because it was something we did together.

When the first *Superman* movie came out, I gave dozens of interviews to promote it. The most frequently asked question was: 'What is a hero?' I remember how easily I'd talk about it, the glib response I repeated so many times. My answer was that a hero is someone who commits a courageous action without considering the consequences. A soldier who crawls out of a foxhole to drag an injured buddy back to safety, the prisoners of war who never stop trying to escape even though they know they may be executed if they're caught. And I also meant individuals who are slightly larger than life: Houdini and Lindbergh of course, John Wayne and JFK, and even sports figures who have taken on mythical proportions, such as Babe Ruth or Joe DiMaggio.

Now my definition is completely different. I think a hero is an ordinary individual who finds the strength to persevere and endure in spite of overwhelming obstacles. The fifteen-year-old boy down the hall at Kessler who had landed on his head while wrestling with his brother, leaving him paralyzed and barely able to swallow or speak. Travis Roy, paralyzed in the first eleven seconds of a hockey game in his freshman year at college. Henry Steifel, paralyzed from the chest down in a car accident at seventeen, completing his education and working on Wall Street at age thirty-two, but having missed so much of what life has to offer. These are real heroes, and so are the families and friends who have stood by them.

At UVA and at Kessler, I always kept the picture of the Pyramid of Quetzalcoatl in front of me. I would look at the hundreds of steps leading up to the clouds and imagine myself climbing slowly but surely to the top. That desire sustained me in the early days after my injury, but during the next couple of years I had to learn to face the reality: you manage to climb one or two steps, but then something happens and you fall back three. The worst of it is the unpredictability. Several times I've made a commitment to appear at a function or give a speech, but the night before, or even that morning, a skin tear, or dysreflexia, or a lung infection suddenly developed and I had to go to the hospital instead.

Climbing up the steps, I've appeared at the Oscars, spoken at the Democratic Convention, directed a film, written this book, worked on political issues, and traveled more extensively than most high-level quadriplegics. But, falling backwards, I've been hospitalized eleven times for dysreflexia, pneumonia, a collapsed lung, a broken arm, two blood clots, a possible hip fracture, and the infection in my left ankle that nearly resulted in the partial amputation of my leg.

I was told by so many 'experts'—doctors, psychologists, physical therapists, other patients, and well-meaning friends and family members—that as time went by not only would I become more stable physically but I would become well adjusted psychologically to my condition. I have found exactly the opposite to be true. The longer you sit in a wheelchair, the more the body breaks down and the harder you have to fight against it. Psychologically, I feel I have established a workable baseline: I have my down days, but I haven't been incapacitated by them. This doesn't mean, though, that I accept paralysis, or that I'm at peace with it.

The sensory deprivation hurts the most: I haven't been able to give Will a hug since he was two years old, and now he's five and a half. This is the reason Dana and I decided not to have another child; it would be too painful not to be able to hold and embrace this little creature the way I did with the others. The physical world is still very meaningful to me; I have not been able to detach myself from it and live entirely in my mind. While I believe it's true that we are not our bodies, that our bodies are like houses we live in while we're here on earth, that concept is more of an intellectual construct than a philosophy I can live by on a daily basis. I'm jealous when someone talks about a recent skiing vacation, when friends embrace each other, or even when Will plays hockey in the driveway with someone else.

If someone were to ask me what is the most difficult lesson I've learned from all this, I'm very clear about it: I know I have to give when sometimes I really want to take. I've realized instinctively that it's part of my job as a father now not to cause Will to worry about me. If I were to give in to self-pity or express my anger in front of him, it would place an unfair burden on this carefree five-year-old. If I were to turn inward and spend my time mourning the past, I couldn't be as close to Matthew and Alexandra, two teenagers who naturally need to turn to me for advice. And what kind of life would it be for Dana if I let myself go and became just a depressed hulk in a wheelchair? All of this takes effort on my part, because it's still very difficult to accept the turn my life has taken, simply because of one unlucky moment.

When I was in California in September 1997 for the dedication of the building that will house the Reeve-Irvine Research Center, I had another MRI. There was concern that a cyst could have developed on my spinal cord, or that there might be a cavity—sometimes the cord splits open long after the initial injury, causing further damage to the nerves. Fortunately, the pictures were clean, meaning that even after two and a half years there had been no more deterioration. This was excellent news and caused a lot of excitement among the doctors who studied the film, but I came away sobered by the comments of the chief radiologist. He showed me that the damage to my spinal cord was only one centimeter wide, and said that if I had landed with my head twisted only a fraction further to the left, I would have been killed instantly. If I had landed with my head slightly more to the right, I probably would have sustained a bruise and been up on my feet within a few weeks. I just happened to hit the rail at an angle that turned me into a C2 vent-dependent quadriplegic. The irony of it hit me very hard, although I kept my emotions to myself. I knew there was no point in dwelling on it. But now I knew on a visceral level how fragile our existence is.

*   *   *

And now I'm sailing again. But this time we're on the *Sea Angel* headed for Maine. It's nighttime and I'm at the helm. Down below Dana and the children are sleeping. The breeze is warm and gentle, and we're sailing down the path of a full moon. For a moment I look behind me, fascinated by the boiling water just astern. Then I look a little further back and see that there are bits of foam, but the water has begun to calm down. When I look even further behind us, our wake has disappeared, and there is nothing to show that we were ever there.

I think this image comes to me out of fear that the best moments of my life are behind me. I look back longingly, hoping that the memories won't disappear. To me they're very vivid, but I cling to them more than I ever would have before my life changed so drastically. At forty-two, still in my prime, I took it for granted that I could look forward to many peak experiences in every aspect of my life. I rarely if ever looked back, because the present was so rich and full of promise. But now, in spite of the pain it causes me, I can't help dwelling on the fact that so many wonderful moments are receding in the distance.

April 11, 1995. Dana and I celebrated our third anniversary by treating ourselves to a huge suite at the Mark Hotel in New York. After an evening out to dinner and the theater, we came back to the room and made love until morning. It was just as exciting as the moment I asked her to marry me and we forgot about dinner and went straight to the bedroom. There will never be another night like it.

It's six years since we filmed *Remains of the Day*; fifteen years since that wonderful summer working on *The Bostonians*; eighteen years since *Fifth of July*. The last time I performed onstage was in *The Guardsman*, at Williamstown in 1992. How can it have been so long? Time collapses in my mind, and suddenly it seems that just the other day Tim Murray and my brother, Ben, and I were taking the *Sea Angel* down to the Chesapeake for the winter. I remember every detail of the trip. But Tim's gone, and my brother and I never speak about it.

Recently I went by our old apartment on Seventy-eighth Street and stopped for a moment to remember, to absorb the atmosphere around a place that was home for more than ten years. I looked up and saw that the cherry trees we had planted on our roof garden were still there, now part of somebody else's life. A block away the asphalt playground of P.S. 77 looked exactly the same. When he was only four years old, Matthew

302

and I used to play racquetball there against the wall. I remember how stiff my back used to get from bending over to hold the seat of his bike as he learned to ride without training wheels on the sidewalks around the Museum of Natural History. Twenty-two years ago I threw caution to the wind and invited all my parents—Franklin and Helen, Barbara and Tris—to the opening night of *A Matter of Gravity* and arranged for them to sit together. Twenty years ago I sat in the middle of a black tie audience at the Kennedy Center and watched *Superman* fly across the screen for the first time. Less than four years ago Buck was stabled at Sunnyfield Farm just down the road, and we worked together with Lendon and enjoyed being part of a group of dedicated riders. Now when we drive by the outdoor ring and the barns, past the horses I used to know turned out in the pastures, I always look away.

I have to stop this cascade of memories, or at least take them out of their drawer only for a moment, have a brief look, and put them back. I know how to do it now: I have to take the key to acting and apply it to my life. There is no other way to survive except to be in the moment. Just as my accident and its aftermath caused me to redefine what a hero is, I've had to take a hard look at what it means to live as fully as possible in the present. How do you survive in the moment when it's bleak or painful and the past seems so seductive? Onstage or in a film, being in the moment is relatively easy and very satisfying; it is an artistic accomplishment with no personal consequences. To have to live that way when 'the moment' is so difficult is a completely different matter.

303

Reluctantly I turn away from my fascination with the wake behind us and concentrate on what lies ahead. But now the boat is damaged, I've been injured, and we've lost our charts. Everyone is fully alert, gathered together on deck, quietly waiting to see if we can navigate to shore. Off in the distance is a faint flashing light; it could be a buoy, another ship, or the entrance to a safe harbor. We have no way of knowing how far we have to go or even if we can stay afloat until we get there. We agree to try, and to help each other steer. In the morning, if we stay the course, our beloved *Sea Angel* will be tied up safely at the dock and together we'll start walking home.

POSTSCRIPT

Dr. Jane was right. About a year after I left Kessler, sensation returned at the very base of my spine. I am, after all, incomplete. The MRI taken at U.C. Irvine in the fall of 1997 also showed that the ventral side of the spinal cord that controls motor function was completely intact. The gap at C2 that prevents messages sent by the brain from being transmitted to the body was only twenty millimeters long. If you were to put your little finger over the site of the injury you would be looking at a picture of a completely normal spinal cord. According to Dr. Schwab, these circumstances make me a prime candidate for the first human trials in regeneration. Because the gap is so small it appears likely that as the nerves regenerate they will be able to make appropriate reconnections. My chances of significant recovery now are greater than anyone could have expected just a few short years ago.

MISSION STATEMENT OF THE
CHRISTOPHER REEVE FOUNDATION

Founded in 1996, the mission of the Christopher Reeve Foundation (CRF) is to raise funds for medical research leading to the effective treatment of and—ultimately—a cure for spinal cord injury paralysis. CRF serves as a source of information and a voice for all people with disabilities. Through grants, CRF also supports programs that focus on quality-of-life issues for all people with disabilities.

To make a donation, or for more information, write or call:

Christopher Reeve Foundation
P.O. Box 277
FDR Station
New York, NY 10150–0277
1–888–711-HOPE

306

CHRISTOPHER REEVE CREDITS

MOTION PICTURES

Village of the Damned	(John Carpenter, director)
Speechless	(Ron Underwood, director)
Above Suspicion	(Steve Schachter, director)
Remains of the Day	(James Ivory, director)
Noises Off	(Peter Bogdanovich, director)
Morning Glory	(Steve Stern, director)
Switching Channels	(Ted Kotcheff, director)
Superman IV	(Sidney J. Furie, director)
Street Smart	(Jerry Schatzberg, director)
The Aviator	(George Miller, director)
The Bostonians	(James Ivory, director)
Superman III	(Richard Lester, director)
Monsignor	(Frank Perry, director)
Deathtrap	(Sidney Lumet, director)
Superman II	(Richard Lester, director)
Somewhere in Time	(Jeannot Szwarc, director)
Superman	(Richard Donner, director)
Gray Lady Down	(David Greene, director)

TELEVISION

Black Fox	(CBS miniseries)
Sea Wolf	(TNT movie of the week)
Mortal Sins	(USA Network movie of the week)
Tales from the Crypt	(HBO)
Death Dreams	(Lifetime)
Bump in the Night	(CBS movie of the week)

Road to Avonlea	(guest star on Disney Channel series)
The Road from Runnymede	(PBS/Constitution Project)
Carol and Company	(guest star)
The Rose and the Jackal	(TNT)
The Great Escape:The Untold Story	(NBC movie of the week)
Last Ferry Home	(WCTVBoston /Hearst Entertainment)
Anna Karenina	(CBS)
The American Revolution	(PBS series)
Love of Life	(CBS)

THEATER

BROADWAY
The Marriage of Figaro
Fifth of July
A Matter of Gravity
The Aspern Papers (London)
OFF-BROADWAY
The Winter's Tale
My Life
REGIONAL
The Guardsman
Death Takes a Holiday
Love Letters (Boston, Los Angeles, San Francisco)
Richard Cory
The Greeks
Summer and Smoke
The Cherry Orchard
The Front Page

Camino Real
Holiday
The Royal Family
John Brown's Body
Troilus and Cressida
The Way of the World
The Firebugs
The Plow and the Stars
The Devil's Disciple
As You Like It
Richard III
The Merry Wives of Windsor
Love's Labour's Lost
South Pacific
Finian's Rainbow
The Music Man
Galileo

DIRECTING

In the Gloaming (HBO; Emmy nomination, won four Cable Ace awards)

APPENDIX

SELECTED SPEECHES

SPEECH AT THE DEMOCRATIC NATIONAL CONVENTION

August 26, 1996

Over the last few years, we've heard a lot about something called family values. And like many of you, I've struggled to figure out what that means. But since my accident, I've found a definition that seems to make sense. I think it means that we're all family, that we all have value. And if that's true, if America really is a family, then we have to recognize that many members of our family are hurting.

Just to take one aspect of it, one in five of us has some kind of disability. You may have an aunt with Parkinson's disease. A neighbor with a spinal cord injury. A brother with AIDS. And if we're really committed to this idea of family, we've got to do something about it.

First of all, our nation cannot tolerate discrimination of any kind. That's why the Americans with Disabilities Act is so important and must be honored everywhere. It is a civil rights law that is tearing down barriers both in architecture and in attitude.

Its purpose is to give the disabled access not only to buildings but to every opportunity in society. I strongly believe our nation must give its full support to the caregivers who are helping people with disabilities live independent lives.

Sure, we've got to balance the budget. And we will.

313

We have to be extremely careful with every dollar that we spend. But we've also got to take care of our family—and not slash programs people need. We should be enabling, healing, curing.

One of the smartest things we can do about disability is invest in research that will protect us from disease and lead to cures. This country already has a long history of doing just that. When we put our minds to a problem, we can usually find solutions. But our scientists can do more. And we've got to give them the chance.

That means more funding for research. Right now, for example, about a quarter million Americans have a spinal cord injury. Our government spends about $8.7 billion a year just maintaining these members of our family. But we spend only $40 million a year on research that would actually improve the quality of their lives, get them off public assistance, or even cure them.

We've got to be smarter, do better. Because the money we invest in research today is going to determine the quality of life of members of our family tomorrow.

During my rehabilitation, I met a young man named Gregory Patterson. When he was innocently driving through Newark, New Jersey, a stray bullet from a gang shooting went through his car window . . . right into his neck . . . and severed his spinal cord. Five years ago, he might have died. Today, because of research, he's alive.

But merely being alive is not enough. We have a moral and an economic responsibility to ease his suffering and prevent others from experiencing such pain. And to do that we don't need to raise taxes. We just need to raise our expectations.

314

America has a tradition many nations probably envy: We frequently achieve the impossible. That's part of our national character. That's what got us from one coast to another. That's what got us the largest economy in the world. That's what got us to the moon.

On the wall of my room when I was in rehab was a picture of the space shuttle blasting off, autographed by every astronaut now at NASA. On the top of the picture it says, 'We found nothing is impossible.' That should be our motto. Not a Democratic motto, not a Republican motto. But an American motto. Because this is not something one party can do alone. It's something that we as a nation must do together.

So many of our dreams at first seem impossible, then they seem improbable and then, when we summon the will, they soon become inevitable. If we can conquer outer space, we should be able to conquer inner space, too: the frontier of the brain, the central nervous system, and all the afflictions of the body that destroy so many lives and rob our country of so much potential.

Research can provide hope for people who suffer from Alzheimer's. We've already discovered the gene that causes it. Research can provide hope for people like Muhammad Ali and the Reverend Billy Graham who suffer from Parkinson's. Research can provide hope for the millions of Americans like Kirk Douglas who suffer from stroke. We can ease the pain of people like Barbara Jordan, who battled multiple sclerosis. We can find treatments for people like Elizabeth Glaser, whom we lost to AIDS. And now that we know that nerves in the spinal cord can regenerate, we are on

315

the way to getting millions of people around the world like me up and out of our wheelchairs.

Fifty-six years ago, FDR dedicated new buildings for the National Institutes of Health. He said that 'the defense this nation seeks involves a great deal more than building airplanes, ships, guns, and bombs. We cannot be a strong nation unless we are a healthy nation.' He could have said that today.

President Roosevelt showed us that a man who could barely lift himself out of a wheelchair could still lift a nation out of despair. And I believe—and so does this administration—in the most important principle FDR taught us: America does not let its needy citizens fend for themselves. America is stronger when all of us take care of all of us. Giving new life to that ideal is the challenge before us tonight.

Thank you very much.

JUILLIARD SCHOOL COMMENCEMENT ADDRESS

May 23, 1997

First of all, I want to thank Dr. Polisi for writing all that down exactly as I dictated it to him [citation honoring Reeve delivered by President Polisi]. It's a real thrill to be here again; I was a student here only twenty-four years ago. And I remember the first production I saw in the Drama Division was *The Night of the Iguana* by Tennessee Williams with an actor named Robin Williams playing an old man. And I thought, If he can do comedy, we're all in trouble. He was absolutely brilliant. I have such warm memories of being here, although I remember we always flattened ourselves against the wall anytime John Houseman went by. It was truly terrifying. And I also remember that at any moment you could be invited upstairs for a little chat and suddenly told that perhaps you should go into computer programming instead. And people suddenly disappeared, and there was nothing left but an empty locker. And yet, if you survived four years here, you emerged as one of the best actors or directors or musicians or opera singers that this country can produce. And while you had to work on technique, while you were often intimidated by teachers, you really had their support. And the most important feeling that you got was that this institution supported you.

Now the difficult part comes, because out in the world institutions basically are against you in too

317

many cases. And in my recent experience I've seen a parallel between the world of disability and the world of the artist when it comes to institutions. Just to give you an example, you may have seen on *48 Hours* last week a mother crying to the insurance company about why her son can't have a [special] chair so that he can take a shower, and being denied by the insurance company. In my own case, when I left rehab I was told that I could have only twenty hours of nursing a week; but I am dependent on a ventilator, and if it fails, I am in very serious trouble. Would they provide a backup ventilator? No. Fortunately, I was able to afford one, but what about all the people who can't? I talk to some of the executives of insurance companies. And I say, Why is this? Why don't you take care of people? People who have paid their premiums, people who are in need. And they say, Well, we're in the risk management business. And I say, You should be in the people business.

For the last nine years or so with The Creative Coalition, I've been working to help save the National Endowment for the Arts. I remember sitting down with some of the opponents of the endowment, people supposedly with IQs in triple digits. And I say, What is your problem with the NEA? Don't you realize what it does for your community, not only in terms of the quality of life but even just economically? And they say, Well, we shouldn't be just giving handouts; if an artist is any good he'll succeed. So, let's follow the logic of that. Have we trained, have we gone through all this so that we can in a calculated way create art to succeed only in the market-place? That would be a tragedy for this country and for the world.

Another opponent of the NEA said, Why don't all of you who make tremendous amounts of money in Hollywood get together and fund the arts? Let's think who the top moneymakers are in Hollywood—that would be Sylvester Stallone, Arnold Schwarzenegger, Jean-Claude Van Damme ... What a wonderful peer-review panel. How would you like to be the artistic director of the Alaska Repertory Company and come before that panel to ask for funding for a season? It's ludicrous.

The point is that in the thirty-year history of the NEA, hundreds of thousands of grants have been given out. It has created arts education in schools. It's brought art, music, dance, and drama to underserved areas, and in all that time there may have been some twenty controversies, twenty or thirty. And yet the NEA is an easy political football.

Back in 1990 there was indignation over Mapplethorpe and Serrano. Now that's past, and instead, the opponents are vitiating the National Endowment for the Arts by just taking away the money. A few years ago $167 million was spent on the arts. That's a mere pittance; it comes out to sixty-four cents per person. In Sweden they spend three dollars per person on the arts. And think of the rich diversity of culture they have. Now the budget is down to about $98 million. So rather than object to content, they just take away the funding. That has to change. We have to fight.

The point I want to make to you, the graduating class, is that the institutions may be against you. As you go out in the world as artists, these institutions, politicians, the corporate world, the people who make policy about what art should be presented and what should not, they may give you a very hard time, much harder than the time you had developing as artists in this place. But never forget that even if an institution is against you, the people are for you. Because the people in this country want the arts. In a recent survey 61 percent of the American public felt more money should be spent on the arts, and in fact over the last twenty years more people have gone to art galleries, to museums, symphonies, opera, dance, and theater than to all sporting events combined.

And so you may not immediately find a chair in the symphony orchestra, or be hired by a great dance company, or find a home in a wonderful repertory theater, because times are tough and money is scarce. But don't lose hope. Don't give it up, don't sell out. Don't let them take your integrity. You are artists, and that is one of the highest and most noble callings that you could possibly attempt in this country today. Stick with it. My hat is off to you. You have achieved something wonderful. Never let go of that vision. We need you. Congratulations. And thank you very much.

TESTIMONY BEFORE THE SENATE APPROPRIATIONS SUBCOMMITTEE: LABOR, HEALTH AND HUMAN SERVICES, AND EDUCATION APPROPRIATIONS

June 5, 1997

Fifty-seven years ago someone struck with a then incurable disease spoke these prophetic words: 'We cannot be a strong nation unless we are a healthy nation. And so we must recruit not only men and women and materials but also knowledge and science in the service of national strength.'

These are the words of President Franklin Roosevelt, taken from his address at the dedication of the National Institutes of Health in October 1940. It's remarkable that even as war was raging in Europe and as the United States stood on the brink of entering that conflict, President Roosevelt had the foresight to recognize the importance of our nation's investment in medical research to its national security.

The question today is whether our current president and the Congress have the vision and wisdom to heed the words of Franklin Roosevelt and recognize the vital role played by medical research in the economic and health security of our nation.

I firmly believe that medical research is key to eliminating disease, reducing human suffering, and reducing health care costs. Heart disease and cancer, the two leading causes of death among Americans, constitute nearly one-fifth of America's health care bill. The costs of Alzheimer's disease—which devastates 4 million Americans and currently costs our nation $100 billion each year—are expected to increase dramatically as baby boomers age.

The economic costs of disease—not to mention the human costs—are truly staggering. Parkinson's disease afflicts nearly a half million Americans and costs our nation at least $6 billion a year. Nearly a quarter million Americans live with varying degrees of incapacity due to spinal cord injuries. We spend $10 billion annually merely to maintain them. A half million Americans suffer strokes each year, costing more than $30 billion for medical treatment, rehabilitation, and long-term care, as well as lost wages. Diabetes, which afflicts nearly 16 million Americans, costs our nation between $90 billion and $140 billion annually and is the leading cause of blindness, kidney disease, and limb amputations.

How do we stop the economic and human cost of these diseases? Research.

When I met with the president in May of 1996, he stated that the ratio of research to clinical results is greater in this country than anywhere else in the world. Money spent on research brings practical results that absolutely justify the investment. Let's look at a few examples.

NIH-sponsored research has resulted in the identification of genetic mutations that cause osteoporosis, Lou Gehrig's disease, cystic fibrosis, and Huntington's disease. Effective treatment for acute lymphoblastic leukemia (ALL) has been developed, and today nearly 80 percent of children diagnosed with ALL are alive and disease-free after five years.

Because of research the nature of medicine is changing. We are approaching disease at the cellular level. We are targeting problems earlier, more specifically, less intrusively, with greater success and fewer side effects. Advances in genetics will soon let us intervene in disease before symptoms appear.

Significant progress is being made in the battle against cancer. As recently as ten years ago AIDS was a virtual death sentence. Now individuals with extremely low T-cell counts are often able to rebuild their immune systems because of new protocols developed at the NIH and NIH-funded laboratories. Scientists are now talking about the possibility of an AIDS vaccine. Just a few years ago that would have seemed like science fiction.

In 1988 the Swiss neuroscientist Martin Schwab discovered two proteins that inhibit growth in damaged mammalian spinal cords, a revolutionary finding. Until then it was believed that the cord's inability to regenerate was due to the absence of nerve growth factors. In 1990 Schwab induced nerve regeneration in the rat spinal cord by blocking the inhibitory proteins with an antibody called IN-1. With adequate funding it is estimated that Schwab's antibody could be adapted for use in humans within the next one to two years.

When we recall that ten years ago a spinal cord injury was considered a hopeless condition, this progress is truly extraordinary. Similar progress is being made in the treatment of Parkinson's, MS, stroke, and other related diseases because research has led to a greater understanding of the complexities of the brain.

We must not stop this progress because we are unwilling to commit enough money to get the job done. It is imperative that the public—and more important our elected representatives—understand that research today is not speculative. It is not a waste of money. It is the only way to relieve suffering while helping to save the American economy at the same time.

Making this a reality demands an investment of real dollars—funds that just don't fit within the constraints of the Budget Agreement passed by Congress this week, which proposes to reduce overall health spending by $100 million next year and by more than $2 billion over the next five years.

That's why I support Senators Specter and Harkin's proposal to establish a National Fund for Health Research to provide additional funds over and above the annual appropriations for the National Institutes of Health. The Specter-Harkin bill proposes taking one penny from each dollar paid in insurance premiums, which would result in as much as a $6 billion increase a year for the NIH.

Some experts say that this bill will never pass because of the strength of the insurance lobby. However, recent experience has shown that even the most formidable lobbyists cannot derail legislation that has bipartisan and public support. The NRA was not successful in repealing the ban on assault weapons.

The American public watched in disbelief as a dozen tobacco company executives testified at a Senate hearing that nicotine is not addictive and denied allegations that nicotine levels were being raised in cigarettes in order to increase addiction.

Now we are witnessing the demise of the Marlboro Man and Joe Camel. There are lawsuits in virtually every state by individuals demanding punitive damages against the tobacco companies. Just this week thousands of government workers petitioned the president to ban smoking in government buildings. I sincerely doubt that the tobacco lobby will be able to stop this initiative.

The religious right led by Pat Robertson, Pat Buchanan, and the Christian Coalition tried twice unsuccessfully (in 1992 and 1996) to hijack the Republican Party and failed in both attempts. Here again was a case when a supposedly powerful lobby did not succeed in promoting their agenda.

I also know from personal experience, as a lobbyist for the National Endowment for the Arts, that in spite of five years of arguing strenuously about the economic benefits of the arts in thousands of communities across the nation, in spite of mobilizing arts groups from around the country annually for Arts Advocacy Day, in spite of showing statistics that 61 percent of the American people believe more money should be spent on federal funding for the arts; we watched in dismay as Congress turned a deaf ear and reduced the NEA budget from $167 million a year to a hopelessly inadequate $99 million. This has resulted in the loss of critical seed money to thousands of orchestras, dance companies, theaters, and museums. It is not only a serious setback to the quality of life in this country but further proof that Congress can and does ignore a strong lobby with tremendous grass-roots support when they so desire.

I have spoken to executives at several insurance

companies about this bill and have been told that their profit margin is so small that the donation of 1 percent of their income is an unreasonable hardship. Personally, I find this about as credible as the tobacco companies' claim that nicotine is not addictive. It is hard to sympathize with insurance companies when you watch a mother in tears begging for a chair so that her quadriplegic son can take a shower. In my own case I have been denied coverage for any physical therapy below the level of my shoulders in spite of the fact that leading researchers repeatedly stress the importance of cardiovascular conditioning and the prevention of osteoporosis and muscular atrophy in preparation for the functional recovery that spinal cord research will very likely achieve within the next few years.

The insurance companies see this legislation as a tax. My question is: Why is that unreasonable, particularly when the insurance companies would save so much money in the long run? Research will keep the American people healthier, resulting in fewer insurance claims. We tax oil companies and use the money to build and maintain highways. In New York State, if you win the lottery you pay a significant tax, which goes to a state fund for education. Most states have sales taxes, which are a major source of revenue for a wide variety of programs and services that benefit the public. Why shouldn't insurance companies be asked to help solve the health care crisis in this country?

Because of the advances to date, we can save millions of lives. Our challenge for the future is not just improving the quality of life of those we save but finding the cures to prevent that suffering in the first place.

Our scientists are on the threshold of major breakthroughs in almost every disease or condition that now causes so much hardship for people across the country and around the world. The insurance companies owe it to our families and our society to make a small sacrifice, which can do so much good. I hope that this excellent piece of legislation, which already has tremendous grass-roots support, will be enacted during this legislative session.

Thank you very much.

SPEECH AT THE NATIONAL ORGANIZATION ON DISABILITY CORPORATE CITIZENSHIP AWARD LUNCHEON

October 8, 1997

Thank you very, very much for that introduction. Again, I want to thank JCPenney and their ad agency for giving me my first job all those years ago. It was kind of a shock. I had never been on camera before. I had been a theater actor, and I got pinned into my dress shirt. They tuck it in at the back so there are no wrinkles. I got out on the floor, and the first thing I heard over the loudspeaker from the director was, 'Makeup, can you do something with his face? It's so bland.' It took me a while, but I bounced back from that little setback.

One thing I want to communicate to you is that I've now spent three birthdays in a wheelchair. At forty-two, I thought the best in life was still ahead of me, and I gave interviews saying that I felt wonderful opportunities were coming my way, both on-screen and off—in my personal life. Everything seemed to be rosier than ever before. One of the last movies I did before I was injured was called *Above Suspicion*, in which I played a paraplegic. I went to a rehab center in Van Nuys, California, to do research on what it would be like to be a paraplegic. I learned how to transfer in and out of a car. I learned how to transfer in and out of bed and onto a rehab mat. And I spent time with a young woman who had been injured in the earthquake in California. A bookcase had fallen on her head, and she was in a halo. She was just learning how to walk. I remember I went about every other day for two weeks to do this research. Every time I would leave and get in my car and drive back to my comfortable hotel, I would thank God that that was not me. Eight months later I had the accident and joined the disability population.

All of you here in this room are leaders—in the corporate world, leaders of foundations, leaders who have tremendous influence in government. The message today is, Just because our company has succeeded, just because our people are doing well, that is no excuse to look the other way and to turn members of our family into strangers. There should never be a sense of being a stranger. We all must be included in the American family.

Those who have the most should give the most, on both the government level and the private level. If we would do that, if we would really work together, if, for example, an insurance company would give one penny of every health premium dollar, that would raise $24 billion for research. It would transform the landscape of the whole health front in America. One penny. You don't need to pass that on to the consumer. There's no insurance company in this country that can't afford one penny of every dollar to help disabled members of the American family. Yet, when this is brought up, they say, 'You're mandating a tax. That's unfair.' I regard that as selfish and un-American. We must do what is necessary, and you can help. We must change that kind of thinking so that all the corporate leaders of these major companies will have the kind of compassion that Mr Oesterreicher and his company have already demonstrated.

So, on behalf of the forty-nine million Americans with disabilities and the half billion around the world, we salute the leadership of companies like JCPenney. Thank you for what you have done. Spread the word. Think of the world as an inclusive family, and let's not leave anyone behind.

The point I'm making is how easy it is to look away. I think that we are all one big family, but in many ways we're a dysfunctional family because we still sometimes see ourselves as separate. We think deep in our hearts, 'Thank God that's not me.' But it is all of us. At any moment some disease or condition of the central nervous system can happen, from Alzheimer's to Parkinson's to MS to the spinal cord. These all are afflictions that will affect us as America grows older. If we can just begin to see that there is no separation between the nondisabled and the disabled, then we will make real progress.

Today we are here to salute those people in the corporate world who realize that they have the leadership potential to promote real inclusion— JCPenney, Merrill Lynch, Bear Stearns—these are major titans of the corporate world, who can set the example and communicate the message that we are all one inclusive family. Whatever happens to me could happen to my brother, or my sister, or my mother, or my grandmother. Once we've realized that connection, then it's easier to say, 'It's not acceptable for someone to be excluded. It's not acceptable for my brother, who may be a person I've never met before, to not get a job. To not be a

331

part of society. It's absolutely unacceptable.' The motivation to include, the motivation to say, 'You, too, can be a part of the real world, not sidelined into a back corner where we merely maintain you and feel sorry for you,' this is the key to a society that can lay claim to being just and being fair.

This sense of equality is what we're really here to celebrate today. You, Mr. Oesterreicher [chairman and CEO], and everyone at JCPenney are leading the way. They need to be followed. The CEOs of insurance companies need to look at what they do and say, 'Why do we deny a young man a shower chair so he can be kept clean? Why do we deny exercise equipment that would allow somebody in my condition to keep himself from atrophy?' Research is leading the way to the day when there will be a significant recovery of function. How can the profit motive overtake the need for compassion? Well, certainly companies like JCPenney put compassion first. Their example must be followed.